CAREERS!

PROFESSIONAL

DEVELOPMENT

FOR RETAILING

AREL

SING

CAREERS!
PROFESSIONAL DEVELOPMENT FOR RETAILING AND APPAREL MERCHANDISING

V. Ann Paulins
OHIO UNIVERSITY

Julie L. Hillery
NORTHERN ILLINOIS UNIVERSITY

FAIRCHILD PUBLICATIONS, INC.
NEW YORK

Coventry University

Executive Editor: Olga T. Kontzias
Acquisitions Editor: Joseph Miranda
Assistant Acquisitions Editor: Jason Moring
Associate Production Editor: Elizabeth Marotta
Art Director: Adam B. Bohannon
Production Manager: Ginger Monaco
Assistant Editor: Suzette Lam
Publishing Assistant: Jaclyn Bergeron
Copy Editor: Donna Frassetto
Interior Design: Stewart Cauley
Cover Design: Adam B. Bohannon

Library of Congress Catalog Card Number: 2004114709

ISBN: 1-56367-357-6

GST R 133004424

Printed in the United States of America

Dedication

For my parents, who always thought I could;
and for Marty and Matt who were patient while I did.
—VAMP

To the students for whom this book is written.
May you find a career that is as rewarding to you, as teaching is for me.
—JLJH

CONTENTS

CHAPTER SEVEN
WORK EXPERIENCES AND INTERNSHIPS

We have, combined, spent over 25 years teaching students the fundamentals of retailing and apparel merchandising. Together, we have worked with thousands of students as they engage in the process of selecting their majors, identifying career goals, seeking work experiences, completing course requirements, and entering their careers. We share a sense of great pride and accomplishment as we watch our former students, who are now graduates, find success in their careers.

The enthusiasm, curiosity, and dedication that our students have displayed over the years motivated us to compile information and materials that are presented in this book. We have observed that the path to a successful career is often tedious. Endless questions abound regarding the "right" way to embark on the career-planning and search process. Our goal in writing this book is to provide a reference guide for (1) students as they initiate career plans, and (2) graduates and entry-level employees as they negotiate the transition from student to professional.

Career development is the theme we emphasize throughout the book. Readers should find the first two chapters helpful in identifying career opportunities and assessing personal characteristics, as a fit between career aspirations and personal strengths, skills, and interests. Chapter 3 introduces the professional portfolio—an instrument that readers are encouraged to continually develop and maintain as a complement to career search activities. As readers progress through the professional development process, subsequent chapters focused on job searching (Chapter 4), interviewing (Chapter 5), and resume and cover letter writing (Chapter 6) should guide the preparation for these activities.

The expectation that students will embark on work experiences is key to well-rounded academic training in retailing and apparel merchandising. Chapter 7 provides a discussion about the value of these experiences and offers advice on seeking high-quality, appropriate positions.

Key to the process of professional development is also the exploration of ethics—in both personal and professional contexts. Chapter 8 presents a discussion of ethics and encourages readers to explore their own ethical constructs. We believe that it is essential for young professionals to develop an awareness of the importance of ethics in the professional arena—particularly before they enter the working world full-time.

Chapter 9 provides information to students as they embark on the transition from student to full-time professional. This, we have observed, is often a difficult transition for students, and one associated with fear, risk, and apprehension. The information we have provided is intended to lessen the risks that are ultimately taken by providing strategies to seek and consider optimal information regarding career plans. By presenting material for aspiring professionals to read and to consider, we hope to allay the fears and apprehensions that often accompany career decisions.

The electronic activities at the end of each chapter correspond to the accompanying CD-ROM. The activities and forms on the CD-ROM are designed to provide students with a sound foundation as they prepare for a career in the retailing and apparel industry.

We realize that the order of topics presented in this book and on the CD-ROM may differ from the order in which these topics are covered in academic courses. This book is designed so that the chapters "stand alone," and hence do not need to be read in progression. We believe that readers will find complete information on the given topic in each chapter.

ACKNOWLEDGMENTS

Without the enthusiasm and great cooperation of so many students, alumni, and industry professionals, this book would not have been completed. We owe a deep debt of gratitude to everyone who took the time to discuss their careers with us. To those who shared examples of their work, we are particularly grateful.

Special thanks are due to the Fairchild team whose thoughtful insights and suggestions have helped make this textbook the best possible—particular recognition is due to Liz Marotta, associate production editor; and Olga Kontzias, executive editor. Your guidance and support throughout this process have been truly invaluable. We would also like to thank Carolyn Purcell, formerly with Fairchild, whose initial edit got us off to a strong start. We also appreciate the work of all the experts who served as reviewers for our book: Teresa Robinson, Middle Tennessee State University; Dr. Tana Stufflebean, University of Central Oklahoma; Mary Boni, Kwantlen University College; Betty Tracy, California State Polytechnic; and Judith Everett, Northern Arizona University. Your advice and direction have made this a better product.

Julie Hillery also wishes to express her deep gratitude to co-author Ann Paulins for letting her join the work in progress. Dr. Paulins' initial vision for this book was the driving force behind its creation. It has been a joy to be a member of this partnership, and the uncanny ability we have had in reading each other's minds is truly amazing!

CHAPTER ONE

CAREERS IN RETAILING AND APPAREL MERCHANDISING

If you don't know where you want to go, you might not get there or you won't know when you have arrived.
— YOGI BERRA

OBJECTIVES

- To provide a brief introduction to the retailing industry.

- To provide a brief overview of the retailing industry as a career choice.

- To identify select entry-level retail and apparel merchandising career opportunities In the areas of sales, management, buying, product development, and promotion.

- To identify skills necessary for success in select entry-level retail and apparel merchandising career positions.

- To identify typical retail career paths.

- To provide real-world examples from young professionals pursuing retail and apparel merchandising careers.

INTRODUCTION TO THE RETAILING INDUSTRY

Retailing is a diverse and exciting career choice—one that is full of endless opportunities for career development. Contrary to popular belief, a career in retailing can entail many more options than working in a store. In the United States alone, it takes millions of sales associates, store managers, buyers, product developers, merchandisers, wholesalers, and designers to sustain this huge industry.

Retailing is the second-largest industry in the United States both in number of establishments and number of employees. It is also one of the largest worldwide. Retail sales in the United States register in the trillions of dollars, with consumers spending hundreds of billions of dollars on apparel, accessories, furniture, and home furnishings alone. Over 23.2 million people are currently employed in retailing, making for more jobs in retailing than the entire U.S. manufacturing segment. Additionally, employment needs are expected to grow at a healthy rate over the next five years despite the current economic environment, which has diminished job opportunities in other fields. It is projected that by 2008, a total of three million new retail jobs will be created ("Retail: Career Futures with Promise," 2002).

There are over one million retail companies in the United States selling items such as building materials, garden supplies, food, automobiles, apparel and accessories, furniture and home furnishings, pharmaceuticals, sporting goods, books, jewelry, and more. In addition to traditional retail stores, merchandise is available from formats such as catalogs, television, and the Internet. On-line retail sales projections call for increases from $7.8 billion in 1998 to over $108 billion in 2003 (U.S. Dept. of Commerce, Bureau of the Census, 2002). Long lists of career options continue to emerge as retail formats are expanded in the marketplace. As well as the employment opportunities with retail firms, professionals are needed to support the design and manufacture, wholesale supply, and promotional requirements of retailers.

Even in an age of corporate downsizing, successful retailers such as Kohl's, Wal-Mart, and Target continue with vigorous plans for expansion. Retailers are also developing new avenues to reach customers, as well as new and improved methods of production, distribution, and acquisition of merchandise. Catalog, television, and Internet retailing have become mainstream, and exciting new employment opportunities related to these retail endeavors are abundant. As long as consumers keep buying, retailers and product manufacturers will have a market and will be looking for quality people to help satisfy those markets.

IS THIS A CAREER FOR YOU?

Whether you have a specific product interest, prefer a specialty store or mass merchandiser's approach, or are intrigued by nontraditional retail formats, there are career opportunities in areas such as sales (both wholesale and retail), buying and merchandising, product development and design, and promotion. In addition to these major career choices, the retail industry provides opportunities in related areas, including distribution, loss prevention, construction and store design, and human resources. Top-performing, ambitious, and goal-oriented employees are afforded numerous opportunities for advancement. Furthermore, because retailing is such a fast-paced and rapidly expanding industry, the pace of advancement can be quite quick. Although some entry-level positions may pay slightly less than the average in other fields, it is quite common in the retail industry for successful individuals to double their salaries within the first five years. Keep in mind that because of the diverse and dynamic nature of retail-oriented careers, many professionals gain experience in multiple paths, and experience smooth transitions from one career specialty to another.

The field of retailing, with its apparel merchandising, selling, and product design components, offers diverse opportunities for career exploration and growth. Another appealing aspect of the industry is that many times it allows individuals to merge a hobby or interest with a career. For example, many apparel-product–development professionals became interested in their field through sewing and designing their own clothing as teenagers. Successful stylists have long had a knack for "dressing" themselves and others. Automobile enthusiasts are apt to find great rewards in selling automobiles, parts, and services. You may have an interest in design or product development, buying, merchandising, sales, manufacturing, visual display, promotion, management, or store planning. Often, experience in one area of retailing, merchandising, or product development leads to opportunities in others. Few career choices lend themselves so well to adaptability toward change from one facet of the industry to another. Many industry buyers began their careers as retail managers, while account executives often have experience as buyers. Careers in human resources are a natural progression from merchandising and management positions. The retail industry is composed of countless interrelated career paths as you will see illustrated later in this chapter. You may wish to develop a niche in some particular area, or to continue to explore options in several career paths.

Due to the special nature of retailing, an industry that largely employs part-time help and hires seasonally, entry into the retailing industry is relatively simple. Most people in retail management positions today likely gained valuable experience working part-time while still students. Such experience may afford you an opportunity to explore exciting careers in areas such as apparel merchandising, buying, promotion, product development, and design. As a student, making good use of your weekend, holiday, and summer breaks can gain you a competitive edge that will prove beneficial to you as you plan your career goals and seek internships and entry-level career positions. In fact, one of the most common items that retail managers look for when seeking entry-level management candidates is prior retail experience. This is because a person with prior experience will have some understanding of what a retailing position entails. From a management perspective, this means that you are more likely to be committed to retailing as a career choice. Many of those without prior retailing experience do not have realistic expectations of what this field involves and therefore are more of a "risk" for management to hire, especially given the costs associated with an executive training program. For those with prior retail experience, the attrition rate is much lower, training is easier, and advancement is generally faster (Polpogian, 2003).

Recently at the National Retailing Federation convention in New York City, H. Lee Scott, Jr., president and chief executive officer (CEO) of Wal-Mart, who was a keynote speaker, included a statement in his introduction about "what makes retailing fun." He noted that retailing is fun because of the people with whom you work and interact, the great relationships you form with suppliers and customers, and the interesting assortment of merchandise to select and sell. He also mentioned that he is proud that working in the retail industry provides a great foundation for any other career path. He went on to say that about 70 percent of Wal-Mart's management team began as hourly workers—proving that experience in entry-level positions with a company really does pay off in terms of career advancement.

WHAT'S IN A JOB?

Most (though not all) retailing and apparel merchandising positions, while customer centered, fit into the areas of sales, management, buying, product development, or promotion and marketing. With this in mind, let's take a look at a few of the more common entry-level positions within these areas.

Sales

At the heart of all of retail job opportunities is the common goal that customers must be satisfied. Although not all positions involve interaction with retail customers, the success of each one depends on the customer's ultimate satisfaction with the product. For this reason, it is important for buyers, designers, and promoters to have a sophisticated understanding of the dynamics of customer service at the retail level.

RETAIL SALES ASSOCIATE. Retail selling is an essential function of all facets of the retail and apparel merchandising complex. Although retail sales positions are often viewed as a starting point to gaining valuable experience, for those individuals who are people-oriented and enjoy the challenges, retail sales can be quite rewarding. In fact, commissioned sales can provide an exciting and lucrative career.

Regardless of your particular career aspirations, you will benefit from some experience in sales at the store level. After all, the retail transaction between a salesperson and customer is the driving force behind the trillion dollar retail industry. As a future buyer, manager, or merchandiser, you will gain valuable insight into the retailing complex through store sales. In fact, most companies will require prior retail experience for those seeking entry-level management or merchandising positions. Entry-level store management positions, which generally involve a good deal of sales, can be opportunities leading to merchandising, buying, and wholesaling positions. Robin Forsythe, a graduate of Ohio University, recognized upon searching for an internship the need to have store experience. She felt that to succeed in buying or merchandising at a corporate level she needed to better understand and experience the selling environment. As she interviewed with several larger retailers, she stated her request to be placed in a store and explained why. Robin's insight into her skills, and the fit between her skills and the needs of the retailer, made her stand out in a competitive job market.

Customer service is the primary responsibility of every salesperson. Customers have come to expect friendly salespeople, and most want to be acknowledged when they enter a store. Customers also expect sales associates to provide product information and to assist them in coordinating merchandise. Many customers desire more personalized service than what they often receive. Successful salespeople recognize the needs and desires of customers, respond appropriately to customer comments and demands, and intuitively offer suggestions that are appreciated by customers. An outgoing personality, good communication skills, and the ability to interact with a variety of people are must-haves for those looking to succeed in retail sales. Of course, a love for the product you are selling always helps, too.

Generally, the training for an entry-level sales position is best done through on-the-job experiences. An effective store management team will provide guidance and suggestions to help their sales staff develop customer service skills. Most retailers will provide written guidelines or manuals on ways to approach customers, tips for suggestive selling, and other general customer service expectations. Additionally, learning about the store product and the target customer would also be included in your training. Successful retailers realize the important role that the sales personnel can play, because oftentimes customers form their impression of the store based on their treatment by the sales personnel. In fact, most times the sales personnel are the only link to the store. All of the planning, merchandising, and product development that the retailer does ahead of time may only be as effective as the sales personnel.

Employees who prove themselves valuable to retailers may quickly enjoy the benefits of wage increases and possibly a promotion to commission sales. Sales of certain merchandise categories, such as shoes, cosmetics, appliances, and technology, typically involve commissions. Increasingly, apparel retailers are offering commissions as an effort to enhance customer service, motivate employees, and increase sales. Successful commissioned sales personnel working at upscale stores can earn an impressive salary and sometimes earn substantially more than those in a more "prestigious" career position, such as a buyer or a visual merchandiser. As an example, it has been reported that some of Nordstrom's most successful commissioned sales personnel earn upwards of $90,000 per year* (Diamond & Pintel, 1996).

MANUFACTURER SALES REPRESENTATIVE. A wholesaler, or sales representative (sales rep), is responsible for obtaining orders from retail stores for the manufacturing company. Sales reps generally work with store buyers to provide merchandise for the store's customers. Some manufacturer sales representatives are referred to as *road reps* because they are assigned geographic territories and usually travel a great deal to their clients—the stores and buying offices—in that territory. A typical territory in the Midwest may include stores in Ohio, Indiana, Illinois, and Michigan. However, sales reps in the garment district in New York City work from a showroom where their clients (e.g., buyers and entrepreneurs) come to them. All manufacturer sales reps also attend numerous trade shows each year in regional or national markets to sell their merchandise. The International Boutique Show, which is held biannually in New York City, is an example of such a show, as is the *MAGIC* show held biannually in Las Vegas.

The position of sales representative is usually not an entry-level one; however, entry-level experience can be gained in a manufacturer's showroom as a showroom assistant or through an opportune internship. Many wholesalers seek to hire retail managers or buyers when filling a position because those with retail store experience have a better understanding of the buyers with whom they will be working. A wholesale representative with a retailing perspective can be invaluable to both the manufacturer he or she represents, and to the buyers who are the rep's customers.

As a showroom assistant, or entry-level sales rep, your duties would usually include general office organization such as reception; scheduling appointments for the sales staff; keeping records; maintaining files; faxing; communicating with buyers in person, on the phone, and through email; and organizing each season's product

---

*For a guide to annual salaries in the retailing industry, see http://www.acinet.org, http://www.careerjournal.com/salaries/industries/retailing/, and http://stats.bls.gov.

lines to ready them for showing and selling to buyers (e.g., receiving, hanging, iron-ing, and ticketing). Occasionally the showroom assistant may even be asked to model garments for clients. Some of these tasks may seem mundane to the recent college graduate, but keep in mind that many employers want you to learn the business "from the ground up." This is especially true in the manufacturer's showroom. The more pos-itive your attitude and willingness to learn, the more quickly you will be given addi-tional responsibility. As this happens, tasks with increased accountability will likely include writing up orders, reordering goods for retail stores, following up on deliv-eries, and analyzing inventory reports. During market week, when the showroom is extremely busy, you may even be asked to "show the line" (or sell) as needed.

As would be expected, a person wishing to pursue a career as a manufacturer's sales rep should have strong interpersonal and communication skills, sales skills, a high energy level, and a math aptitude. Sales reps should also be highly flexible and well organized. As mentioned previously, retail experience, and an understanding of retail store assortment planning, is also a definite plus. Generally training for manu-facturer sales rep positions occurs on-the-job. Salaries of manufacturer's reps range dramatically, depending on the sales volume generated. Successful and ambitious sales reps earn upwards of six figures once clients are established and accounts are effi-ciently and successfully maintained. The *Careers Up Close* profiles on pages 8–12 provide a real-world look at the manufacturer sales rep position and the key account position, which is an upper-level sales position.

Retail Management

If you thrive in the retail environment and are successful in retail selling, store man-agement may be just the job for you. Store managers are responsible for intra- and inter-store operations. They must ensure that merchandise is properly stocked and dis-played within their stores, and that employees are efficiently assigned and adequately informed to assist customers. Managers organize and supervise people, as well as products, and are responsible for enforcement of policies and expectations of the store or business. The smooth operation of any type of store or business depends largely on the effectiveness of the manager. Although entry-level management positions will vary by type of retail store, they generally include management trainee, department or area manager, and assistant store manager.

MANAGEMENT TRAINEE. Most department stores and many specialty stores require managers to complete a training program that typically lasts from 3 to 12 months. Trainees are most often recent college graduates and are viewed by

(continued on page 13)

MOLLY SIMON & *Careers Up Close*
Accessories Sales Representative ANGIE GARDNER
PAM DELUCA, LTD. Accessories Sales Representative
MAUREEN SHINNERS CONTEMPORARY
ACCESSORIES, LTD.
GRADUATED IN 1997 FROM
NORTHERN ILLINOIS UNIVERSITY
MAJOR: TEXTILES, APPAREL,
AND MERCHANDISING

MOLLY SIMON BEGAN HER CAREER IN STORE

management for The Limited. However, while a student at Northern Illinois University (NIU), she completed an internship with the Chicago Apparel Center, where she worked as an assistant to the fashion director. Her primary responsibilities included answering the phone, general office duties, and assisting with all fashion events at the Apparel Center and in the Chicago-land area, such as fashion shows, market weeks, and other promotional events. A major part of her internship requirements included picking up merchandise from manufacturers' showrooms and delivering it to the location of the fashion show or event in which the items would be featured. Much of the time this involved hauling hundreds of pounds of clothing and accessories around 14 floors of the Apparel Center and sometimes even miles away to off-site destinations. However, Molly maintained a positive attitude, did whatever was asked of her, and found that she was able to network with many different manufacturers' sales representatives. During her summer internship she became a familiar face at the Apparel Center. The sales reps came to know that they could trust Molly with several thousands of dollars worth of merchandise at a time.

One day toward the end of her internship, Molly was running an errand that required an elevator ride to a lower floor of the building. When the elevator stopped on another floor, an accessories sales rep stepped on, and when she saw Molly in the elevator, the rep offered Molly a sales position on the spot. Although Molly did not personally know the sales rep, it was apparent that her strong work ethic had earned her a widespread positive reputation. Because Molly's internship was unpaid, she had continued to work at The Limited. Once her internship was completed, Molly decided to stay

Both Molly and Angie agree that it is essential for sales reps to possess both "people skills" and presentation skills.

at The Limited—in part because The Limited offered her a set salary rather than a less stable commission-based income, as the sales position would have required.

A year later, after working for The Limited for over six years, Molly decided to take a chance and accept the same sales position in the accessories showroom that she had previously been offered. Molly began as the showroom assistant and was quickly promoted to a manufacturer's sales position. After four successful years in that position, a new and upwardly mobile opportunity presented itself, and she decided to move on to a sales position with a gift manufacturer. Before leaving, however, and in keeping with her strong work ethic, Molly hired and trained her replacement, Angie Gardner. Molly and Angie had become friends several years earlier while serving as officers in the Fashion Industries Student Organization at NIU. Molly immediately thought of Angie because she knew that Angie's strong work ethic matched her own. Also, through networking, Molly knew that Angie was interested in leaving the retailing side of the industry. When asked why she felt the obligation to fill her own vacancy, Molly explained that she wanted to do everything she could to ensure a smooth transition for everyone concerned. Molly also wanted her boss to know how appreciative she was for the opportunities she had been given.

Today, Molly is a successful manufacturing rep for Pam Deluca, Ltd., a showroom based in the Chicago Merchandise Mart that represents numerous accessories manufacturers. Angie also continues to be successful in her sales rep position with Maureen Shinners Contemporary Accessories, Ltd. Together, they currently service over 3000 accounts (in an eight-state territory) and travel extensively throughout the Midwest selling their accessories lines to buyers and retailers. They help these retailers maintain

One of the things that Molly and Angie like the most about their positions is the relationships they have established with their customers.

inventory and identify items that best match each store's target customers. Both Molly and Angie agree that it is essential for sales reps to possess both "people skills" and presentation skills. Furthermore, they feel it is extremely important to be honest and to build trust with each retailer because repeat business is absolutely essential to their success. In fact, one of the things that Molly and Angie like the most about their positions is the relationships they have established with their customers. Knowing their customers allows them to recommend the best items for each of the stores each season. Also, their extensive retailing experience has been invaluable because they both understand the challenges that retailers are faced with on a daily basis.

Molly and Angie hope to team up someday and own their own showroom that offers wholesale accessories and small home-decorating goods. Recently, they have also been exploring the idea of manufacturing their own lines. This activity will be very different from the sales-oriented positions they currently hold and will involve sourcing and production. As undergraduates, Molly and Angie were advised to work in the retail industry while they were in school. They both heeded this advice—Molly worked at The Limited, Angie at Wal-Mart—and offer it to aspiring students of retail merchandising. Their experience in retail, they insist, contributes directly to their success in manufacturer sales.

GINA BASICH
Key Accounts Manager
LION BRAND YARN COMPANY

GRADUATED IN 1996 FROM OHIO UNIVERSITY
MAJOR: RETAIL MERCHANDISING

AS AN ENTRY-LEVEL ASSISTANT DESIGNER, GINA

Basich was responsible for assisting in all aspects of operating the showroom and design studio at Kiki & Pooky, Ltd. Sales and Manufacturing Company, a women's apparel manufacturer in New York City. (Kiki and Pooky Ltd. has since relocated to Westport, Conn.) Gina's job entailed clerical duties such as answering telephones, responding to messages, and making appointments, as well as contacting contractors and sewers, assisting in organizing production of the merchandise, cutting samples, constructing trim sheets, and sourcing fabric. Gina completed an internship with Kiki & Pooky, Ltd. prior to her college graduation and credits her college courses—including Flat Pattern Design, Retail Math, Buying and Negotiation, Fashion Illustration, and Costume History—for preparing her well for her current position. While a college student, she worked as a costume curator for Ohio University's Mary C. Doxsee Historic Costume Collection and gained valuable sales experience by working at JC Penney and the May Company during university breaks. These sales experiences, she claims, provided excellent customer relations experience through exposure to customers as well as helpful sales experience and some knowledge of distribution. Gina offers these words of advice to prospective professionals: "Keep an open mind, be ready and willing to work; it's constant work that is not easy, but you have to be open minded to opportunities."

Gina built on her experience as an assistant designer when, five years ago, she became the administrative assistant to the vice president of the Lion Brand Yarn Company. When the retail analyst left the company, Gina asked to assume that role along with her current duties. After demonstrating professional development and competence along with an open-minded attitude, Gina moved into her current position as key accounts manager. Her varied responsibilities now include such things as managing the work flow to resolve day-to-day issues centered around key mass-retail customers;

Gina states, "Take healthy risks that promote learning, don't be afraid to leave your 'comfort zone,' and take every opportunity to network and to meet people both in and outside of your industry."

reviewing, analyzing and using data in product and promotional decision making and planning; and coordinating promotional presentations for key accounts. Gina is involved in product development, promotional strategy, and sales. She continually seeks to advance her knowledge of her customers in order to better understand and help them achieve their goals.

As for the future, Gina's own goal is to continue her professional development while making a positive contribution to the organization where she is employed. In the near term, she plans to stay in her current position at Lion Brand Yarn, which offers opportunity for growth in new geographical markets for her current customers. Although sales is exciting, challenging, and has provided Gina with tremendous opportunities for developing interpersonal communication skills, her ultimate career goals center around management and organizational behavior. She plans to earn an MBA with a focus on organizational behavior and psychology, then move into executive-level management on the operations side, ultimately achieving the position of vice president of a medium-sized corporation. Eventually, Gina would like to own and operate her own business. Gina credits her excellent college experience in getting her off to a good start in New York, but acknowledges that, along with formal education, experience remains one of the best "teachers." Gina shares the following advice with aspiring merchandising professionals: "Take healthy risks that promote learning, don't be afraid to leave your 'comfort zone,' and take every opportunity to network and to meet people both in and outside of your industry." She suggests that students plan to continually take steps to further their knowledge, such as attending business seminars and conferences and reading industry periodicals. Finally, she says, "If you want more responsibility or a promotion, ask for it. Don't wait around for someone else to figure out what you want." After all, that is how Gina found herself in this exciting and challenging position!

the company as potential buyers or managers. Because the competition for department store training programs is stiff, a bachelor's degree is necessary, as is a high grade point average and prior retail experience.

During their training period, management trainees are exposed to all aspects of the retail business, including merchandising, advertising, human resources, distribution and logistics, marketing, budgeting, and sales. Training usually consists of a combination of formal classroom instruction and in-store training. As an example, the 16-week training program at Saks Incorporated includes the classroom topics of retail math, inventory management, merchandise processing systems, assortment planning, pricing, and leadership. The "hands-on," in-store training covers operations of the store, staffing, visual merchandising, business analysis, and customer service. By the completion of training, the Executive Trainees at Saks Incorporated are provided experience with systems' operations, the buying office, corporate support, and time in the stores ("Store Management" n.d.).

In general, training periods not only give the company a chance to evaluate the trainee, but can also help the trainee identify his or her particular area of interest within the retail store or the company. Once the training program is complete, some companies may offer the trainee options on their particular placement within the company. However, it is more typical for the trainee to be placed in a department, or store, depending on the needs of the retailer and the potential they see for the trainee based on his or her performance during the training period. A promotion to that of department manager, or an entry-level buying position, is typical upon completion of the training program. For example, at most major department stores, the executive trainee may choose one of two career paths. A typical merchandising (buying/planning) career path is illustrated in Figure 1.1, and a store management career path is illustrated in Figure 1.2. Figures 1.3 and 1.4 illustrate the merchandising career path and the store management career path opportunities available with Kohl's Department Store.

To be successful, manager trainees will possess strong organizational and analytical skills, good communication skills, leadership ability, computer proficiency, and a high level of energy and motivation. Because of the varying demands of the job, a manager trainee must also be extremely flexible, thrive on some level of stress, and operate daily with a "sense of urgency."

DEPARTMENT OR AREA MANAGER (DEPARTMENT STORE). In addition to having a store manager, department stores and big-box retailers, such as Target, also have managers for each department or area within the store. The department/area manager position is generally the first position available after completing the man-

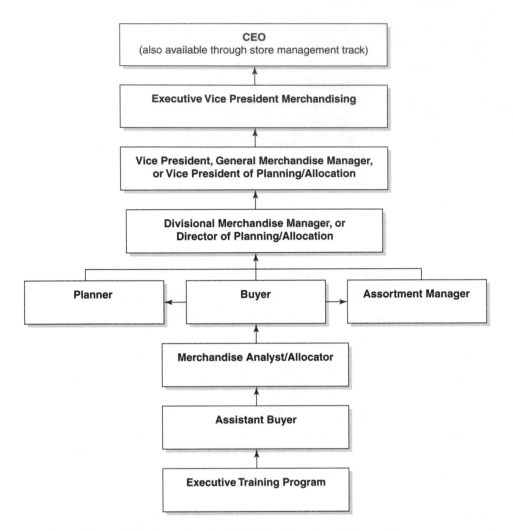

FIGURE 1.1   Typical Merchandising Career Path at Department Store

agement trainee program. However, some companies fill these positions directly by hiring recent college graduates or other individuals with prior retail experience. Likened to an entrepreneur, each day these managers are responsible for a diverse collection of duties within their particular department or area. Varied responsibilities include selling, visual merchandising, opening and closing the registers, receiving, stocking, inventory control, loss prevention, public or customer relations, and the training, supervision, and retention of all associates. Department managers also often communicate with the stores' buyers concerning sales and inventory.

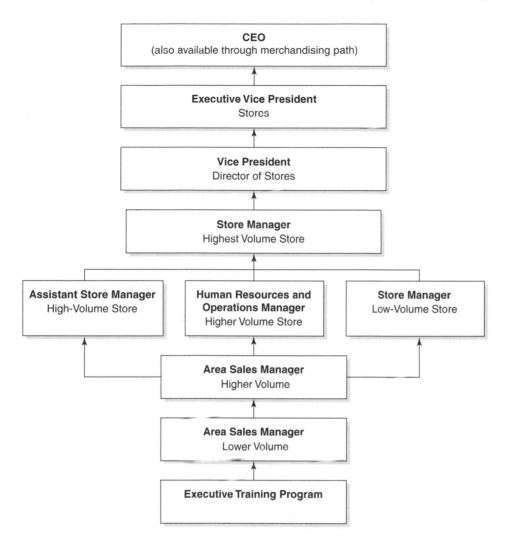

FIGURE 1.2   Typical Store Management Career Path at a Department Store

On a store management track, as illustrated in Figure 1.2, the department or area manager is typically promoted to an increasingly higher volume department or area, after which he or she becomes an assistant store manager, then the store manager. However, some department stores give department managers the opportunity to follow a merchandising career path that eventually leads to a buying position. Skills needed for a department or area manager are essentially the same as those for the management trainee position.

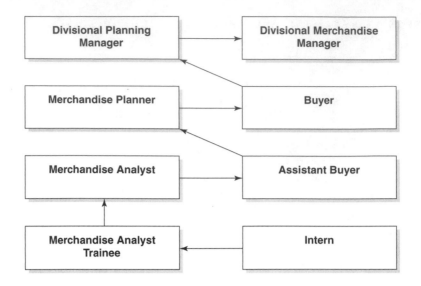

Merchandise Analyst: Responsible for analyzing, reviewing and reacting to sales, turnover and margin opportunities for their assigned business areas. By identifying trends, key items and other business opportunities, they can react and drive sales by placing the appropriate amount and type of merchandise in the appropriate markets.

Assistant Buyer: Assists Buyer with product assortment, pricing and merchandising strategies based upon history, current trends and future forecasts. Analyzes business trends and opportunities that could improve merchandising strategies. Highly involved with the advertising process to ensure that products are effectively advertised.

Merchandise Planner: Responsible for determining high level financial goals such as financial plans, open – to – buy management and new store budgets. Responsible for the planning and monitoring of key items, analyzes assortments and provides recommendations to optimize breadth, depth and profit. Coordinates merchandise exit strategies, including recommendations on purchase quantities, timing, and markdown strategies to improve transition and maximize profitability. Develops strategies for maximizing profitability of the inventory through analysis of planogram, fixture, and floor capacity.

Buyer: Responsible for all facets of product assortment, financial planning and vendor partnerships for the departments they manage. Develop the seasonal merchandise assortment, determine pricing and advertising strategies, coordinate with vendors to ensure seasonal plans are met. The Analyst, Planner, Assistant Buyer and Buyer all work together as a team to develop a successful game–plan to drive and manage their business.

The **Divisional Merchandise Manager (DMM)** is responsible for an entire division of merchandise representing a wide span of related departments. A DMM assumes the role of a general manager. Working with his or her buying team, the DMM builds the overall business strategy for the division focusing on merchandise assortments, promotional strategies, product life-cycle planning and seasonal transition. Key measures include sales, gross margin, and inventory turnover. They play a key role in talent development. In a national retail operation, DMM responsibilities can easily exceed one billion dollars in annual sales volume.

Like the DMM, the **Divisional Planning Manager** is responsible for an entire division of merchandise representing a wide span of related departments. This position works in tandem with the DMM to accomplish the business goals of the division. While the DMM's primary focus is on merchandise, the Planning Manager's focus is on seasonal financial management and inventory planning. Like the DMM, the Planning Manager serves in a general management capacity, developing and integrating various business strategies to accomplish the overall team goals. People development is a key focus.

Source: Reprinted with permission of Kohl's Department Stores. For more information on the Internship and Merchandise-Analyst Trainee programs, see www.kohlsoncampus.com

FIGURE 1.3   Kohl's Merchandising/Buying Career Path

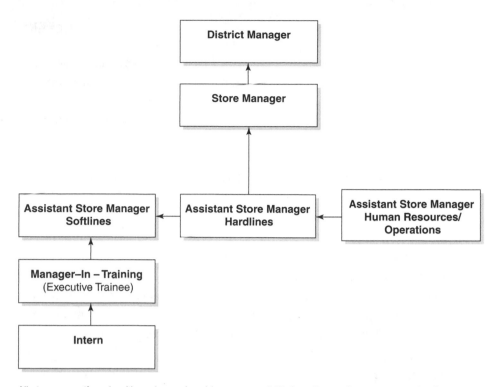

All **store executives** (positions shown above) have responsibility for sales, credit, customer service, inventory turnover, human resources, expense management, and supervision of all Associates throughout the building. Although each executive may have designated primary duties, they work as a team to achieve the store goals.

The primary focus of the **Assistant Store Managers** in both the apparel and accessories area and the children's/footwear/home area relates to the selling floor areas. These positions play an integral role in the store management team. Executive responsibilities include providing leadership for the store in the areas of: Associate development; execution of merchandise sales areas according to Kohl's best practices; communications; analysis of business operations; expense management; and general management of the store as part of the store management team.

The Assistant Store Manager in the Human Resources Operations area has primary responsibility for recruitment, training, staffing, payroll, receiving and freight processing, stock rooms, store maintenance, store systems, customer service, and cash office processes. This executive works closely with his/her peers to ensure that the store is staffed to meet the needs of the business.

The **Store Manager** is the general manager of the building and is ultimately responsible for sales and operating profit, managing payroll and other controllable expenses, inventory management and shortage, merchandise presentation standards, Associate training, and development of people.

National retailers subdivide geographic regions of the country into business units called districts. For many retailers, a **District Manager** is accountable for between 8 to 14 stores, based upon issues relating to territory management. Such issues may include population density, traffic patterns and drive time, relative proximity of one store site to the next, size and complexity of various stores, and the experience level of the District Manager. District Managers are responsible for the sales and profitability of his/her assigned district. As such, they play a lead role in identifying sales opportunities, creating consistent store standards, and providing an enticing shopping experience for customers throughout all of their stores. District Managers must be able to relate to a broad range of people, motivating, inspiring, and recognizing their performance. District Managers are keenly aware of the need to identify and develop top talent. In addition, they are vital in communicating with the corporate office, partnering with many areas to refine merchandise strategies or improve business operations.

Source: Reprinted with Permission of Kohl's Department Stores. For more information on the Internship and Manager-in-Training programs, see www.kohlsoncampus.com

FIGURE I.4   Kohl's Store Management Career Path

At the store manager level, in addition to a base salary, compensation is also given in relation to the volume of business the store produces. Effective store managers can earn attractive bonuses—sometimes as much as 30 percent of their annual salary. In fact, many successful department or big-box store managers earn six-figure incomes.

ASSISTANT STORE MANAGER (SPECIALTY STORE). This entry-level position is offered by stores such as The Limited or the Gap. Responsibilities in this position vary somewhat by company but generally involve assisting the store manager in all aspects of store operations. The duties are generally the same as those of the department or area manager; however, the assistant store manager is responsible for an entire store rather than one specific area. Although the responsibilities of a specialty store manager are similar to those of a department or area store manager, their career paths are somewhat different. Figure 1.5 shows a typical specialty store management career path. Note that this career path does not lead to a buying position, which may be an option in department stores. As shown, a typical promotion for a specialty store manager would be to that of district or regional manager, which would involve overseeing the growth operations for several stores in a given area.

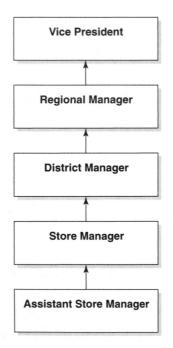

FIGURE 1.5   Typical Specialty Store Management Career Path

Buying Office

Many merchandising students aspire to become buyers. This rewarding, yet demanding, career choice is not an entry-level position. The role of a buyer is key to the success of a retailer, and the buyer's judgment is constantly scrutinized as each season progresses. The buyer uses forecasting ability and analyzes trends to produce an assortment of merchandise that appeals to the targeted market of the store. With advances in technology and an increased emphasis on private label merchandise, the buyer's responsibilities continue to evolve. Although many buyers today still buy merchandise from well-recognized name-brand manufacturers, many also find themselves involved in the product design and development of the retailer's exclusive private label merchandise. Professional skills that are absolutely essential for buyers include negotiation, organization, analysis, and a strong math aptitude. Two of the more traditional and common entry-level opportunities that lead to a career as a buyer are those of an allocation analyst or planner or an assistant buyer.

ALLOCATION ANALYST OR PLANNER. This position is commonly the starting point for a career in buying. The primary purpose of an allocation analyst, or a planner, as this position may also be titled, is to control inventories and allocations for a particular department or classification of products. The goal of the allocation analyst is to ensure that inventory at the retail level meets customer demands in order for the company to meet sales and profit plans. Primary responsibilities for the allocator include developing and reviewing actual and forecasted sales to determine distribution models, timing and quantities of purchases, and initial inventory demand quantities. The allocation analyst or planner continually reviews data generated at the retail level to identify specific market segments and store needs, which will drive distribution orders. It is the analyst who ensures that items are shipped at the right time, in the right quantity, and in the right assortment. Related responsibilities include analyzing and reporting on test merchandise and promotional activities, preparing store assortment plans based on trends, reviewing sales projections to determine merchandise flow through the company distribution center, and moving merchandise between stores as needed to meet customer demand. The allocation analyst must possess strong organizational and communication skills because he or she maintains effective documented communication among many areas of the company, including planning, allocation, distribution, buying, and the stores. At the basic level, the allocation analyst's goal is to prevent any out-of-stock situations at the retail level, which is a primary cause of customer dissatisfaction. Chances are that if you have ever gone shopping for a particular item and found that the item you wanted was out-of-stock, the company's allocator or planner is to blame. The *Careers Up Close* profile on page 20 provides a real-world look at the allocation analyst position.

MISSEY HOPKINS

Allocation Analyst

CLAIRE'S ACCESSORIES, INC.

GRADUATED IN 2000 FROM NORTHERN ILLINOIS UNIVERSITY
MAJOR: TEXTILES, APPAREL, AND MERCHANDISING

WHILE A STUDENT, MISSEY HOPKINS GAINED valuable retail experience as a part-time sales associate with Chernin's Shoes. As part of her college requirements, she later completed a visual merchandising internship between her junior and senior years at the corporate headquarters of Claire's Accessories. As a visual assistant, Missey's responsibilities consisted of maintaining the model store at corporate headquarters, pulling markdown merchandise from the stores, and preparing the store planograms. She also frequently visited stores "in the field" to make sure the planogram had been implemented correctly, and to help store personnel with any merchandising problems they might have encountered in doing so.

In considering the value of her internship, Missey states: "My internship was instrumental in helping me choose my career path because I was able to learn about the other career paths offered at the corporate level. After working at the corporate level it opened my eyes to opportunities that I didn't even know existed." Although Missey enjoyed her time as a visual assistant, she realized through networking at the corporate offices that she was more interested in allocation and planning. During her senior year in college, she kept in touch with the human resource director at Claire's and expressed her interest in an entry-level position in allocation. When such a position became available, Missey was thrilled to interview for the job and to have it waiting for her upon graduation.

Missey has recently been promoted to the position of allocation analyst. Her primary responsibilities and duties consist of reporting product demand based on sales, allocating products to maximize sales and turnover opportunities, and developing and reviewing actual and forecasted sales. Based on her observations and reports, she also

Missey states, "My internship was instrumental in helping me choose my career path because I was able to learn about the other career paths offered at the corporate level."

develops allocation models, including the timing for and quantities of purchases, and forecasts preseason demand quantities. While completing these multiple tasks, she must ensure and maintain effective and documented communication between the allocation and planning areas, the buyers, Claire's stores, and the distribution center.

For her current position, in addition to needing great communication and organization skills, Missey states that learning Excel in a college computer class has been a big help to her since the majority of her reports are created as spreadsheets. Also, the Retail Math portion of her Buying class has been invaluable because much of her work is number and formula oriented. For example, she looks at inventory turn, sales, and sell-through percentages on a daily basis in order to effectively allocate merchandise to the stores.

Until she completed her internship, Missey never considered a career in store planning and allocation. However, she is now looking forward to her next promotion, which will be to a senior allocator position. After that, she aspires to become an associate planner and then a planner. If her interests change, Missey also has the option of pursing a buying career. If she so chooses, her next position would be as assistant buyer, followed by associate buyer, and then the position of buyer. (Similar career paths are outlined in Figures 1.3 and 1.6.) Missey's advice to anyone pursuing a career in retailing and apparel merchandising is to learn as much as you can about the different options and career paths that are available and then to follow your dreams!

Typically, as Figure 1.6 illustrates and explains, an allocation analyst can follow one of two career paths: one that leads to store planning, the other that leads to buying.

ASSISTANT BUYER. Assistant buyers are directly responsible to the buyer, and therefore must be familiar with the buyer's role in a given organization. As the title suggests, their primary purpose is to provide assistance to the buyer. Responsibilities of the assistant buyer will most likely include analyzing weekly business reports with the buying team, preparing and expediting purchase orders, competitive shopping, inspecting merchandise for quality, assisting allocators with new merchandise distribution, and sourcing new products. Identification of top-selling items—and items that are not moving is another important task. An assistant buyer communicates with vendors as well as with the buyer and often must serve as mediator between the two. In this capacity the assistant buyer may be required to place reorders of merchandise, negotiate with vendors for price and delivery, confirm orders with vendors, and advise the buyer of any potential problems with the orders. Organization of the buyer's files and knowledge of the buyer's goals are other essential duties required of an assistant buyer. If the development of private label merchandise is involved, the buyer's duties may become more closely aligned with those of a technical designer, which are explained later in this chapter.

When asked about the skills necessary for success in this position, an assistant buyer for a nationwide specialty store chain replied that first and foremost an assistant buyer must possess patience. This is, he claims, because assistant buyers must often calmly communicate with angry or frustrated vendors and buyers. Furthermore, assistant buyers must be able to take criticism well, and to be able to keep calm when things seem to be in crisis. It is important to be adaptable, because one minute you may be assigned one task and two minutes later asked to do something else. Personal qualities that are helpful for assistant buyers include self-confidence, creativity, and an ability to look at problems objectively. Buyers, he continued, must be able to see the needs of the target market and not be swayed by their own taste in apparel: "It might not be your style, but it may suit thousands of people just right!" Figures 1.1, 1.3, and 1.6 provide an overview of buying career paths.

Design and Product Development

With the emergence of private label merchandise in most department and specialty stores, design and product development career opportunities have grown. Merchandise

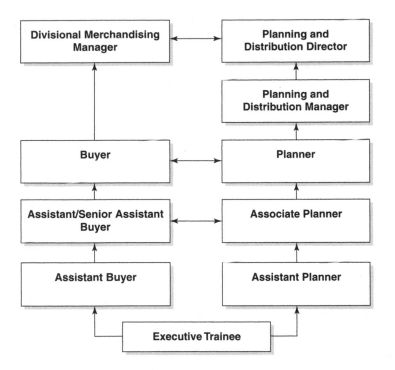

Executive Trainee. The executive trainee position is the entry-level position for assistant buyers and assistant planners. Typically, the trainee will complete a ten to twelve week training program designed to teach him or her about selecting, buying, and assorting merchandise to capture emerging trends. Working directly with buyers, planners, store executives, vendors, and advertising, the trainee will learn how to execute a specific business strategy.

Assistant Planner. This is an entry-level planning position responsible for the execution of a specific business plan. The assistant planner also assists with office management duties.

Associate Planner. Major responsibilities include assisting the planner with a specific area of merchandise. Takes ownership of a specific classification or group of merchandise, overseeing its planning and distribution.

Planner. Based on historical data and forecasting trends, the major responsibility is to develop seasonal plans by store for a specific area of business.

Planning and Distribution Manager. Provides leadership, direction, and support at the merchandise division level. Responsible for appropriately planning, distributing and monitoring inventory level, by location, to ensure the maximization of sales, turnover, and profitability.

Planning and Distribution Director. Supervises the management of merchandise at the location level to maximize and achieve financial objectives and profitability for specific area of business.

Assistant Buyer. This is an entry-level buying position responsible for the execution of a specific business plan. The assistant buyer assists with product assortment, pricing and merchandising strategies, analysis of business trends and opportunities that could improve merchandising strategies, and office management duties.

Associate/Senior Buyer. Major responsibilities include assisting the buyer with a specific classification of merchandise and taking ownership of it. Manages the processes needed to achieve sales and margin objectives for that classification.

Buyer. The buyer is responsible for maximizing sales and profitability for a set area of business. Develops and implements the business strategy including analysis and reaction to sales trends. The buyer also provides overall support for the company's sales, turnover objectives, and gross margin.

Divisional Merchandise Manager. Supervises the execution of merchandise selection and procurement for a specific family of business. Also sets the strategy for profitability, marketing, and overall business performance while ensuring that the product mix meets, and exceeds, customers' expectations.

FIGURE 1.6   Typical Planning/Buying Career Path at a Corporate Office. Adapted from www.macysjobs.com.

that traditionally had been designed and then produced exclusively by manufacturing companies is now often influenced and developed for the specific needs of retailers. Although designing in the traditional sense is a popular and feasible career option, many retailers offer opportunities for design-oriented employees to work directly with manufacturers to produce unique and cost-effective private label merchandise. Typical entry-level positions in design and product development include those of technical designer and quality assurance assistant.

TECHNICAL DESIGNER. The technical designer is the person who takes the designer's idea and translates it into the actual product. A primary responsibility in doing so is ensuring that the product can be manufactured efficiently and within a particular budget. Because the cost of making the product determines the retail price, technical designers need to know how much their particular customers are willing to pay, and whether that price will be enough for the retailer to make a profit. The technical designer helps develop a prototype for which subsequent products are made and, at the entry-level position as an assistant to the technical designer, your training would be multifaceted. For example, in the apparel industry, this would involve learning about fabrics and findings, fitting techniques, pattern making, garment construction, sizing, specification writing, and computer applications. Once promoted to a technical designer, your primary responsibility would be the development of a particular category of clothing, such as ladies' knit shirts or men's sport jackets. Technical designers are found at recognized brand-name manufacturers (e.g., Levi's) as well as major retailers, where they develop private label merchandise (e.g., Sonoma for Kohl's). According to the Web site *www.wetfeet.com*, buyers who have product development and private label experience will be one in a position for which demand will grow. The *Careeers Up Close* profile on page 25 provides an overview of the position of technical design assistant.

QUALITY ASSURANCE ASSISTANT. With the vast assortment of merchandise being produced for retailers all over the world, quality assurance is an important issue. Customers expect that merchandise they purchase will hold up to normal use and will perform as expected. Retailers and product developers, therefore, must implement quality assurance programs to reduce the chances of having large amounts of merchandise returned due to shoddy manufacture. Quality assurance personnel work to guarantee the quality of the goods their firms produce. Working in a laboratory setting, their responsibilities include verifying dimensions, color, weight, texture, strength, or other physical characteristics of their products.

BRAD THOMAS
Design Assistant–Reaction Ladies
KENNETH COLE PRODUCTIONS
GRADUATED IN **2003** FROM OHIO UNIVERSITY
MAJOR: RETAIL MERCHANDISING

BRAD THOMAS CURRENTLY WORKS AS A DESIGN
assistant for Kenneth Cole Productions. He has held this title for about five months. After
earning a Bachelor of Science degree with a major in Retail Merchandising and a minor
in Business Administration, Brad entered the company as an intern. When he graduated,
Brad observed that the job market was "not the greatest," so he took a gamble on an
unpaid postgraduate internship with Kenneth Cole Productions. Brad reflects that he
knew Kenneth Cole Productions hired many of their interns, so he relocated to New York
City and put his time and effort into an internship position. Brad's gamble—paired with
hard work, determination, and appropriate career skills—paid off, and he was eventually offered a permanent position. He knew that he needed to venture out beyond his
hometown to obtain a career position that fit his goals, so he took a risk and headed to
New York City to begin his career.

In his position with Kenneth Cole Productions, Brad believes that classes such as
Professional Development, Design and Illustration, Color Theory, Textiles, Retail
Math, Strategic Merchandise Planning, and his internship best prepared him for his daily
responsibilities. He notes that personal characteristics that helped him obtain his career
position were a determination to follow through on his personal goals and a lack of fear
about the unknown.

Reflecting on the aspects of his job that he really enjoys, Brad notes that he has a
wide range of responsibilities and that he does not do the same things over and over. His
biggest responsibility is dealing with the entire confirmation sample process. The purpose of confirmation samples is to check all colors and styles of a certain product for
aesthetics standards (material, color, construction, etc.) before it goes into mass

Brad advises, "Stay true to yourself and follow your dreams."

production. So Brad needs to make sure that Kenneth Cole Productions receives these samples in time to approve them, or to have revisions done and not delay delivery to their customers. In addition, Brad assists with most aspects of the design process, such as trend forecasting, producing color palettes, and developing sales and production specs. He also acts as a liaison among the sales team, design team, and overseas factories. Brad notes that communication is extremely important—especially the challenge of a language barrier when dealing with overseas constituents.

Brad advises retailing and apparel merchandising students to "stay true to yourself and follow your dreams." Brad notes that he switched majors during his junior year and consequently had to stay in school a little over five years. In his own words, "I do not regret a thing because I was very unhappy in my previous major and would not have found a career that made me happy. It was a dream of mine to work with a major fashion company in New York City, so I did what I had to do to make that happen. I was also very lucky to have a great friend in the company who really went out of her way to help me out, which is why you should always try and network as much as possible."

Soft goods must be tested to determine whether they will shrink or fall apart in the wash, and whether they are colorfast. Depending on the product being produced, other tests may include those for flammability, moisture resistance, seam strength, and wrinkle resistance. Often, in addition to the material used for clothing products, a variety of findings—zippers, thread, and buttons—must also be tested. For example, quality assurance may conduct tests to determine what happens to the buttons on a garment after repeated washing and ironing.

One student recalled a quality assurance problem that arose during her internship as a merchandise coordinator. A flannel sleepwear item had been designed with pant legs each of a different fabric. A customer, she noted, returned a pair because one leg had shrunk more than the other. This is a typical quality assurance matter. The challenge for employees of the quality assurance department is to identify and solve problems before the merchandise is distributed for sale in the stores.

The person wishing to work in a quality assurance position should possess knowledge of the performance properties of various fibers and textiles and also have an understanding for garment construction techniques. Attention to detail and good communication skills are of utmost importance, especially when conducting and reporting on product testing.

Promotion

Promotion includes display, store layout, event planning, coordination of merchandise, trend analysis and presentation, and marketing. The goal of the promotional department is to create an environment in which the merchandise is appealing to the customer. Knowledge of the store environment, channels of distribution, and current trends, as well as an ability to construct displays and create interesting space are all important components of effective promotion. A thorough understanding of the store's target market is also essential. Common positions in the promotion area include display and visual merchandising assistant, merchandise coordinator or merchandiser, marketing coordinator, fashion coordinator or director, and stylist.

DISPLAY AND VISUAL MERCHANDISING. Most department stores and specialty stores have a display and visual merchandising division whose employees are responsible for creating the stores' floor plans as well as eye-catching displays that highlight the merchandise. Visual merchandising specialists not only set the entire store image, but they also are responsible for the physical placement of merchandise. How the racks and fixtures in a store are placed has a huge impact on customer traffic flow and the resulting sales. An effective visual merchandiser knows how to place the merchandise to positively influence sales and promotions. Additionally, the merchandising must be done with adherence to regulations such as fire codes and the Americans with Disabilities Act (ADA).

Specialty stores, particularly large chains, typically house their visual merchandising departments within the corporate headquarters. For example, at Claire's Accessories, the visual team plans the merchandising of their stores through the use of a model store replicated at their corporate office. Visual teams are responsible for communicating the stores' merchandising plans via promotional manuals, or planograms, which are distributed to the stores and implemented by the managers and sales associates. A planogram, which can be computer generated or hand drawn, is a visual plan detailing where merchandise is to be placed in each store. Most times it will also outline instructions for building in-store and window displays. Most chain stores implement a uniform planogram in every store to ensure that the store image is maintained no matter which store their customers shop in.

Although creativity is important to this position, there is much more to a visual merchandising job than making the store look nice. As the visual merchandiser, your primary goal is to create appealing displays that will generate sales. To be effective, you should have an understanding of consumer behavior, be familiar with the different floor layouts and traffic patterns, know about various store fixtures and display items, be comfortable working with technology (most planograms are computer generated), and realize the importance of attention to detail. An understanding of the principles and elements of design is also essential. The *Careers Up Close* profile on page 29 provides an overview of this position.

MERCHANDISE COORDINATOR OR MERCHANDISER. A merchandise coordinator, sometimes known as a merchandiser or sales coordinator, is responsible to a particular manufacturing company for ensuring that appropriate merchandising is occurring at the stores where the products are offered. Therefore, this is a somewhat unique position because it provides the opportunity to work with both the retailing and the wholesaling aspects of the industry. Typically a merchandiser services one chain of stores within a particular area (e.g., Marshall Field's stores located in the Chicago-land area). Brands such as Nautica, Polo, Tommy Hilfiger, Nike, and Guess are offered by retailers who have agreed to contract conditions regarding the manner in which the merchandise will be displayed, priced, and promoted. The merchandise coordinator is the liaison between the manufacturing company and the retailer. Merchandise coordinators spend most of their work weeks traveling among the

(continued on page 31)

IMMEDIATELY FOLLOWING HER GRADUATION FROM

Colorado State University, Tracy Poole Tracy worked as a Display Merchandiser for West Marine, a boating retailer located in California that has recently expanded across the nation and increased its merchandise offerings and brand recognition. Tracy was responsible for merchandising products from water skis to motor parts to apparel. The challenge of working with both hard and soft goods appealed to Tracy who created displays, photographed them, and distributed them along with store plans to all West Marine stores. West Marine, at the time rapidly expanding, depended on the visual merchandising department to serve as a new store support system. Twice annually Tracy's department oversaw the new product rollout as the soft goods in the stores were completely re-merchandised.

Tracy recalled, "As a college student I didn't have a clear understanding about opportunities in the retailing and apparel field. Once I got into the corporate environment, it happened that an opportunity came up in visual merchandising." This experience allowed her to consider upward career moves in visual merchandising and buying. Visual merchandising, Tracy asserts, provides a good background for the entire field. "You can see the big picture—working with stores and buyers you see all sides of the industry." Ultimately, Tracy has been able to apply her knowledge of retail operations, visual merchandising, and buying toward an entrepreneurial venture. She owns and operates Cambridge Creek Outfitters, an apparel store located in historic downtown Cambridge, Maryland.

Tracy encourages prospective merchandisers to take advantage of opportunities to make presentations and learn all they can about the industry. She emphasizes that

Tracy asserts, "You can see the big picture—working with stores and buyers you see all sides of the industry."

working in groups and undertaking realistic course projects gave her some hands on experience that has proven valuable. "You can't expect to know everything going into a job," says Tracy, "but I have learned the details as I go, building on my overall industry knowledge gained from courses at Colorado State University."

various retailers who sell their products, communicating the needs and goals of the manufacturer, recruiting sales associates for the designated product areas, instructing them regarding selling strategies and product knowledge, displaying and merchandising the products according to manufacturer's policy, putting stock on the floor, taking inventory, delegating projects and assignments, trouble-shooting, and problem solving as conflicts are anticipated or become apparent. The merchandise coordinator also provides extra sales help when special promotions occur at the store. One of the merchandise coordinator's most important jobs is to make sure the allotted number of square feet assigned to a product is maintained. Competitors are always more than willing to take away floor space if the opportunity presents itself.

Training for this position usually takes place on the job and is provided by a regional merchandise coordinator or the manufacturer's sales representative for the particular store. The entry-level merchandise coordinator may also obtain some product-knowledge training from the manufacturer's showroom. Skills that are particularly important include sales and negotiation, creativity for merchandising and promotion of the merchandise, attention to detail, strong interpersonal and communication skills, self-motivation, and a high level of energy. Typical promotions from this position would be to that of a regional merchandise coordinator or a manufacturer's sales representative. The *Careers Up Close* profile on page 32 provides an overview of this position and its requirements.

MARKETING COORDINATOR. The marketing coordinator ensures that the retailers' advertising and promotion program is developed and implemented at the local and national level. Generally, the marketing coordinator develops advertising campaigns by selecting the media through which the advertising is done, determining the copy, and indicating the frequency of the message. Overall, it is the marketing coordinator's job to create an image for the store that will stimulate business with new and existing customers. Of course, this all has to be done within the department's budget. Thus, the marketing coordinator has to be both creative and analytical. This position also requires a great deal of organization, considering what is involved in implementing the comprehensive marketing strategy. The marketing coordinator may be supervising magazine, newspaper, and television advertising; direct-mail promotions; Web site design and development; and in-store events—all at the same time. Although the marketing coordinator position is not an entry-level job, all retailers, usually at the corporate level, have entry-level marketing positions such as a marketing coordinator assistant or advertising assistant. Other titles for entry-level positions in a marketing department may include assistant copy writer and layout assistant.

EMILY ELLERBROCK KETCH
Sales Coordinator
TOMMY HILFIGER

GRADUATED IN 1995 FROM OHIO UNIVERSITY
MAJOR: FASHION & RETAIL MERCHANDISING

THE SUMMER AFTER HER JUNIOR YEAR IN COLLEGE,

Emily Ellerbrock Ketch completed an internship with a merchandise coordinator for Tommy Hilfiger. This experience gave her a foot in the door with the company, and after graduation the following year, she was offered the position of merchandise coordinator. This position title has since changed to sales coordinator. While a student majoring in Fashion and Retail Merchandising, Emily was unsure of the direction she wanted to take in her career. Following her internship she felt more confident of the opportunities in the field. A trip to the market put "everything into perspective," claims Emily. "The roles of the buyer, sales reps, and merchandisers all came together. I can see now why the buyers want to hear from merchandisers and I better understand the role of each position in the industry." Her primary responsibility as a sales coordinator is to make sure that all areas of Tommy Hilfiger within each store—shoes, men's, and children's—are merchandised correctly. A further responsibility of the sales coordinator is to train the sales associates, who are actually employees of the stores, to achieve the highest sales possible for Tommy Hilfiger. The merchandise coordinator, Emily explains, is the liaison between the company and the store, and serves as the eyes and the ears of the operation. Because she is responsible for a number of stores within a geographic area, Emily travels almost every day and communicates with many people—managers and merchandisers from each store, and her supervisors at Tommy Hilfiger.

A student who interned with Emily recalled her responsibilities as communicator between Tommy Hilfiger and the retailers. "It was important to talk to the sales associates about the merchandise and its standards. We needed to let them know how important it was to merchandise the clothing a certain way, especially since we could not

According to Emily, networking is a key strategy in career development: "talk to as many people as you can to find out about opportunities," she advises.

be there every day. For example, many of Tommy's clothes include a great deal of detail. It may appear on the back, front, or sleeve. In order for customers to recognize the name wherever the details were, the clothing needs to be hung or folded a certain way. If the details are on the back of a shirt, the shirt needs to be either hung or folded backwards. If the name was down the sleeve, the merchandise had to be hung sideways so customers could recognize it from a distance. We would convey this message to the sales associates, department managers, and the store manager so when merchandise arrived in the store, the associates would know how to merchandise and place the clothing where it could be seen."

Emily advises prospective merchandisers to pay attention in the Retail Math course. As a sales coordinator, she recognizes the value of understanding the calculations performed by buyers, and she believes that experience in buying would be helpful for her position. A course in negotiating proved helpful to her career, as cordial relationships with store and department managers enhance the negotiated position of Hilfiger merchandise. Emily has recently been promoted to an area of larger volume stores. The next career step for Emily will be either to the position of regional coordinator, responsible for supervising 10 to 18 merchandise coordinators, or to a wholesale manufacturer sales representative position. According to Emily, networking is a key strategy in career development: "talk to as many people as you can to find out about opportunities," she advises.

In addition to a retailing or apparel merchandising degree, those interested in this area may consider a minor or a double major in one of the following fields: marketing, advertising, or journalism.

FASHION DIRECTOR. Large companies with a fashion-forward image often have a fashion office that is overseen by the fashion director. Merchandise marts and many consumer magazines also have fashion offices run by a director. Buyers look to the fashion office for advice on product trends. Store image is shaped and tweaked in the fashion office. Fashion information is collected, compiled, and disseminated through the fashion office. The fashion director oversees the entire process of trend identification and promotion. It is the responsibility of the fashion director to coordinate store presentation, advertising, catalogs, and Web site messages so that the company is effectively promoting its image and communicating a consistent fashion message. Knowledge of world events, factors that affect the economy and fashion trends, and a willingness to travel the world to identify emerging fashion trends, as well as an understanding of the history of fashion and its influences on the future, are essential for success as a fashion director.

Although this is not an entry-level position, individuals with a keen interest in fashion trends, strong leadership, superb communication skills, and an ability to multitask may aspire to the position of fashion director. The assistant fashion director and others who report to the fashion director are responsible for analyzing and presenting trends that will be promoted within their companies. Amy Herriot, assistant fashion director for AmericasMart Atlanta, has among her career duties coordinating and producing all fashion-related events held at AmericasMart, including the women's, children's, and men's apparel market fashion shows. She also serves as a booking agent for runway and showroom models. In addition, Amy is highly involved with many colleges and universities in regard to internship programs and experience-related opportunities at the Mart.

STYLIST. Did you ever wonder who dresses the actors on your favorite television show or the characters in commercials? Have you thought it would be exciting to select clothing for a movie star—or perhaps the news anchor at a local television station? The role of a stylist is to do just that.

Typically a stylist is self-employed as a freelance agent. Producers in the movie, television, or advertising industries hire stylists to select clothing—and in some cases build costumes—for the characters in their productions. Good listening skills are essential as stylists work with producers and directors to create the right "look" for each part in the production. Knowledge of fashion trends, both current and historic, is important so that the look that is created fits the setting that is being created. Stylists and their assistants put in long days and must demonstrate high energy levels, excellent customer service and communication skills, and extraordinary patience as directors make changes and production plans evolve. Successful stylists have regular clients and impressive networks of industry contacts. They also have a lot of work and are generally looking to hire assistants who are interested in learning the business and contributing to the projects at hand. The best way for aspiring stylists to break into the industry is to seek an internship or work experience with an established stylist.

While studying at the American Intercontinental University in London, Karen Davies had the opportunity to work with stylist Robin Dutt. Dutt has been featured in magazines and on television, and has authored *Gilbert and George: Obsessions and Compulsions*, published by Wilson Philip Publishers, Limited. To prepare the students in Davies' class for work as stylists, Dutt directed them into teams that prepared models for photo shoots focused on particular topics and themes. To prepare for the photo shoots, the student teams brought "tear sheets," or magazine cut-outs, with ideas for a shoot and they discussed the "look" they wanted to play on or achieve while in the studio. In addition, they visited museums and art galleries for inspiration. They brought items they owned, or purchased suitable items at vintage markets such as the Portabello market. At the studio, they brought everything they had collected together and set up the entire shot, including the selection of lighting and props. These activities reflect the procedures that stylists follow as they work with clients. As a result of her experiences with Robin Dutt, Karen Davies was able to compile a portfolio that portrays the photo shoots her class presented as well as her own contributions to the presentations. Karen plans to return to London, armed with experience and industry contacts, to pursue a career as a stylist.

Successful stylists typically begin their careers in this manner. Contacts within the advertising, television, movie, and fashion industries are essential for stylists to secure work. Referrals from professionals already active in the industry who are familiar with your abilities and work ethic are equally important for securing projects. Creative problem solving and strong communication skills will enhance your probability of success as a stylist.

GETTING STARTED

Although the entry-level job opportunities and the career paths described in this chapter are the more common ones, they are by no means all-inclusive. Rather, they are meant to spark your interest so that you will be motivated to learn more about these and other opportunities that are available. You can get started by working through the activities in this textbook, which include speaking with professionals, networking at career fairs, resume writing, and exploring internship and work opportunities. In completing these activities, regardless of your particular career interests at present, remember to keep an open mind to the professional opportunities that await you. Soon you will find your niche and be headed toward an exciting and rewarding retail merchandising career!

PROJECTS

1. You want to find a career that is best suited to you. Toward that end, you are trying to find out what *that* career feels like and what the job entails. One way to go about it is by doing what's known as an informational interview. Here's how it works:

   a. Identify at least two people in your locality who actually do the work in which you are interested. If you do not know of anyone, ask your friends, neighbors, fellow classmates, parents, and professors for their help in identifying someone.

   b. Call or e-mail the persons you identify to ask for an appointment with them. Ask for only ten minutes of their time and be sure to stick to that time limit once you meet.

   c. At your meeting, ask the following questions:
      • How did you get started in this work?
      • What do you like the most about it?
      • What do you like the least about it?
      • Where else can I find people who do this kind of work? (You should always ask them for more than one name, so that if you run into a dead end at any point, you can easily visit the other people they suggested.) If it becomes apparent to you, during the course of this ten-minute visit, that this career, occupation, or job definitely *doesn't* fit you, then the last question can be turned into a slightly different query: Do you know anyone else I could meet with to discuss my skills and interests (favorite subjects), so I can find out what other careers they might point to? If they can't think of anyone, ask them if they know anyone who *might* know. Then go visit the people whose names they give you.

  d. Write a thank-you note or letter to the persons you interviewed.

  e. Upon completion of your informational interviews, prepare a separate report for each. Include the following information: name of person interviewed, position, company or organization, and his or her responses to the interview questions. Also provide a summary of your reaction to the information you collected in each of the interviews, including why this does or does not sounds like a position suited to you.

2. Identify an entry-level position that you find interesting and would perhaps like to pursue. Prepare a three- to five-page report about the position, including a summary of the responsibilities of the position, specific companies offering such a position, the skills needed for success, and your qualifications for such a position. If you currently do not have the needed skills or qualifications, provide a brief discussion as to what you can do while a student to develop these skills prior to graduation. You should also include in the report a flowchart illustrating the typical career path based on the entry-level position.

QUESTIONS FOR DISCUSSION

1. What positions do you find especially interesting? Why? How could you find out more information about them?

2. Are there particular positions that you would not like? Explain why.

3. Pick three of the entry-level positions discussed in the chapter. What are five skills, or personal characteristics, that you think would be especially important for those positions? Why would they be important?

4. What are five required courses in your major, and how will they be important to a retail-merchandising career?

5. Based on the career paths, can you identify particular advantages of working for a department store rather than a specialty store?

6. What are some other areas in retail merchandising that you would like to know more about? How could you find out about them?

7. What are some specific stores that you would like to work for? Why are you interested in them?

ELECTRONIC ACTIVITIES

Refer to the accompanying CD-ROM. The key elements are:

1. Summary of Chapter 1 text

2. Informational interview activity

   a. Initial contact letter

   b. Informational interview question form

   c. Informational interview report form

   d. Thank you letter template

3. Career path links

REFERENCES

Diamond, J., & Pintel, G. (1996). *Retailing* (6th ed.), Upper Saddle River, NJ: Prentice-Hall.

Polpogian, L. (2003). *Retailing principles: A global outlook.* New York: Fairchild Publications, Inc.

Retail: Career futures with promise (2002, January). In: *Careers in retailing.* New York: DSN Retailing Today, pp. 4, 6–7.

Store management. (n.d.). [On-line]. Retrieved March 15, 2002 from http://www.saksincorporated.com/careers/storemanagement.html.

U.S. Department of Commerce, Economic and Statistics Administration, Bureau of U.S. Census. (2002, May). *Annual benchmark report for retail trade and food services: January 1992 through March 2002,* Table 2, Estimated Annual Retail and Food Services Sales by Kinds of Business: 1992 through 2001. Washington, DC: Author.

CHAPTER TWO

PREPARING TO BECOME A PROFESSIONAL

Be willing to work hard, do what you do well, volunteer, and give more than 100 percent!
—JODIE TUCHMAN, SALES ASSOCIATE, H. STERN

OBJECTIVES

- To identify the personal qualities of a professional.

- To evaluate one's own personal qualities with respect to professional standards.

- To set goals, both personally and professionally.

- To recognize and practice appropriate behaviors in professional situations.

- To learn to adapt to various situations as they are presented in professional settings.

- To establish a plan to practice professionalism.

- To identify specific professional skills necessary for success in the broad retail industry, particularly in the areas of retailing, apparel merchandising, selling, and product design careers.

- To explore the relationship between essential professional skills and specific professional positions in the retail, apparel merchandising, and design complex.

- To identify a plan for obtaining an entry-level position leading to a successful career.

- To understand productivity factors for professionals in retailing, apparel merchandising, selling, and product design careers.

DEVELOPING A PROFESSIONAL PROFILE

As a college student you are preparing for a fulfilling and satisfying career, full of exciting employment opportunities. As a future professional, you are wise to develop yourself both personally and professionally, as well as academically. The transition from full-time student to career-track professional is significant and challenging. Preparing to make this transition will position you well to accept the challenges and opportunities that await you.

Professionalism—a word that describes the personal behaviors, standards, knowledge, and presentation of a person who has an identified role within an organization—is usually associated with a career position. A professional seeks employment as a career, with expectations of gaining experiences that contribute to advancements and greater responsibilities. Furthermore, professionals expect to find personal satisfaction throughout their careers.

When seeking employment, particularly at the entry level, aspiring professionals should be conscious of the value of the experiences that they will encounter. There is no substitute for experience, particularly in an industry as dynamic as the retailing and apparel merchandising complex. Whether aspirations are toward product development, sales, merchandising, manufacturing, or management, experience in as many facets of the industry as possible not only will increase your knowledge of the interdependence of the industry, but also will provide the advantage of learning first hand about career possibilities that you might not otherwise have considered.

Professionals, according to *Webster's Dictionary*, are "engaged in, or worthy of the high standards of a professional." Drawing upon this generic definition, the following section explores several criteria that contribute to professionalism. Box 2.1 highlights ten behaviors that exemplify professional actions and attitudes.

Body of Knowledge

Professionals have developed skills and expertise that allow them to show leadership in their organizations and make their own advancement in the industries where they work. As a future professional, you are acquiring skills and knowledge that contribute to your mastery of the retailing and apparel merchandising disciplines. Knowledge of retailing principles, textiles, manufacturing processes, merchandising mathematics, promotional strategies, and so on, prepares you to interact successfully in the merchandising industry. Although basic knowledge of these and related areas positions you to embark on a career in this industry, advanced knowledge that comes with experience will enable you to grow in your career and accept greater responsibilities as time goes on. The knowledge that you gain academically, as evidenced by an earned degree from a college or university, is likely to be viewed by recruiters as an "entry ticket" to your life-long career.

BOX 2.1

INVESTOR'S BUSINESS DAILY'S TEN SECRETS TO SUCCESS

1. **How you think is everything.** Always be positive. Think success, not failure. Beware of a negative environment.

2. **Decide upon your true dreams and goals.** Write down your specific goals and develop a plan to reach them.

3. **Take action.** Goals are nothing without action. Don't be afraid to get started now. Just do it.

4. **Never stop learning: Go back to school or read books.** Get training and acquire skills.

5. **Be persistent and work hard.** Success is a marathon, not a sprint. Never give up.

6. **Learn to analyze details.** Get all the facts, all the input. Learn from your mistakes.

7. **Focus your time and money.** Don't let other people or things distract you.

8. **Don't be afraid to innovate; be different.** Following the herd is a sure way to mediocrity.

9. **Deal and communicate with people effectively.** No person is an island. Learn to understand and motivate others.

10. **Be honest and dependable; take responsibility.** Otherwise, Numbers 1–9 won't matter.

Value for Lifelong Learning

We live in a dynamic world. When you leave the academy and embark on a career full-time, the educational process will continue in a new setting. New technologies, new management theories, changes in global environments and attitudes, and corporate restructuring all provide new opportunities for learning. As you progress through your career, you should expect to observe the environments around you, learn about new innovations, and grow in your knowledge and leadership abilities. You should seek opportunities to become educated with respect to cutting-edge technologies, and you should be able to adapt to change as it occurs. Professionals not only anticipate but embrace new opportunities for learning throughout their careers and lives.

Commitment to the Company and the Industry

Loyalty is an important characteristic of a professional. When you make employment decisions, you should be committed to that organization. Although it is expected that you will seek additional employment opportunities in the future, you should exercise discretion regarding the commitment you have to your current employer. In fact, your loyalty to a current employer is likely to be evaluated by future employers as you pursue career advances.

Personal Contribution to the Field

Mentoring is a way of giving back—to the profession, the industry, your alma mater, and those who aspire to reach the goals that you have already achieved. You are likely to have many mentors who guide your professional development and, in turn, you should plan to provide mentorship to others when you have reached a certain level of professional status. In fact, as an upper-class student, you may have multiple opportunities to be a mentor to students who are less experienced than you. Professionals look for ways to make positive contributions to their companies, the industry as a whole, and aspiring professionals. This process includes contribution in professional organizations, where conveniently, much networking and mentoring occurs. Organizations such as the National Retail Federation, the Fashion Group, and the American Marketing Association provide venues offering leadership and educational seminars. Individual professionals who take advantage of these industry events are afforded great networking and information-gathering opportunities that benefit themselves as well as the companies they represent. Memberships in professional organizations enable you to develop a set of credentials that allow you to give back to your company and to the profession.

Career Advancement

Ambition is a character trait associated with professionalism. As you negotiate growth strategies for your career, you should keep in mind that complementary values such as loyalty, commitment, life-long learning, and knowledge are associated with career advancement. Your ability to set goals will enable you to assess the progress of your career growth. Valuing advancement as opposed to settling for the status quo in a career is a positive reflection of one's professional profile. Career advancement can take many forms. Examples of career advancement include expansion of a sales territory, consistently increasing personal sales and your client base, promotion to a new position, and taking on additional supervisory roles. All of these examples reflect personal improvement, continual progress, and acceptance of new challenges.

QUALITIES FOR SUCCESS

Whether you aspire to enter the retail management, sales, apparel merchandising, product design and development, or promotion and marketing area of retailing, certain key professional skills should be developed as you prepare yourself for a successful career. Developing these skills, and being able to recognize them and to market yourself based on your mastery of them, will serve you well as you seek work experience, an internship, or an entry-level position. Regardless of the particular aspect of the retailing or apparel business that interests you, key personal qualities are essential. These qualities are not exclusive to any one career focus and are certainly applicable to the retailing and apparel merchandising professions. In fact, whatever career ultimately awaits you, these qualities will contribute to success. Future employers expect you to have these qualities and will scrutinize you during the interview process as they seek to recognize them in you. Furthermore, these capabilities will be observed and evaluated as you make your way in an entry-level position. The successful demonstration of these qualities will be instrumental in your career advancement. Box 2.2 lists the top ten qualities that employers seek, as published in the 2004 Job Outlook of the National Association of Colleges and Employers.

Being successful doesn't mean that you will never fail. Most successful leaders can cite numerous failures that have paved their roads to success. H. Lee Scott, president and chief executive officer (CEO) of Wal-Mart Stores, announced at the 2004 National Retail Federation Annual Convention and Expo that "it is more dangerous not to test than to test and fail." He noted that one can never know what opportunities might be missed due to a lack of risk. Being able to recognize "successful failures" is an important process of growth and development. The experiences that come from failed endeavors, and the ability to learn from one's mistakes, are of tremendous value.

BOX 2.2

TOP TEN QUALITIES EMPLOYERS SEEK

1. Communication Skills (verbal and written)

2. Honesty/Integrity

3. Interpersonal Skills (relates well to others)

4. Motivation/Initiative

5. Strong Work Ethic

6. Teamwork Skills (works well with others)

7. Analytical Skills

8. Flexibility/Adaptability

9. Computer Skills

10. Detail-oriented

SOURCE: Reprinted from *2004 Job Outlook*, with permission of the National Association of Colleges and Employers, copyright holder.

Analytical Skills

Analytical skills, which typically relate to your adeptness at manipulating numbers and using formulas, are an important component of your problem-solving ability. Although mathematical acumen and an ability with numbers generally come to mind when analytical skills are mentioned, this concept actually involves much more. Buyers in particular must be skilled at manipulating numbers in order to determine stock levels, reorders, markup on merchandise, and so on. All professionals in retail-related fields need to understand how to calculate the bottom line—that is, profit. Designers and product developers must determine product and materials costs, as well as understand measurements for the products. The technical design field requires careful precision when entering and interpreting computer-generated data. Merchandisers will need to calculate sales per square foot, selling cost percent, and sales increases and decreases from year to year. Managers are responsible for interpreting sales figures for their associates and departments, as well as working with planned sales in their areas.

Managers and sales associates also need to be able to use analytical skills to assess store environments, interpret consumer behaviors, and evaluate promotional strategies. Knowledge of computer applications, such as Excel, that involve creating and using spreadsheets, will enhance your personal marketability. The better you are at math, logical thinking, and data analysis, the more effective you are likely to be as a retailer, merchandiser, or product designer.

Assertiveness

Assertiveness is an asset for many positions in retailing and apparel merchandising. The fast-paced nature of the industry requires that successful professionals speak up and act with confidence. Roles you may hold within the industry may require you to convince others to purchase products or services, or to buy into concepts you have created. You will often have a limited time to make a meaningful or memorable impression. If you don't speak up or state your case with gusto, you may miss the opportunity entirely.

As a retailer, you will represent the company employing you. You must exude confidence in this role. Your body language and verbal behaviors speak volumes about your confidence and assertiveness. Walking and sitting with excellent posture, offering your hand for a handshake when being introduced to people, speaking clearly and in a strong voice when you talk, and simply being willing to speak up when you have an important contribution to make in a meeting or conversation, are all indications of assertiveness. You may need to take control of a situation, offer leadership in a crisis, or communicate at a crucial moment. Assertiveness will enable you to be the person who can handle these tasks.

Willingness to Accept Challenges

When the task-at-hand seems impossible to complete, that is the time to decide you are just the person to see the project through. Kelly Rademacher Schur, who completed an internship with Victoria's Secret, was advised by her supervisor to, "Go in with a positive attitude, be willing to jump into anything, and always give 150 percent." Throughout her internship, Kelly was given opportunities to make decisions that affected 700 stores. She accepted the challenge and emerged from the experience with a high confidence level and a feeling of "I can do this!"

As a new entry-level employee, it can be intimidating to supervise 30 employees, assume responsibility for a multimillion-dollar inventory, or make a trend presentation to the CEO and board of directors. If you establish a track record of accepting challenges—and preparing yourself to reach success—you will be much more comfortable moving into roles of greater responsibility as your career progresses.

Communication

Every successful executive must be able to communicate effectively. This ability includes informal communication with colleagues, written communication, and presentation skills. A terrific idea may never be realized if you are not able to communicate it effectively to the people who are responsible for implementation. Often, you will be the "front person" for the company—the one who interacts with customers, clients, vendors, or manufacturers. The ability to adapt your communication style to best accommodate a given situation will serve you well. Tracy Poole Tracy, former Display Merchandiser for West Marine in Watsonville, California and currently entrepreneur of Cambridge Creek Outfitters in Cambridge, Maryland, emphasizes the importance of making effective presentations. She recalls as an Apparel and Merchandising student at Colorado State University she was often required to deliver presentations as components of course projects. Looking back, she recognizes the value of these presentations and encourages other students to embrace the opportunity to practice presentation skills. She notes that communication skills are used daily on the job.

Not only should you be able to communicate clearly, but you also should remember to keep your communication professional at all times. You are a representative of the company that has hired you, and your actions are a reflection of the company. Customers, clients, account holders, and other acquaintances will base their perceptions of your company on your ability to communicate. Co-workers, too, are influenced by your communication skills. While completing her internship at a corporate headquarters of a large national specialty store, one student observed the importance of professional communication within the company. As an intern who had been advised to be professional at all times, this student was surprised at the lack of professional behavior she saw exhibited at a department meeting. She observed people gossiping about co-workers and carrying on conversations while the speaker was talking. The unprofessional environment left the intern with a poor impression of the company, and the inability of corporate leaders to communicate and model appropriate professional demeanor was likely to negatively influence the morale of their employees. It certainly reduced the level of respect for the organization held by this particular intern.

Whether you are being interviewed, performing your job with colleagues, or working with company clients, your communication style will be evaluated. Gina Basich, key account manager for Lion Brand Yarn Company, notes that in addition to the technical skills you must possess, social skills involving professional, clear, and personable communication are essential. Most young professionals observe that communication is one of the top priorities in any business. On an average day, merchandisers are likely to speak to many different people within the business. These people might include sales reps, buyers, sales associates, department managers, and store managers, as well as customers. The professionalism of your communication abilities will affect your growth in a company and is a highly visible, continually scrutinized component of your professional profile.

Creativity

Design, product development, and merchandising depend on creativity to differentiate one product or store from the next. Creative promotions encourage consumers to take a second look at products and consider purchasing them. Aesthetically pleasing environments enhance the consumer appeal of a store or showroom, brands, and products. Careers in visual display and design require knowledge of design principles and elements, and a particularly good understanding of color theory. Individuals who can "see" products or store layouts in new and exciting ways enable their companies to effectively position themselves within a special niche. Although obvious for visual fields such as merchandising, display, and design, creativity is an important skill for other retailers, too. Merchandising professionals must solve problems creatively in order to keep their customers happy. For example, buyers may not be able to receive orders that they request from vendors, producers may desire an outcome that the stylist cannot build, or customers may not be satisfied with the environment or selection of a given store. As a result, merchandisers must be creative with suggestions for alternative solutions so that the customers, clients, and company being represented all end up satisfied with the business transaction.

Ethics

The topic of ethics is so important to the process of professional development, that we have devoted an entire chapter of this book to it. Employers want to employ people who have values that match those of the company, who will be honest in their dealings both inside the company and with external constituents, and who uphold principles of fairness and trust.

Flexibility

A successful professional must learn to always be willing (and ready) to implement Plan B. In other words, "be" flexible. In a fast-paced, ever-changing working environment, the plan that was set to roll last night is often outdated or inappropriate by morning. This is a fact with which we all must live. People with rigid, unyielding plans will end up watching the world pass them by. Fortunately, people who have a knack for adapting to change will thrive in today's business and creative environments.

Elisha Siepser, merchandise analyst for Lord and Taylor, recalled a situation when, during her internship in the visual merchandising department of DKNY, a window display was planned in which dry cleaning hangers would be the main props. It was Elisha's responsibility to research the availability, cost, and sourcing of the hangers. After learning that a certain minimum order would need to be placed with the hanger supplier—resulting in significantly more cost than was budgeted for the window—the initial window display was scrapped and an alternate display concept was used. The visual design team must be ready with more than one idea and must be flexible to adapt to changing merchandise, availability of props, and evolution of themes that will best fit the store's promotional strategy.

Initiative

Are you a self-starter? Your ability to initiate activities and bring closure to your tasks is valued by employers. Look for tasks that need to be done and volunteer to do them. Step up when opportunities arise. Many of the jobs you take on will not be glamorous, but the initiative you show by doing what needs to be done will be noticed. Darcie Rae, independent broker for Wellspring sales and marketing, cites self-motivation as a key qualification necessary for sales reps. She notes that her boss lives in a different city and couldn't possibly check up on her on a regular basis. Furthermore, as a sales rep, Darcie does not have a time clock that keeps track of her work hours. She must travel extensively and set her own schedule. Therefore, Darcie's success is dependent on her personal initiative.

Leadership

Employers not only expect you to be able to follow directions, they expect you to be able to lead others in the event that you will be giving directions. Effective leadership involves taking initiative, providing motivation to complete tasks, accepting responsibility regardless of the outcome, and rewarding members of your team. Many new college graduates fall short in the area of leadership as they are evaluating their skills and producing their resumes. Don't let this happen to you. Take opportunities to be a leader. Become involved in professional, extracurricular, and academic organizations. Don't be content to simply join organizations, because anyone can become a member. Accept the challenge of holding an office, organizing an event, or implementing a new program. Employers are particularly interested in hearing about leadership skills that you have developed in addition to your academic endeavors.

An important area of leadership that is becoming increasingly important to employers is volunteerism. Make an effort to become involved in your community. Employers want to know what you have done to improve not only your life, but the lives of other people. Most corporations encourage their employees to participate in volunteer activities and will be impressed to know that you have taken the initiative to get involved on your own. There is no better indication of leadership than evidence that you have given of yourself. Volunteering may be just the thing that differentiates you from many other applicants for a position. It says something about your character and work ethic, and indicates an unselfish, team-oriented, outcome-based value system.

There are many books available at bookstores and in libraries that focus on the topic of leadership. Opportunities to learn about leadership and gain experiences in leadership roles are widely available through workshops, college courses, and extracurricular organizations. Take advantage of the resources available to you, and strive to assess your leadership acumen and improve your leadership skills.

Loyalty

Employers desire employees who are trustworthy and loyal. Loyalty involves maintaining confidentiality of records, fairness to clients and constituents, and integrity as you interact with customers and co-workers. A good way to demonstrate loyalty to prospective employers is to choose your words carefully when you speak about former employers. How do you refer to the company or to a former supervisor? Do you speak highly of the opportunities that you were offered there, or are you negative about the experience? Recruiters are likely to assume that the attitudes you develop toward them will be similar to the attitudes you display toward others. Another important way to demonstrate the characteristic of loyalty is through the work that is displayed in your portfolio. Be certain that you exhibit only those examples that are approved for wide distribution. Many company documents are considered secure and privileged information. You need to carefully honor the trust that has been extended to you during work experiences.

Loyalty doesn't necessarily mean that you must make a long-term commitment to work exclusively for a certain company. Loyalty does, however, mean: "Don't burn bridges." Although long-term commitment might be a trait associated with loyalty, you should keep in mind that you can exhibit loyalty even in a short-term professional relationship with a company. You can do this by exercising discretion, being honest about your plans for the future and your goals for the present, and maintaining confidentiality of records whenever appropriate. If you part ways with a company, leave on good terms, issue your resignation with plenty of notice, and behave professionally through your very last day of work. Familiarize yourself with the expectations of your company, and be aware of practices in which you can engage, that demonstrate loyalty.

Negotiation

Related to communication, successful negotiation skills lead to a win-win situation when resolving conflict and making decisions affecting your company. Successful negotiation requires that you know the facts, the position of your company, and the bottom line concerning terms you have the authority to agree to or approve. Win-win negotiating requires that you consider the needs of those with whom you are negotiating and may require that you compromise occasionally, and generate creative solutions often. Good listening skills, creative problem solving, and an ability to anticipate alternate outcomes all contribute to successful negotiation skills.

Generally, the process of buying comes to mind when mentioning negotiation skills. Although buyers and sales representatives need to be particularly skilled at negotiating, other retail-oriented professionals negotiate as well. Emily Ellerbrock Ketch, sales coordinator for Tommy Hilfiger, regularly negotiates space. As a merchandiser, she is responsible for positioning her company's merchandise in the best possible location in each store. She must convince store managers and buyers that her merchandise needs the space she desires, and negotiations must be effective because a cordial relationship between her company and the store is essential.

Organization

Recruiters and human resource managers continually link the success (or failure) of employees to organizational skills. In the fast moving, ever-changing field of retailing and apparel merchandising, professionals must develop a "sense of urgency" and organize their daily schedules accordingly. Most successful young professionals cite good organization as a top priority contributing to their effectiveness on the job. Not only must you be able to organize your tasks, you must appropriately prioritize them.

A popular interview technique involves an in-basket exercise in which the interviewee is asked to assess the items in the in-basket and prioritize them according to their urgency. Are you confident in your ability to prioritize effectively? If not, begin now to practice this important skill.

If learning to be organized is a challenge for you, there are numerous strategies that you can develop to improve your organization. One effective practice is to carry a small notebook or personal digital assistant (PDA) with you and use it to record important information. Keeping a record of what needs to be done, and often how to do it, will provide a point of reference, enabling you to record your progress as well as serving as a reminder that you need to stay on task. A student who completed an internship in the corporate office of a large apparel retailer reflected upon the completion of her experience that the notebook she used throughout her internship was her most valuable resource every day. She knew that she would be overwhelmed with all of the details and new information for which she would be responsible, and she did not want to overburden her supervisor and co-workers with repetitive questions. So, she wrote notes about everything in her notebook. She found this tool to be infinitely valuable in keeping her organized, and she recognized the added benefit of having a detailed log of her work. She had information—and often answers—right at her fingertips.

Darcie Rae advocates using a planner to keep organized. She stresses the importance of documenting everything—from phone calls and shipment dates to important details about each account and buyer. In sales, Darcie notes that she has a responsibility to follow through with all obligations that she has made. In order to do this, it is essential to write information down.

Physical and Emotional Fitness

Stamina is essential for a successful career in retailing, merchandising, and design! As with most exciting professions, you will periodically work long hours and need to be able to handle a fairly heavy dose of stress. Many people thrive in a physically and emotionally demanding environment. Preparing for a week of work is accurately compared to training for an athletic event—or at least getting fit. Full working days can be tiring, and you may find that the first several weeks of a full-time job or an internship are exhausting. Be prepared for this, and recognize that you may need additional physical "training."

An exciting career can also be emotionally demanding. Your ability to handle stress will directly affect your emotional and physical fitness for any job. The adage "don't bring your problems to work" truly applies to the retailing and apparel merchandising.

It is important for you to anticipate the stress that is likely to come with a full-time work experience. The change from being a full-time student to a full-time professional employee is significant. You will face more structure throughout your day and increased responsibilities, particularly involving supervision of other people. These changes are often accompanied by geographic moves and shifts in your support network. Anticipation of these major life changes should allow you to introduce coping mechanisms that will help you adjust to the career phase of your life.

Planning and Execution

Are you able to conceive of an idea, plan for its implementation, and then carry it out? This process of planning and execution will serve you well as you enter the professional arena and are required to identify or troubleshoot problems, generate workable solutions, and ultimately solve existing problems. Many of the projects that you complete as a college student will require these abilities. As you complete such projects, document the strategies you have identified that contribute to your ability to plan and execute. These opportunities will serve you well as you seek to relay evidence to prospective employers that you posses such skills.

Willingness to Relocate

Many opportunities for advancement depend on location and ability to relocate. Being willing to live in new geographic areas will open possibilities for your career growth that are not possible if you are geographically limited. Certain locations have an abundance of career opportunities in a variety of retailing and apparel merchandising niches. New York City, Chicago, Los Angeles, Dallas, and Atlanta are cities in which career positions from stylist to buyer to showroom sales abound. Many more opportunities for career growth and variety can be found in a large city than in a small town. Although opportunities exist in the retailing and apparel merchandising industry in virtually every location on the globe, the scope of opportunities changes with respect to the geographic location. Furthermore, the specific company you are working for may limit your geographic choices. Wal-Mart's corporate office is in Bentonville, Arkansas; The Target Corporation is headquartered in Minneapolis, Minnesota; the J. C. Penney Company corporate office is in Plano, Texas; and offices of The Limited Brands are in Columbus, Ohio. Specific corporate office positions will require that you live within commuting distance from the office sites.

Selling Ability

In a retailing or apparel merchandising career, you may be required to sell a product, sell an idea, or, in the case of an interview, sell yourself. Successful selling ability may be the single most important professional skill, at least for getting your foot in the door.

Retailing is the level at which products and consumers meet. When retailing is successful, products are sold to consumers. Product designers and merchandisers, as well as retailers, must be able to recognize how to sell their products. Future executives need to be able to sell. Sales will take place at every corporate level and in every company division in some form. Designers and product developers must sell the production team on their ideas, sales representatives must persistently appeal to buyers as they compete with other labels for store space, buyers must convince managers that merchandise is exciting and salable, visual merchandisers use displays to enhance and encourage sales, and so on.

As a sales rep, Darcie Rae emphasizes the importance of product knowledge to effective selling. From the ingredients in the health food products she sells to both wholesale and retail pricing, to current specials offered by the manufacturer, Darcie's credibility as a salesperson—and ultimately her success in her career—depend on her product knowledge. In addition to product knowledge, Darcie must cultivate personal relationships with each of her clients. People skills, according to Darcie, are absolutely crucial to effective selling. She notes that "people buy from people they like," so she makes an effort to learn about her clients and show attention to detail regarding their preferences. Darcie identifies several key strategies that improve selling skills. First, she practices the ABCs of business—"Always Be Closing!" She observes that closing the sale in outside sales is different from a store close, because the outside sales close takes more initiative on her part. Second, upselling is another great skill to acquire. For example, if a store client currently carries only one or two SKUs (stock-keeping units) from Darcie's line, she makes an effort to get the top selling items into that store. Third, patience is important in selling. Darcie has observed that it takes some people a while to warm up to a new salespeson, so don't give up! Finally, always assume the sale. Darcie advocates talking to buyers as if they are already going to bring the product into their stores.

Experience in sales is essential to success in any aspect of this business. Future professionals should seek opportunities to develop and refine selling skills. Selling merchandise directly to customers is an excellent way to enhance communication skills and to gain an understanding of retailers, corporate structure, the retail calendar, and other professional positions available within the company.

An abundance of sales opportunities exists. Check the classified advertisements in your local paper, the signs posted in many retail establishments, and the Web sites of retailers. Many positions are available for part-time employment and for summer and holiday breaks (which are great opportunities for students). Keep in mind that a sales associate's primary role is to offer service to the retailer's customers. Customers will appreciate friendly store employees who can communicate with them by acknowledging their presence in the store, providing accurate and informative information about the products, offering suggestions to the customer and coordinating merchandise items. Knowledge of this ultimate goal for all products—sales—will enhance your ability to design, produce, promote, and buy. Sam Walton (1992), founder of Wal-Mart Stores promoted his customer-oriented philosophy in his book *Sam Walton, Made in America* (1992). According to Walton, the customer is the boss in a retail operation, and giving the customer what he or she wants is the key to success in a retail operation. Mr. Walton effectively argued that everyone involved in the retail operation must understand the importance of the interaction with the customer.

Problem-Solving Ability

Overall, retailers are looking for employees who can solve problems. Whether the quality is expressed as analytical ability, effective teamwork, or innovative and creative thinking, the bottom line is that a successful employee must be able to solve problems. In retailing and apparel merchandising careers, problems occur every day. Each day's problems are different, requiring unique and creative solutions. Problems range from dealing with difficult customers, to determining how to increase sales, to dealing with a shipment that has been damaged in transit. What do you do when you can't deliver goods to your customers, or for reasons beyond your control you can't follow through on an agreement with a client? Regardless of the specific solution that you propose, you must solve problems. Effective problem solving develops through experience, teamwork, good listening skills, and knowledge-based competencies. It is important to think reflectively, recognize long-term implications, and communicate ideas when solving problems.

Problems present themselves on a regular basis to stylists in the advertising industry. One stylist in particular has one rule to follow when working with clients, "never tell them no!" You can suggest another idea, but you cannot say "no" when you are working with producers. This is a good rule of thumb for other facets of the retailing and apparel merchandising industry. Problem solving involves creating alternative solutions that meet the needs of your customers or clients, and ideally result in repeat business.

Ability to Work with People from Diverse Populations

In addition to basic communication skills, your comfort level in working with people who are different from you should be high. The retailing, merchandising, and product development complex is a global industry. Workplace environments are composed of individuals from diverse cultural backgrounds and representing various nationalities. Furthermore, today's workplace environments recognize and value the infusion of diversity of race, physical ability, and sexual orientation among their employees. Depending on your own background and life experiences, you have a unique perspective on life, interpersonal relationships, and values. Your ability to approach interpersonal relationships with co-workers, clients, and customers in an open-minded fashion that exhibits respect for others and appreciation of diversity will enhance your career progress in this industry. If you have the opportunity to seek international study or travel, interact with diverse populations, and learn about languages and cultures that are not native to you, you should definitely make an effort to do so. Most colleges and universities offer global diversity–focused courses and international markets courses. These academic offerings can expand your knowledge regarding diverse populations.

In a presentation entitled "Leadership in a World of Extremes" at the 2004 National Retail Federation Convention and Expo, Ming Tsai, global vice president of retail for IBM, cited the trend "Diversity Runs Deeper." He noted that household norms are changing. We no longer expect households to be composed of a mother, father, two children, and a dog. Ethnicity has different meanings today than in the past, and the layers of ethnicity run wider and deeper than ever. Additionally, age is increasingly a diversity factor, with individuals living longer, activities changing throughout active life spans, and market power shifting as baby boomers age and new generations of young people grow up accustomed to affluent lifestyles.

Keep in mind that fashion evolves through a diffusion process. Furthermore, the retailing industry is increasingly global, requiring cross-cultural communication and international trade for optimum productivity and competitive advantage. The greater your knowledge of global issues and your understanding of cultural, racial, physical, and social issues, the better prepared you will be to function successfully in an environment of diverse populations, especially in an industry that thrives on rapid change.

Ability to Work Under Pressure

Retailers often have many important tasks that seem to all need to be completed at once. An ability to develop a sense of urgency means that you can prioritize which tasks must be done right away, which tasks you need to do yourself, and which tasks can be delegated for others to complete—and you can carry those out in a calm and effective manner. Christine Wittenbrink learned the importance of working under pressure while she was an intern at the Fashion Office in AmericasMart, the Apparel Mart in Atlanta, Georgia. Particularly during market weeks, she needed to complete everything that needed to be done in preparation for fashion shows while the environment in which she worked was hectic and people around her were often frantic. Her ability to work under pressure allowed her to take care of the business at hand, complete tasks in a prioritized manner, and present a final product that was an impressive reflection of her professional talents. She notes that one's personality is an important element in this characteristic. An enthusiastic and outgoing individual with a high energy level is best suited to work in an environment that requires working under pressure. In addition, she emphasizes the importance of being able to exert authority when appropriate, delegate work when necessary, and think on your feet when things get hectic.

MAKING THE MOST OF THE QUALITIES YOU POSSESS

You should continually assess your strengths and your experiences so that you can readily identify the qualities that are most characteristic of you. Seek opportunities that will enable you to practice the professional characteristics that you haven't yet fully developed. Note those qualities that are particularly reflective of you, and begin to establish goals for the future that capitalize on your greatest strengths. The more familiar you are with the personal qualities that you possess, the better able you will be to set goals that are realistic for you and that will yield satisfying outcomes as you pursue them.

Identify a mentor who can provide constructive feedback to you as you exercise your talents and skills. Having someone who is more experienced than you, and whom you can trust, to offer advice and to listen to your plans and questions will provide focused opportunities for you to excel in your plans.

SETTING GOALS FOR YOURSELF

Once you have explored work experience opportunities and career options, identified areas of interest to you, and considered your strengths, the practice of setting goals will enable you to maximize your potential. Living without goals is similar to planning a trip without a road map. You are much better able to plan your strategy to reach an end when you have identified where you want to go and how you can go about getting there.

Goal setting often presents itself as an overwhelming task for students, but keep in mind that your goals can, and probably will, change. If you have some idea of what interests you, or of what you think you might like to try, investigate that area. Identify what you like to do and what you don't like to do. Consider how you might implement activities that are enjoyable into your career plans while simultaneously eliminating those you find unpleasant (but keep in mind that all jobs have some distasteful aspects). Plan a strategy for the present. As your goals change and evolve—which they should—modify your strategy. The important thing is to begin with a plan by setting goals. Your life experiences will shape the path of your goal planning, and you should strive to be open-minded with respect to new, previously unearthed possibilities. Regardless of your ultimate career position, clearly established and well-thought-out strategies leading to identified goals will serve as a road map for your climb up the career ladder to success.

Short-Term versus Long-Term Goals

Goal setting should be a continual process. To maintain ongoing progress in personal and professional development, new goals should be identified as other goals are being met. Regardless of the complexity of your goals and the length of time involved in accomplishing them, identifying specific tasks necessary to realize the goals will be helpful in your progress to complete them.

Short-term goals are typically defined as goals that can be realized within one year's time. Some short-term goals, such as completing a term paper, may be accomplished within a matter of weeks. Typical tasks associated with this goal would include conducting research on the topic, developing a thesis for your paper, organizing your thoughts, and producing a series of drafts. Other short-term goals may be more complex, involving a greater number of specific tasks toward their completion. For example, the goal of securing an internship for the summer would likely involve researching a number of opportunities, developing a cover letter and resume, contacting the representatives of potential internship sites, coordinating interviews, waiting for offers, and selecting from among the options that are ultimately presented. Short-term goals are associated with clear timetables and concrete outcomes. If you complete the tasks necessary to meet your short-term goals, the results (completion of the goals) are predictable.

The outcomes associated with long-term goals tend to be more abstract. Long-term goals might be presented for a period of five to ten years, or might be lifetime achievement goals. A long-term goal for today's college student might be to become a buyer or a fashion director. Short-term goals can be set and accomplished in the near future that will position you to make progress toward a long-term goal. For example, academic course choices, summer work experiences, strategic networking opportunities, and information gathering can be strategically directed toward the long-term goal of becoming a fashion director. Many aspects of life are apt to change as the time frame for long-term goals unfold—such as technologies, personal interests and responsibilities, knowledge of career requirements, opportunities, and attitudes toward lifetime priorities. For these reasons, long-term goals should be continually reassessed. It is reasonable to expect that long-term goals will be revised, refined, and restated numerous times. Short-term goals should be set to coincide with progress toward long-term goals.

Goals can be used as conversation points with prospective employers, academic advisors, and mentors. When you interact with others, share your short-term and long-term goals. Simply having such goals demonstrates your initiative and work ethic. Experienced professionals with whom you interact will likely be able to offer helpful advice regarding ways to achieve your goals—and may even suggest additional goals to include in your list. You will also be positioned to determine whether opportunities that are presented to you will be instrumental in helping you achieve your goals. Without goals, it is impossible to assess a given opportunity's merit toward achieving your lifetime ambitions.

Personal versus Professional Goals

Typically, college students are facing major transitions in life. It is likely that you are considering both goals that include extra-curricular and personal interests and professional goals, which are work and career related. Both are important and should be addressed. Eileen McDargh, author of *Work for a Living and Still be Free to Live*, notes that "there is as much 'success' in catching a trout, comforting a friend, or kneeling before whatever Higher Power you profess, as there is in making a killing on Wall Street, heading up a corporation, or closing a crucial sale" (1999, p. 112). McDargh advocates exploring those things that make you feel "alive" with the same passion that you explore those things that make you "successful." In fact, it is counterproductive to work toward a successful career at the expense of one's personal life. A balance between career and personal activities is usually more fulfilling and less stressful than a career-dominated life plan.

PROJECTS

1. Refer to the accompanying CD-ROM for a step-by-step process to analyze your competencies with respect to the qualities for success listed in this chapter. What are your areas of strength? What are your challenges for improvement? How can you capitalize on your strengths? How can you improve your areas of weakness?

2. Set goals (activity and related forms on CD-ROM):

    a. Begin with a self-assessment, or SWOT analysis. SWOT stands for "strengths, weaknesses, opportunities, threats." You should continually evaluate your strengths and weaknesses, and also the opportunities that are available to you and the threats that serve as barriers to your progress.

    b. Ask your instructor, academic advisor, employer, and peers to review your SWOT, and ask for their reactions. Do they agree with your stated assessment? Do they offer a different, yet insightful perspective? Take the opportunity to reflect on the content of the feedback that has been offered to you.

    c. Articulate a set of long-term goals. Include a timeframe within which you will work to accomplish these goals. Consider which short-term goals will be important for you to achieve as you progress toward these long-term goals.

    d. Make a list of short-term goals. Define specific tasks that will enable you to accomplish these short-term goals.

    e. As you continue your academic studies and embark on work experiences, document your achievements and make plans for improvement with respect to your strengths, weaknesses, and progress toward goals.

QUESTIONS FOR DISCUSSION

1. Which professional skills do you demonstrate on a regular basis? Explain how you demonstrate these skills.

2. In evaluating your professional skills, which skills have you best developed? How have you developed these skills? Which skills do you most need to improve? What evidence can you offer that leads you to know that you need improvement? What strategies can you implement to achieve improvement?

3. Identify your ideal work environment. Does this environment have a good fit with any of the career paths described in the previous chapter? What are your top priorities in the environment of your job?

4. As you think ahead toward a work experience, internship, or postgraduation career position, what geographic locations provide the most opportunity for you?

    a. Is geographic location a factor in your career success?

    b. Are you limited by geographic restraints in reaching your career goals? If so, what plans do you have to confront this limitation?

5. How will you combine your personal and professional goals? Are there any conflicts you can identify between these two areas? If so, what are they and how will you deal with them?

6. How do you see loyalty as a factor in your career plans? How will you demonstrate loyalty yet seek new opportunities for career growth?

7. Can you be too flexible? Explain.

ELECTRONIC ACTIVITIES

Refer to the accompanying CD-ROM. The key elements of this chapter are:

1. Summary of Chapter 2 text

2. Personal qualities assessment: This exercise will enable students to match their strengths and interests to specific professional opportunities

3. Goal-setting exercises:

   a. SWOT analysis

   b. Long-term goals

   c. Short-term goals

4. Opportunity Plan "A" (regarding goals)

REFERENCES

McDargh, E. (1999). *Work for a living and still be free to live* (revised ed.). Wilsonville, OR: BookPartners, Inc.

Walton, S. and Huey, J. (1992). *Sam Walton: Made in America: My Story.* New York: Doubleday.

CHAPTER THREE

DEVELOPING YOUR PROFESSIONAL PORTFOLIO

A visually pleasing portfolio generates interest and is a great way to get an employer to be excited to turn the page and ask more questions.
—JODI FOERTSCH, ASSISTANT MERCHANDISER,
POLO RALPH LAUREN

OBJECTIVES

- To identify various types of portfolios used to promote your professional growth and profile.

- To identify appropriate uses of portfolios for personal assessment, career search, and professional advancement.

- To participate in the process of self-assessment using a portfolio.

- To develop a personal, professional portfolio suitable for presentation to employers.

- To initiate an ongoing portfolio development process that will enhance your professional career.

THE PROFESSIONAL PORTFOLIO

A portfolio is an organized collection of documents that provides evidence of personal accomplishments. Traditionally, designers and others whose careers require visual examples have compiled portfolios. Today, most professional people recognize the benefits of portfolio use. Both the process of coordinating the elements comprising the portfolio and the presentation of the portfolio (during an interview or employment review) are important contributors to professional growth. Alyssa Dana Adomaitis, assistant professor of Apparel Merchandising and Management at California State

Polytechnic University, Pomona, advocates that merchandising students use a portfolio to visually communicate their abilities. She notes (2003) that a visual presentation of work increases students' abilities to sell their talents, beyond simply discussing their work. Adomaitis points out that abilities such as organization, management, following directions, and creativity can be illustrated in a portfolio.

Why Create a Portfolio?

As you prepare yourself academically for a career in the retail and apparel merchandising industry, you are amassing excellent examples that you can use to document your skills, knowledge, and personal strengths. Creating a portfolio provides you with a systematic mechanism for evaluating your work. You can identify the specific skills for which your work provides documented examples, such as management, retail math, and trend analysis. Your portfolio can also reflect knowledge that you possess—for instance, with respect to application of color theory, historic dress, and global apparel industries. Personal strengths that can be emphasized in your portfolio might include attention to detail, organization, leadership, and perseverance. Your portfolio allows you to assemble and organize a comprehensive presentation of your professional profile.

In an interview situation, a prospective employer will want to see evidence of an entry-level applicant's success through internships and other practical experience as well as academic course work. A well-planned and neatly presented professional portfolio is a useful vehicle for personal promotion. As you continue to gain experiences and develop professionally, updating the portfolio as well as the resume will be important. The portfolio is, essentially, an expanded resume that provides the documentation for accomplishments you will list on your resume and discuss in interviews. You should review your portfolio regularly and use it as you evaluate your progress toward goals, set new goals, and consider upwardly mobile career moves. In addition, your portfolio can be used for periodic employment evaluations as well as during interviews for new positions. As with any personal accomplishment, the sole person responsible for compiling its documentation is the author—you. You may be the only person who, at a later date, remembers and has evidence of your work. Your portfolio is an ideal way to document your career and academic progress.

We recommend that students begin to develop a portfolio documenting academic and practical experiences and accomplishments early in the collegiate experience. Portfolios are works in progress. It is important that you allow the portfolio to develop by adding new elements and deleting outdated items as progress is made through college and into a career. Initially as you begin your portfolio, include as much information as possible. It is advisable that all projects, papers, exams, and other academic assignments be saved for possible inclusion in a portfolio. As the portfolio develops, it should be streamlined so that it becomes a positive reflection of appropriate elements of your work. From all of the work that you save, you can determine which items to include, and which to leave out.

Types of Portfolios

There are three basic types of portfolios; assessment portfolios, interview enhancement (career search) portfolios, and performance review and evaluation (career enhancement) portfolios. Most students will benefit from preparing both assessment and interview enhancement portfolios. Each of these should be used separately as appropriate. Familiarity with the portfolio development process will enable you to transition your interview enhancement portfolio into a performance review and evaluation portfolio as you embark on your career.

All three types of portfolios may be maintained and presented electronically or in hard-copy form. You may wish to construct both—one portfolio that you can carry with you and use to keep original documents, and another, electronic, version that is available on the World Wide Web or burned to a compact disk. An electronic version allows you to create multiple copies that can be left with the portfolio reviewer. You can even purchase a compact disk that is shaped like a business card—and can be labeled as such. This is an ideal way to promote yourself at career fairs and during the interview process.

ASSESSMENT PORTFOLIOS. Assessment portfolios are compiled primarily to demonstrate growth and accomplishments over a period of time. Students are increasingly required to compile assessment portfolios in their programs of study so that universities can measure the student learning that is taking place (Paulins, 1998; Paulins & Graham, 1999). You may be required to complete an assessment portfolio as a component of your coursework. This is a useful tool for self-evaluation, as well as a collective tool for program faculty to evaluate the progress of their students. Items compiled in an assessment portfolio should be representative of early and later work so that changes in depth of knowledge, application of information or theory, and experience can be demonstrated.

For example, an effective assessment portfolio may contain versions of resumes from sophomore, junior, and senior years, each of which demonstrate growth of experience and improved resume-writing skills. Students may wish to include examples of papers that indicate improved writing ability over time. Illustrations of designs from an introductory class contrasted with a senior project would provide evidence of mastery of skill.

What is the benefit, for students, of compiling an assessment portfolio? Alexis Clinton, an Apparel Merchandising and Management student at California State Polytechnic University, Pomona, has used her portfolio for self-assessment. She acknowledges that her portfolio allows her to look at herself in a "different" light. Her portfolio not only provides immediate access to examples of her best work, but also guides her through the process of evaluating her personal accomplishments. Alexis notes that she is keenly aware that there is always room for improvement. In fact, she states, "The day that you feel your portfolio is done is the day that your self-growth has stopped. Your portfolio should always be something to improve upon and work on." She advises fellow students, "Don't get discouraged when you receive a negative comment about your portfolio. Take constructive criticism as a positive thing that will only help you in the long run."

Although it is true that portfolios used primarily for assessment will not be presented at interviews, you will have the potential to gain a tremendous amount of insight with respect to your personal knowledge through compilation of such a portfolio. The concept of reflection, which is a process of taking the time to review, consider, and evaluate experiences, is key to the benefit of assessment portfolios. The process of compiling past and current documents that represent your learning experiences is a valuable self-reflection tool. Self-reflection is an important exercise prior to presenting yourself in an interview. Interview questions, such as "What did you learn in college?," "What are your most valuable personal skills?," and "Why should I hire you?," will be easier to answer after completing an assessment portfolio.

INTERVIEW ENHANCEMENT PORTFOLIOS. Traditionally, portfolios have been prepared to enhance an interview presentation during a career search. Designers, models, and professionals in other visually oriented career paths have long recognized the advantage of displaying examples of their work. Today it is recognized that virtually all professional people can successfully use a portfolio as an extension of the personal interview. The nature of the retailing and apparel merchandising profession lends itself particularly well to portfolios because so much of the work professionals do involves visual presentation and creativity. The potential is great for successful retailers and apparel merchandisers to present exciting, interesting, and visually appealing work in a professional portfolio.

If a portfolio has been developed for the purpose of interview enhancement, it must be extremely well organized, of a reasonable size, and presented appropriately in the interview. When presenting yourself through a portfolio, only high-quality and error-free work should be included. You want to be careful not to clutter your "message" with extraneous examples. Most interviewers will not want to be handed the portfolio without explanation. You should be prepared to offer specific explanations of work in the portfolio and articulately relate the item to skills needed for the position in question. Students have indicated that with a portfolio in hand, they feel prepared to go through the interview process because the portfolio serves as a starting point for conversations and provides illustrations of their abilities that are applicable to the fashion industry (Adomaitis, 2003). According to Adomaitis, portfolios should be used to showcase your best work. The portfolio serves as a record of your work and can help you prepare for interviews by providing a means of reviewing your work and noting the skills and talents that enabled you to complete that work. During the interview, the career search portfolio can serve as a starting point for conversations about your skills. For example, reviewing a particular document in your portfolio with a prospective employer might lead to a conversation about your problem-solving abilities. Adomaitis encourages students to make portfolios competitive by presenting them well and then being prepared to discuss abilities and document talents in the portfolio.

Jodi Foertsch, a 2003 graduate of Ohio University's Retail Merchandising program, used a portfolio when she interviewed for her position as an assistant merchandiser at Polo Ralph Lauren. Her portfolio illustrated her internship experience, her ability to communicate with vendors, and to complete tasks. When the career offer was made, Jodi was informed that her portfolio gave her the edge over other applicants. Jodi explains that her portfolio gave her prospective employer something to look at that was a "hands-on example of my work experience instead of a verbal explanation." She further notes:

> Interview questions transitioned immediately from those difficult generic interview questions to questions about things I had in my portfolio. This made the interview easier for me because I was easily able to talk about anything and everything in that portfolio. I believe this creates a more relaxed interview for the interviewer as well because he or she is able to break away from questions on a piece of paper—and actually get a chance to engage in a more conversational type of interview.

PERFORMANCE REVIEW AND EVALUATION PORTFOLIOS. Similar to an interview enhancement portfolio, an updated portfolio can and should be used for periodic evaluations with your supervisor. As you take on new responsibilities and gain new skills and knowledge, you should maintain the process of portfolio development. Your interview enhancement portfolio can transition into a portfolio that can be used to document specific work you have accomplished in your career. When it is time for performance review and evaluation, the use of a portfolio that served you well when interviewing will again give you an edge in documenting your career performance. It is unlikely that anyone other than you will note each of the specific contributions that you make to the company in your career position. Your ability to organize your accomplishments, illustrate them in your portfolio, and present them to your supervisor will reflect the level of commitment you have to your career growth. Your ability to identify your accomplishments will demonstrate to a prospective supervisor an affinity for self-analysis and improvement. Box 3.1 offers a list of guidelines for portfolio development.

BOX 3.1

GUIDELINES FOR PORTFOLIO CONSTRUCTION

- Make the initial investment in a high-quality portfolio case. Opt for real leather over imitation. Look at artists' portfolios, such as those used by photographers.
- Search for professional-looking acetate sleeve covers to protect the pages. Those without printing (such as manufacturer's information) and with smooth edges (that don't show the manufacturing process, such as heat sealing) are preferable.
- Avoid using standard, office-type dividers or anything that makes your portfolio look like a book report.
- The layout of your portfolio should be consistent to provide a good flow between sections.
- You may want to consider a title page dividing each section that *briefly* describes the project or assignment.
- Don't be afraid to add a simple graphic element to improve the continuity of your portfolio, but make sure that it doesn't overpower the material itself.
- Minimal uses of color or special papers are acceptable; you can tie those elements in with the color and style of your portfolio.
- Be sure that any pictures or visuals you use are of a high quality and neatly trimmed and mounted to fit the format of your portfolio.
- Reduce the size of items on a color copier or scan and edit the material on a computer for a professional and finished look.
- Remember, it's a fashion-forward industry—be creative!

SOURCE: J. Michelle Price, assistant professor, Ohio University.

ORGANIZATION AND PRESENTATION
OF THE PORTFOLIO

Just as a resume must be customized to fit the career path and specific position for which you are applying, portfolios should be organized to promote the most appropriate items that you wish to exhibit for each situation. Items for the portfolio must be selected with care. Only work that is relevant to the purpose of the portfolio (assessment, interview, or career review) should be presented. Assessment portfolios should include benchmark documents that demonstrate growth and learning. You should include only your best work in a career search portfolio that will accompany you on interviews. When preparing a portfolio for an employment review process, focus on work that you have completed for that company, and contributions that you have made in your career at your current position.

Because a portfolio, as a reflection of your professional growth and abilities, is a work in progress, it must be updated often. Alexis Clinton looks at her portfolio as a work-in-progress. She notes that when she began working on it, her major challenge was to include items that represented her best work. Now that she has a portfolio that she is proud of, she is motivated to keep updating and adding to it. She expects to continue to update her portfolio once she graduates and plans to use a career-enhancing portfolio throughout her career.

Each item that you include in your portfolio should be positioned in such a way that the reader can easily identify its purpose. Portfolio content will vary, depending on the type of position and company that you are targeting. Employers in general want to see evidence of work—both academic course work and on-site experiences that fits with their needs and desires for employees. Michelle Price, former line designer for American Greetings Corporation and currently assistant professor in Ohio University's retail merchandising program, suggests that students identify their audiences as they develop their portfolios. She notes that the manner in which your portfolio is presented is a reflection of you. Furthermore, your portfolio can indicate the fit that you bring to the position you are seeking. If you are applying for a visually oriented position, the design of your portfolio is particularly important.

Generally, items such as examples of trend and concept boards that you have created, reproductions of work you have done that demonstrate your visual display ability, and documents such as spreadsheets that show your analytical ability and knowledge of specific computer programs are appropriate to include and are of interest to recruiters. Documents that highlight your creativity and problem-solving skills will enhance your portfolio. The portfolio itself becomes a product that demonstrates many of the skills and professional characteristics that are desirable to recruiters. As you compile and organize your portfolio's contents consider the whole package that you will be presenting. Brief explanations accompanying your projects and documents will help guide the reader—and will prompt you to offer more detailed explanations in an interview.

Format of the Portfolio

Portfolios, because they may contain items of nonuniform size and shape, should be created with convenience, organization, and neatness in mind. Michelle Price encourages students to remember that it is difficult for recruiters and potential supervisors to see the quality of the work in your portfolio if the presentation is sloppy or unprofessional. It is important for a portfolio to have an attractive presentation, with items appearing in an orderly fashion to "tell a story" of your accomplishments, knowledge, and skills. Jane Kenner and Rebecca Greer (1995) offer the following guidelines for preparing a portfolio:

- First, establish the purpose and goals for the portfolio.
- The portfolio should look professional and attractive.
- Portfolio materials should be clearly written in concise language and with an eye-appealing format.
- Materials in the portfolio should be focused on the purpose intended.
- The portfolio should be of a convenient size, large enough to show work but small enough to carry easily.
- The portfolio should have consistent page orientation, either vertical or horizontal.

Box 3.2 lists several resources for portfolio supplies.

Contents of the Portfolio

Once the purpose of the portfolio has been determined, the contents must be identified. Each person possesses an individual set of goals, personal strengths, knowledge base, skill set, talents, interests, and experiences. Each of these items shapes the portfolio that will be created to exhibit a professional profile. Therefore, there is no set rule to follow that will tell you what, exactly, to include in your portfolio. Michelle Price encourages students to continually set aside possible additions to their portfolios. She notes that if you wait, the task of compiling portfolio documents becomes over-

BOX 3.2

RESOURCES FOR PORTFOLIO SUPPLIES

- http://www.fastportfolio.com
- http://www.quincyshop.com/porandbin.html
- http://www.dickblick.com/categories/portfolios/
- http://store.artcity.com/

Note: As you prepare to invest in portfolio materials, be sure to look at the size before ordering. Order a standard size for which you will be able to obtain refill sheets. Additionally, be sure that you can remove the sheets from the portfolio.

SOURCE: J. Michelle Price, assistant professor, Ohio University.

whelming, and it is easy to forget all of the projects that have been completed over time. Furthermore, Michelle suggests that you be prepared with an updated portfolio at all times, because you never know when you might need to present your work unexpectedly.

How do you determine what your portfolio should contain? Remember that the portfolio is in essence an expanded resume. You should use the portfolio to:

- **Demonstrate examples of your work.** This can be done through photographs, letters of thanks or commendation, and examples of course projects and work experiences that emphasize your skills.
- **Illustrate growth and development in your professional preparation.** As you gain work experiences and refine your career goals, your professional portfolio will evolve. Keep in mind that each person who reviews your portfolio may have a different approach. Some people will want to peruse the visual elements, such as pictures; others will want to read explanations of your work. Your task is to present all of the items that might be desired for review in a manner that allows the reader to easily access the element of interest to him or her.

Ask your professor, peers, and even interviewers for feedback about your portfolio. Strive to improve yourself and your portfolio presentation by considering constructive criticism as you continue to develop your portfolio and seek experiences in the retailing and apparel merchandising industry.

We recommend that you begin your portfolio with a summary of your strengths and skills, a reflective goal statement, and an updated resume, and then progress to course projects, evidence of work experience, a statement emphasizing your ethical base, and letters of recommendation.

SUMMARY OF STRENGTHS AND SKILLS.   After compiling your portfolio elements, you should be able to assess the themes emerging with respect to the strengths and skills you are documenting. A summary that describes these strengths and skills, and that refers to the specific documents that further illustrate them, provides the reader of your portfolio with an introduction and overview to your professional profile. The summary should tie all of the visual elements of the portfolio together, present a theme for your portfolio, and guide the reader to specific items in your portfolio that document your experiences, strengths, and skills.

Even though this is a summary of the work that is included in your portfolio, it should appear near the front, as an introduction to your work. The summary should be written clearly and concisely. Correct grammar and sentence structure are important components of a high-quality summary. The summary should be proofread and error-free.

REFLECTIVE GOAL STATEMENT.   Prospective employers realize that goal setting is an important step in career growth. Your documented ability to set and articulate goals can enhance your professional profile. Establishing a plan to accomplish your goals will provide direction in your professional development and will inform prospective employers about your plans for the future. Keep the goal statement at a professional level. While we all must also recognize our personal goals, these are not appropriately shared in a professional portfolio.

Through review of your portfolio, employers will have the opportunity to consider whether your goals can be met through the opportunities that they offer, so be certain that your goals are fully developed but do not limit your employment options. On the other hand, clear communication between you and prospective employers will enable you to be fully informed with respect to the degree to which your goals can be met with each employment option.

UPDATED RESUME.   Although your resume should be presented to prospective employers separately, including a copy in your portfolio is a good idea. In fact, you may wish to keep extra copies of your resume in your portfolio so that you can distribute them efficiently.

As you progress toward your educational and professional goals, your resume will change to reflect updated work experiences and skills. The latest edition of your resume should be presented in the professional portfolio. Resume development is thoroughly covered in Chapter 5.

COURSE PROJECTS. Many of the projects and assignments that you complete in classes offer valuable evidence of your accomplishments and skills. Prospective employers will welcome the opportunity to view your work, and the projects that you include will offer a catalyst for you to discuss yourself in an interview.

For example, you can begin a dialog about your ability to work with others or as a member of a team by describing a group project that you have included in your portfolio. You could expand on your leadership ability by describing how you took a leadership role in the project. You could talk about your affinity for figures by describing the six-month plan that you have included in your portfolio. This might lead to a discussion about your goal to become a buyer. A portfolio sample page describing a team project is illustrated in Figure 3.1.

EVIDENCE OF WORK EXPERIENCE. As you gain work experience that will enhance your professional profile, include evidence of such in your portfolio. You may wish to include photographs illustrating visual displays you developed, letters of appreciation from customers or supervisors, and supervisor evaluations.

Be certain to avoid including proprietary information that you may have had access to during an internship or work experience. This might include information about vendors, sales figures, design sketches, or color swatches. Companies typically forbid employees to share these items—sometimes such information may not be removed from the premises—and it would be unethical to include such information in your portfolio. Nevertheless, you can demonstrate your ability to complete appropriate and informative documentation of your on-site career preparation. If you have any doubts about whether to include evidence of your work with an employer, be sure to ask the appropriate company representative before completing (and especially distributing) your portfolio.

STATEMENT OF ETHICAL BASE. Character education has been a hot topic in higher education for the past decade. It is likely that you have completed courses that focused on ethics or had ethics components. In this age of corporate scandals and questionable practices at the workplace, employers are interested in learning about your ethical perspective. You may choose to write a personal work philosophy, incorporate a statement addressing ethics in your goals, or construct a personal code of ethics. It is recommended that some form of your work that speaks to the topic of ethics be included in your portfolio.

Trend Analysis Project

The Trend Analysis and Forecasting Team Project was designed to provide a team experience in the compilation and presentation of information acquired in the retail industry, particularly in the apparel and home furnishings industry. In addition, the experience of making a timed presentation before a class was an important aspect of the project.

Three Upcoming Fashion Trends for Home Furnishings

1. **Bring the outside in:** The great outdoors is coming inside! From specialty grasses grown in fanciful pots on the coffee table to gentle creatures from nature displayed as folk art throughout the home (picture wood-carved ducks "flying" through your living room and ceramic chickens perched on your kitchen counter), consumers will be seeking ways to live outside, even when they enjoy the comforts of their cozy homes.

2. **Home entertainment reaches new heights:** It is no longer enough to have a big-screen television and a home-wide speaker system. Consumers are looking for entertainment that rivals the movie theaters, upscale restaurants, and cozy coffee houses. Homes will be offering "dining centers," "movie centers," and "conversation centers" that will sport extraordinary comforts.

3. **Master bedrooms for all-day living:** Home is where the heart is, and busy people will be seeking master bedrooms that provide all-day comforts. From personal entertainment centers that include cozy couches, easy chairs, and large-screen televisions to attached amenities such as porches, balconies, and home offices, a whole new function is being discovered for master bedroom suites. Promotion of home furnishings to match these day-long functions will find great success in the upcoming season.

SOURCE: Introductory paragraph by Tracy Thomas, reprinted with permission.

FIGURE 3.1   Sample Portfolio Page: Trend Analysis Project

LETTERS OF RECOMMENDATION. Letters of recommendation can offer additional support for you by emphasizing your abilities and expertise. Professors and previous employers may be in a position to write a letter of recommendation on your behalf. Positive letters can point out skills and talents that might not be otherwise evident in your portfolio, such as your tendency to work hard and never be absent. Authors of recommendation letters often speak to the character of their subjects and can offer insight into the attitudes, values, and behaviors that you exhibit.

Refer to Figure 3.2, which demonstrates examples of introductory statements to accompany the documents that you will include in your portfolio. Table 3.1 and the CD-ROM contain an evaluation rubric that you may wish to refer to as you assess the contents and presentation of your portfolio.

Code of Ethics

The purpose of my Personal Code of Ethics is to identify and explore the relationship between professionalism and ethics. Through this statement, I explain how I will develop accountability by encouraging acceptance of responsibility, while establishing awareness of relationships and the role ethics play in the work place.

Work Experience

The experience gained at The Other Place gave me an opportunity to obtain a realistic hands-on experience in a retail environment that was fresh, new, and challenging. I was able to develop my creative skills by practicing promotional exhibits, clothing mannequins, and supervising window displays.

Budget and Buying

Through the use of advanced spreadsheets and merchandise mathematics, I was able to incorporate computer simulations and case studies of various merchandising techniques.

SOURCE: Tracy Thomas, reprinted with permission.

FIGURE 3.2   Sample Portfolio Introductory Statements to Accompany Student Work

TABLE 3.1
RUBRIC FOR PORTFOLIO EVALUATION

PORTFOLIO OBJECTIVES	BELOW STANDARDS	MEETS STANDARDS	EXCEEDS STANDARDS
Evidence of ability to **set goals**	No goal statement is evident	Goals are presented; statements are brief and nonspecific	Goals are presented in a logical order with clear, specific personal expectations noted
Evidence of ability to **evaluate personal strengths**	No strengths are noted; no reflection of personal strengths is provided	Strengths are noted; brief descriptions are noted that demonstrate strengths	Reflective personal evaluation of strengths is presented in a clear and logical manner
Evidence of ability to express **ethical base**	No statement of personal ethics is presented	An Ethical Code is presented, but there is limited reflection or insight	An Ethical Code that reflects insight and thought is presented
Evidence of ability to **analyze and forecast trends**	Neither trend analysis nor forecasting ability and experience is documented	Basic evidence of experience and ability to analyze and forecast trends is documented	Strong documentation is presented of high-level competency with trend analysis and forecasting
Evidence of effective **communication skills** (written, oral, graphic or visual)	There is lack of evidence of multiple types of communication skills	Evidence of basic interpersonal and visual communication skills is included	Documented evidence of strong ability to communicate in multiple ways with reflective analysis of personal skill is provided

Evidence of **creative and conceptual problem solving**	There is lack of evidence demonstrating creative problem solving	Evidence of ability to solve problems is included	Strong evidence of ability to apply creative solutions and strategic planning to problem-solving opportunities is provided
Evidence of ability to work with **diverse populations**	Neither evidence of attitude toward nor stated value of working with diverse populations is included	Evidence is presented that indicates an understanding of the importance of diversity	Evidence of positive attitude toward diversity and demonstrated ability to work with diverse populations is provided
Evidence of appreciation for **lifelong learning**	There is no evidence of appreciation for lifelong learning	Evidence is presented that indicates an appreciation for and ability to engage in lifelong learning	Evidence of positive attitude, demonstrated ability, and plan for continued engagement in lifelong learning is provided
Evidence of **leadership** ability	There is no evidence of leadership ability, and no leadership experience is noted	Documented leadership experiences are presented	Multiple leadership experiences are documented with reflection on experiences and indications of future leadership presented
Evidence of **industry experience**	There is no evidence of industry experience, and no plans are presented for future industry experience	Evidence of work experience is presented, and a connection is made between academic preparation and work experience	A variety of work experiences is documented with reflection of the relative value of the experiences and connection of experiences to academic work and personal goals

ON-LINE AND ELECTRONIC PORTFOLIOS

There are several advantages to creating an on-line or electronic version of your portfolio. Portfolios that are posted at a URL (Universal Resource Locator, available on-line) may be viewed any time by readers who have access to the Internet. Distributing a URL or a compact disc (CD) version of your portfolio allows the reader to view your work at his or her leisure. People who view your portfolio may want to keep it for further review or pass it on to others for their perusal. Providing a URL or a CD with your portfolio is a great strategy to keep you and your professional skills in the forefront of employers' minds.

You may establish long-distance correspondence with a prospective employer, and distributing your portfolio electronically is an efficient and risk-free way to present your portfolio. Although you cannot include original work in this format, scanners and digital photography allow electronic reproductions of excellent quality.

Electronic portfolios, particularly those burned onto CDs, are not as easy to update as hard copies, so you must be prepared to face this challenge. You should carefully label and date all of the work that you include in an electronic portfolio. A good strategy is to produce a personal, hard copy of your portfolio and then reproduce that in an electronic format.

COPYRIGHTING YOUR PORTFOLIO

Because your work is disseminated worldwide when your portfolio is posted on the Internet, it is worthwhile to give notice regarding the copyright of your work. All original unpublished works of which you are the author are recognized under the authority of copyright (as long as you did not produce the work for hire or as part of your employment). In other words, your original unpublished works are automatically copyrighted, and technically you do no need to indicate the copyright on your work. However, it can be difficult to distinguish what work has been published and what hasn't when work is copied and distributed electronically. Essentially, once you copy and distribute your work you have published it.

It is simple to give notice that your work is copyrighted, and your notice will indicate publicly that your work is owned by you and should not be copied. Therefore, we recommend that you publicly copyright your unpublished portfolio and your electronic and Web-based portfolio versions. This can be accomplished by noting on your cover page: Unpublished work © 2004 Your Name. Notice of copyright should be made on a CD version of your portfolio and each page of your Web-based portfolio should carry notice of copyright such as: © Your Name. Refer to Box 3.3 for additional guidelines.

BOX 3.3

GUIDELINES FOR COPYRIGHTING YOUR PORTFOLIO

Copyright is a form of protection provided by the laws of the United States to authors of "original works of authorship." When a work is published under the authority of the copyright owner, a notice of copyright may be placed on all publicly distributed copies. The use of the notice is the responsibility of the copyright owner and does not require permission from, or registration with, the Copyright Office.

Use of the notice may be important because it informs the public that the work is protected by copyright, identifies the copyright owner, and shows the year of first publication.

What Is Publication?

The 1976 Copyright Act defines publication as "the distribution of copies or phonorecords of a work to the public by sale or other transfer of ownership, or by rental, lease, or lending." An offering to distribute copies of phonorecords to a group of personas for the purposes of further distribution, public performance, or public display also constitutes publication.

Copyright Notice Is Not Required
On Unpublished Works

The copyright notice has never been required on unpublished works. However, because the dividing line between a preliminary distribution and actual publication is sometimes difficult to determine, the copyright owner may wish to place a copyright notice on copies or phonorecords that leave his or her control to indicate that rights are claimed. An appropriate notice for an unpublished work might be: Unpublished work © John Doe.

Form of Notice

The form of the copyright notice used for "visually perceptible" copies—that is, those that can be seen or read, either directly (such as books) or with the aid of a machine (such as films)—is different from the form used for phonorecords of sound recordings (such as compact disks or cassettes).

(continued)

BOX 3.3 continued from page 79

Visually Perceptible Copies

The notice for visually perceptible copies should contain three elements. They should appear together or in close proximity on the copies. The elements are:

1. **The symbol** © (the letter C in a circle)

2. **The year of first publication.** If the work is a derivative work or a compilation incorporating previously published material, the year of first publication of the derivative work or compilation is sufficient. Examples of derivative works are translations or dramatizations; an example of a compilation is an anthology. The year may be omitted when a pictorial, graphic, or sculptural work, with accompanying textual matter, if any, is reproduced in or on greeting cards, postcards, stationery, jewelry, dolls, toys, or useful articles; and

3. **The name of the owner of copyright in the work,** or an abbreviation by which the name can be recognized, or a generally known alternative designation of the owner.[1] **Example:** © 1999 Jane Doe.

Position of Notice

The copyright notice should be placed on copies or phonorecords in such a way that it gives reasonable notice of the claim of copyright. The notice should be permanently legible to an ordinary user of the work under normal conditions of use and should not be concealed from view upon reasonable examination.

The Copyright Office has issued regulations, concerning the position of the notice and methods of affixation (37 C.F.R., Part 201). To read the complete regulations, request Circular 96 Section 201.20, "Methods of Affixation and Positions of the copyright Notice on Various Types of Works," or consult the *Code of Federal Regulations* in your local library.

Complete information about copyrights can be found at *http://www.copyright. gov.*

---

1 The United States is a member of the Universal Copyright Convention (the UCC), which came into force on September 16, 1955. To guarantee protection for a copyrighted work in all UCC member countries, the notice must consist of the symbol © (using only the word "Copyright" or the abbreviation are **not** acceptable), the year of first publication, and the name of the copyright proprietor. Example: © 1999 John Doe. For information about international copyright relationships, request Circular 38a, "International Copyright Relations of the United States."

PROJECTS

1. Review the goals that you identified in Chapter 2. For each goal, identify documents that need to be included in a portfolio to supply evidence that these goals have been achieved.

2. Review the top five professional strengths that you identified previously. How will you document these strengths in your portfolio?

3. Make a list of items that you should include in an assessment portfolio.

4. Make a list of items that you should include in a professional enhancement portfolio.

5. Begin the project of portfolio development:

   a. Define your purpose.

   b. Select the items that you will include in the portfolio.

   c. Compile the items in your portfolio and organize them appropriately.

   d. Write a summary for the introduction of your portfolio.

6. Analyze the portfolio that you have created. Does it have a professional look? Are the items well organized, clearly labeled, and easy to access? Do all of the items make sense in terms of reflecting your professional profile and helping you meet your goals?

7. Transform your portfolio into an electronic format.

QUESTIONS FOR DISCUSSION

1. Review your assessment portfolio, or the items that you would include in one. What are your strongest areas of growth over time? In what areas can you set goals for improvement? How did you determine these responses?

2. Create a list of criteria that you would expect to see in a professional portfolio. How would you evaluate the quality of those criteria?

3. Review the portfolio that you have created. How did you decide what to leave in and what to remove?

4. Describe in detail the skills, talent, and knowledge that you have represented in your portfolio. Are those items clearly evident to others who review your portfolio? How did you arrive at this conclusion?

5. How do the documents that you have chosen to include in your assessment portfolio differ from those in your professional enhancement portfolio?

6. What changes do you need to make in order to successfully transform your hard-copy portfolio into an electronic format?

ELECTRONIC ACTIVITIES

Refer to the accompanying CD-ROM. The key elements of this chapter are:

1. Summary of Chapter 3 text

2. Portfolio development

3. Portfolio components

    a. Examples of portfolios

4. Portfolio evaluation

    a. Rubric

REFERENCES

Adomaitis, A. D. (2003, November 10). Retail merchandising portfolio: Preparing students for industry. Paper presented at the annual meeting of the International Textiles and Apparel Association 2003, Savannah, GA. In: *Proceedings of the International Textiles and Apparel Association 2003*. [On-line]. Available: http://www.itaaonline.org.

Kenner, J. O., & Greer, R. (1995, Spring). The portfolio concept: Make it work for you. *The Candle*, 10–11.

Paulins, V. A. (1998). Assessment through portfolios in retail merchandising. *Journal of Family and Consumer Sciences, 90*(4), 82–87.

Paulins, V. A., & Graham, A. (1999, June). An assessment plan for family and consumer sciences programs: Using portfolios. Paper presented at the annual meeting of the American Association of Family and Consumer Sciences, Seattle, WA.

CHAPTER FOUR

THE JOB SEARCH

The person with the best job search skills will typically get the
job over the most qualified person.
— UNKNOWN

OBJECTIVES

- To identify significant resources available for conducting a successful job search.

- To identify the advantages and disadvantages of each job search resource.

- To identify networking opportunities available for your job search.

- To compile a list of contacts to aid in your job search.

- To conduct and analyze current research on a prospective employer.

- To develop guidelines for professional behavior at an employer job fair.

- To develop a strategy for conducting a job search in a market different from your current one.

- To identify alternatives methods for the job search when having difficulty finding a job.

- To formulate a plan for conducting a successful job search in the retailing and apparel-merchandising field.

IDENTIFYING RESOURCES FOR FINDING A JOB

Two of the most fundamental questions that students have concerning their job search are what to do and where to begin. Consider the job search proverbs provided in Box 4.1 and then proceed with the chapter, which is designed to help you get started with your search.

BOX 4.1

JOB SEARCH PROVERBS

- Only you can find your dream job. Don't depend on anyone else to hand it to you on a silver platter.
- Your college owes you nothing other than a great education. Your diploma does not come with a guarantee of a great job. That is something you will have to secure on your own.
- Seek work you love. You will be spending the greater portion of your life working. Make it an enjoyable experience.
- You are infinitely better off making $25,000 and happy than making $50,000 and miserable. No, the extra $25,000 is really not worth the misery. Happiness is priceless.
- Extracurricular activities count. Whether a club or athletics, it shows you are a well-rounded person. And it may be your best opportunity to exhibit leadership skills.
- Experience is experience. You gain new experiences every day. You do not have to be paid for it to be considered valid experience.
- A part-time job during school is a great way to pay the bills and gain some experience. But don't let it take priority over your education or your eventual entry-level job search. Remember what you came for.
- Grades do matter. If you are reading this early, keep your grades high. If late, you will need to provide potential employers with a very good reason if you have not maintained at least a 3.0 ("B" average) or above.
- Keep your ethical standards high and this will soon become one of your most admired qualities, because very few remain honest to such standards. Do not let yours down. Be the exception rather than the rule.
- The truth is still the truth even when everyone else abandons it. Stand for honesty and truth in all you do.
- Don't be afraid to ask questions. Many people may be willing to help, but first you must be willing to ask for their help.
- Develop the necessary computer skills for your field or industry of interest. If you are not sure what they are, check out current job postings.
- Thoroughly research each employer you pursue. It is not enough just to show up for the on-campus interviews and hope for the best.

- The most qualified person does not necessarily get the job. The person with the best job search skills will typically get the job over the most qualified person.
- Job search is a game, complete with a defined set of rules. You need to play by the rules. But to win, you will need to push those rules to the limits.
- Remember that managers hire people who are like them. Do your best to reflect common attributes.
- Always think about meeting the needs of others. This is the only way to meet your own personal needs.
- Nervousness is common and to be expected. It helps you stay on your toes.
- You are unique. There is no one else out there exactly like you. Learn to recognize your unique strengths so that you can communicate them to others.
- A smile will carry you a great distance in your job search. A warm, friendly attitude communicates the message that you are enjoyable to work with.
- What you lack in experience, compensate for with enthusiasm.
- The better you become at your job search, the easier it becomes. And when you have finally mastered the process, it is over. But it is a life skill that you will return to again and again.

SOURCE: *http://www.collegegrad.com/jobsearch/1-15.shtml*. Used by permission of author and publisher. Copyright © 2004, Collegegrad.com, Inc. Additional career information is available at *www.collegegrad.com*.

In the current economic conditions, the job search may not be as easy as it was recently, but as a college student, you have many resources available to you. You should take advantage of all of them, because once you leave campus, your support system may be lessened significantly. Following is a discussion of some of the more common resources available to college students.

College Placement Offices

When it comes to a job search, one of the major advantages you have, as a college student, are the resources available at the college placement office. Here you will often find items such as books, magazines, company reports, videotapes, alumnus lists, and a database of prospective employers looking for people in your major. It is likely that this office will also have listings of companies scheduling on-campus interviews for soon-to-be graduates. Generally, a career counselor is available who specializes in your specific major and entry-level employment opportunities. If you have not visited this office on your campus, now is the time to do so. Do not wait until you are in the last semester of your senior year to familiarize yourself with their services.

Employment Fairs

Most college campuses hold career fairs. Common career fair themes include internship fairs, summer employment fairs, or entry-level employment fairs. Regardless of the type of fair, prior to attending one, find out what companies will be there and do your homework. Research each company and prepare a short introduction of yourself, including your name, major, and career interests. Practice your introduction with friends; include looking them in the eye, giving them firm handshakes, and handing them copies of your resume, just as you will the recruiter.

Because a career fair can be somewhat intimidating to first-time attendees, it is never too early to begin attending them. The more fairs you attend, the more comfortable you will be when meeting the recruiters, and the more information you will have about different companies and the careers they offer. Also, by speaking with the recruiters each time they come to campus, you will establish a rapport with them, which can give you an advantage over others when you are ready to interview for a position.

In addition to career fairs on campus, you should be alert to fairs held near your college or university that are specifically aimed at fashion merchandising and retailing students. For example, the Fashion Group International (FGI) sponsors career days that provide students with the opportunity to bring their resumes, complete applications, hear speakers, and compete in fashion shows. Needless to say, these days provide excellent networking opportunities for those who attend. Examples of such fairs include the FGI Career Day Chicago each fall, and the Dallas Market Career Day, both of which are attended by about 1,000 students a year. If you do not live near a major city, you may still be able to attend. Ask your professor for more information, or visit the Fashion Group International Web site at *www.fgi.org*.

The activities section at the end of this chapter, as well as the accompanying CD-ROM, provides an in-depth activity to guide you through participating in a career fair. Also check with your college placement office to see if they offer workshops to help prepare students for a career fair.

Professors

Although some students would rather walk over a bed of hot coals than visit a professor's office, your professor may prove to be a valuable resource in your job search. In

BOX 4.2
TOP TEN MOST EFFECTIVE METHODS FOR EMPLOYER RECRUITING

1. Organization's internship program

2. Organization's co-op program

3. On-campus recruiting

4. Employee referrals

5. Career and job fairs

6. Faculty contacts

7. Internet job postings (company's own Web site)

8. Job postings to career offices (printed)

9. Student organizations and clubs

10. Internet job postings (campus Web site)

SOURCE: Reprinted from *2003 Job Outlook*, with permission of the National Association of Colleges and Employers, copyright holder.

fact, Box 4.2 illustrates that employers, including alumni, often find new hires through college faculty. Many times alumni and others in the community call professors for referrals to fill vacancies in their companies. Your professors will be best able to match you with an employer if you have made yourself and your career interests known to them. As a courtesy, you should also provide your professors with a resume so that they will have ready access to your experiences and your career objectives when employers call. Professors are interested in seeing their students succeed and most are willing to help with a career search.

Professional and Student Associations

Most majors on campus have student associations, clubs, or honor societies serving the interests of their members (e.g., American Marketing Association, Kappa Omicron Nu). In addition, depending on the locale of the university, there are often professional associations nearby that accept student members (e.g., Fashion Group International, which has chapters in many major cities across the country). Join organizations both on- and off-campus whenever possible because they can provide invaluable experience in building a professional network. Keeping in mind the truth of the adage "it's not what you know, but rather whom you know," you should take advantage of every opportunity that membership in such a group offers. Services often include a directory with contact information for each member, seminars, workshops, and guest speaker events. Many times your membership also includes the particular trade publication for that association. Such publications not only contain the latest trends in the industry, but also may include a classified section listing job opportunities. If you are unsure of the groups that are active on your campus, most colleges have a student association office that can provide this information. You could also ask your fellow classmates or your professors for help, or check your college Web site for a listing. It is quite common that the contacts and friends you make through student organizations while in college will provide job leads for you well into the future.

Your membership in any of these groups, particularly professional organizations, will greatly increase your chances of a successful job search when the time comes. As Brian Krueger, author of the *The Networking By Association Technique* (2003) states, meetings of professional organizations are a networking contact dream. All of the people at the meeting are walking, talking, breathing network contacts and they are all in your field. Additionally, most of these professionals will feel a certain obligation to help others like you get started. Of course, you will have to do your part by effectively interacting with them, but the more meetings you attend, the more comfortable you will become with talking to others about yourself and your career goals. The more people you can talk to, and get to know, the better your chances will be of landing that perfect job. Remember, too, as emphasized below, that the best time to look for contacts is when you do not *need* to look for contacts. In other words, don't wait until the last term of your senior year to start networking. Three rules of networking are:

1. The best time to look for contacts is when you are not looking for contacts.

2. You never know who you are really talking to.

3. *Always* ask for names of other contacts.

As you become skilled conversing with others and gathering contacts, make sure that you follow up on each contact given to you by your network associates. When contacting a potential job lead, you should state your name and also give them the name of the person who referred you. Remember that you are now making a "warm call" rather than a "cold call," which should make you feel more comfortable and also make the person you are calling more receptive.

Internships

The number one place that employers find new hires is through their company internship programs. Therefore, the chance to complete an internship or co-operative education experience, as they are sometimes called, is arguably one of the most valuable opportunities available to college students in terms of their professional development. In fact, given the competitive nature of today's job market, it is not uncommon for a student to complete more than one of these experiences. You should talk with your academic advisor about such opportunities early in your college career. (Note: Recognizing how important the internship experience is for you as a college student, we have devoted Chapter 7 to a discussion of these experiences; however, they cannot go without a brief discussion here in terms of the job search.)

Many retailing and apparel merchandising programs offer college credit for completing an internship, or co-op, because they are the best way to gain "real-world" experience while exploring opportunities in a chosen field of interest. An internship may also be your "in" to a company, as is illustrated in Box 4.2. It is quite common for companies to extend offers for permanent positions to students who successfully complete an internship. Because many students complete their internships between their junior and senior years of college, imagine the pressure that is eliminated by coming back to school for your senior year with a job offer already in place.

It bears mentioning that while internships are designed to help you identify what you want to do upon graduation, they can sometimes be even more valuable by helping you identify what you do not want to do. This is a common occurrence, and it is far better to find out during an internship that a particular position is not for you, than to realize this three months into your first job. Heather Holoubek, associate buyer for Claire's Accessories, Inc., who completed her internship at a specialty maternity-clothing store explains, "My internship was very valuable in that it taught me right away what I didn't want to do. I realized that I did not want to work in the specialty maternity market. I found it very hard to relate to my customers because I had never been in their situation of expecting a baby!" However, as Heather did, you should remain in your internship and learn everything that you can. For example, Heather was able to develop both her management and organization skills in the specialty-store setting, and these skills serve her well in her current position.

Remember, if you find yourself in an internship that is not interesting or challenging, you should still maintain a positive attitude and strive to do the best job possible. You never know when you may again encounter the people you are working for, or with, during your internship! The retailing and apparel merchandising field tends to be a "small world" even in big cities. Also, keep yourself open to exploring other opportunities within the company that may interest you. Perhaps you have found during the internship that buying is not a career for you. However, in working with the marketing department, you have discovered that you are quite interested in promotion. In that case, find out who is in charge of the marketing department and let your interests be known to them. Another excellent source for job leads during your internship experience is through the relationships you may build with the vendors and manufacturer reps servicing your internship site. Some of the most successful manufacturer reps were recruited out of a retail or merchandising setting.

If you are doing your internship for college credit, and you find yourself unhappy, you should discuss your discontent with your college internship supervisor. Your supervisor will be able to offer advice and may even be able to speak with the company's internship coordinator to identify other tasks for you. Regardless, keep your positive attitude and remember that the main purposes of the internship are to explore different career opportunities and gain real-world experience.

The Internet

Although not exclusive to college students, the Internet is fast becoming the most popular resource for a job search. Web sites such as http://www.monster.com and http://www.hotjobs.com offer multiple job listings in a variety of fields. The appendices at the end of this book provide a list of some of the Web sites dedicated to the job search. In addition, most company Web sites now include a section on employment opportunities. Company profiles available on-line are a good place to begin your research. Refer to the activity at the back of this chapter for guidelines on how to conduct research into a prospective employer. A particularly good site to use in conducting research while completing this activity is http://www.hooversonline.com.

Although the Internet makes it particularly easy to fire off cover letters and resumes via e-mail, you should view the Web as just one tool in your job search and not as an exclusive means to an end. As is true with any of the previously discussed job-search resources, you will greatly increase your chances of success by using all methods available to you. Most openings posted on-line will elicit a phenomenal amount of responses, so it may be unrealistic to expect that this is how you will find your job.

Newspapers and Trade Publications

In examining Box 4.2, you will notice, interestingly, that newspapers and trade publications are not popular choices for employers looking for new hires. However, you should not discount these sources completely when conducting a job search. Just ask people who have found jobs through newspaper ads if they would recommend that method. That is, if you can find someone! It is not uncommon for newspaper ads to generate 200 responses per ad. Major newspapers such as the *Chicago Tribune* sometimes receive up to 2,000 responses to a single ad. This means your chances may be 1 in 2000 of landing that job. Given these odds, newspapers and trade journals should definitely not be your sole source of job leads. If you do want to use them, remember that most major newspapers now provide both printed classified sections and postings on the paper's Web site. Usually, the electronic version contains more job postings than the printed version. Also, there is usually a particular day of the week that focuses on careers, so be sure to get that day's newspaper. These career sections not only offer job postings but also contain valuable articles related to conducting a successful job search. If nothing else, perusal of the classified section will give you a good idea of who is advertising positions and the types of positions within a company. Classified ads in trade journals, such as *Women's Wear Daily* or *Daily News Record*, may also help you identify positions that you either may not have considered or did not know existed. If you find something that is new to you, and that sounds interesting, do your research to find out what such a position entails, and the qualifications needed.

Other Contacts (Your Personal Network)

As previously discussed, networking is one of the most effective ways to find a job. In fact, you are more likely to find a job through someone you know than through any other means discussed in this text. According to Kevin Donlin, author of *The Last Guide to Cover Letter and Resume Writing You'll Ever Need* (2003), 70 to 80 percent of your success in finding a job hinges on your ability to build and use a network of contacts. Included in your network should be not only professional contacts but other people, such as friends and their family, people you have worked with, people you meet socially, those serving as your references, neighbors, and even your own family members. When you begin your job search, you should let everyone know about your search and the career goals you have set for yourself. Meet with people and ask for their advice. Also, ask for the names of other people who might be able to assist you. The more people that you have looking out for you, the better. You may be surprised at who will offer that one lead you need.

BOX 4.3

YOUR JOB SEARCH NETWORK—62,500 STRONG, BY KEVIN DONLIN

In this economy—or any other—all my research and experience points to one fact. It's this: Up to 70 to 80 percent of your success in finding a job hinges on your ability to build and use a network of contacts—people who can alert you to new job openings and help you get hired. When you are referred to a hiring manager by one of their employees, you benefit from the trust that exists between them. And it gives you an almost unfair advantage over other job seekers who come in via the classified ads or the Internet. It's like cutting to the front of the checkout line.

You may have already known that. But did you know there's an army of volunteers—62,500 people strong—sitting right under your nose, waiting to send you job leads? It's true.

Now. Do you think you *might* get an interview or two every week if you had 62,500 pairs of eyes and ears on the lookout for job openings? Well, you do! Because, according to most research, the average person is acquainted with about 250 other people. And those 250 people know 250 more. Multiply the two and you get 62,500 people, enough to fill Ross-Ade Stadium at the University of Purdue. This huge figure is the true value of your network. Because it's not just who *you* know, it's who *they* know that counts.

So right now—today—please do these three things:

- **Step 1.** Write down the name of every single person you know, from friends and family to casual acquaintances. That includes your CPA, attorney, hair stylist, manicurist, dentist, banker, real estate agent, neighbors and pastor, to name just a few. Put special emphasis on listing affluent people (most wealthy people own their own businesses or know someone who does) and centers of influence (local leaders who know the movers and shakers in town, like pastors, superstar real estate agents, and attorneys). Don't stop writing until you have at least 250 names.

- **Step 2.** Contact 10 people a day for the next 25 days and say these words when you call or write: "I'm looking for a position where I can help a _____ company with my expertise in _____. Who do you know that I could talk to?" Try to get at least three names from each person. Be sure to *thank* your contacts for every name they give you. Then, ask each contact to please pass your name and phone number on to anyone they think of later whom you might be able to help. (Notice, you're not begging for a job here. You're offering to help a company with your expertise. Big difference. And it gives you the enthusiasm that encourages others to respond.)

- **Step 3.** Pick up the phone, call each potential job lead and follow this script: "My friend, Joe Jones, in Chicago told me to give you a call. I'm a manufacturing manager in Minneapolis and Joe said you would know who to talk to for advice. For the past _____ years I've specialized in _____ and I'm looking for a company that needs to get the most out of its _____. Who do you know that I should be talking to?"

If that person can't help you directly, he or she should be able to give you the name of someone who can. Using a script is important, because you can practice until it flows naturally. And be sure to stand up when you make your phone calls—this gives your voice an extra dose of vitality, a definite plus.

Remember, the worst that can happen when you make a networking call is that someone you approach won't be able to help. But that just puts you one step closer to someone who can. Networking is simply a numbers game, one with 62,500 people on your side.

Box 4.3 contains an article and an activity designed to help you generate a list of contacts. Because a personal network of contacts is so important, there is also another activity included at the end of the chapter to help you generate such a list. Also refer to Table 4.1 which provides an overview of the types of contacts found in a typical network, and what their role can be with regard to helping you with your job search.

WHAT TO DO IF YOU CAN'T FIND A JOB

Recently the job market for college graduates has fallen off slightly compared to what it was in the late 1990s. This means that you may have to work a little harder to find a job, and it may also take you somewhat longer than you expect. If you find yourself in this situation, it is extremely important that you remain optimistic and not give up on

TABLE 4.I

TYPES OF CONTACTS FOUND IN YOUR NETWORK AND WHAT YOU CAN ASK OF THEM

CONTACT	WHAT THEY CAN DO	WHAT THEY CANNOT DO
Friends and family	Give you names Comment about your personal characteristics	Give leads for every industry Serve as professional references
Professional references	Identify leads for you Comment about your work ethic and key skills	Give leads for every industry Increasingly, laws are limiting references as to what information can be legally shared—check with each reference concerning this
People with whom you have worked	Comment about your work ethic and skills Refer you to others	Know a lot about all the companies in which you are interested
People you meet socially	Refer you to others Refer to you as a likeable person Provide on-the-spot informational interviews	Comment about your work ethic Always do what they say they will do

your efforts. For those seeking careers in the retailing and apparel merchandising industry, there is some encouraging news. In a recent survey conducted by the National Association of Colleges and Employers (NACE), findings indicated that the service industry, of which retailing and apparel merchandising is a part, holds the most promise for the hiring of recent college graduates. It is also important to note that employers representing the service sector constituted 50 percent of the survey participants. Service-sector employers reported an expected 16.1 percent increase in hiring for Spring 2004 as compared with a 12.6 percent increase and 4.5 percent decrease for manufacturing and government–nonprofit sectors, respectively (National Association of Colleges and Employers, 2004).

Interview As Much As Possible

In the same survey, when asked to give some additional advice to students seeking jobs, the employer members of NACE reported that students were not signing up in great numbers for on-campus interviews. Indications were that this was happening because students had simply "given up." The fact is that there are employers interviewing on campus and students need to take advantage of every opportunity available. Remember that each interview, regardless of the outcome, provides a learning opportunity, and will also better prepare you for the next interview.

Assess Your Job Search Efforts

If you find yourself becoming discouraged with your job search, now is a great time to assess your search efforts to date. This assessment allows you to ask yourself if you have really done everything you can do to find a job. Take a critical look at what you have done and what you may have missed. (The accompanying CD-ROM for this textbook provides a career search quiz to help with your assessment.) In your assessment, you should also ask yourself if you are expecting too much or being too demanding. For example, recently a student asked us to review her resume because she was having a hard time getting an interview even though she had a very high grade point average (GPA), great leadership experiences in student associations, and quite a bit of practical experience. One had only to look as far as the second line of her resume, under her name, where it stated: *Will not consider any positions starting at under $30,000 a year!* Of course, this type of demand would not be appropriate even in a good job market. In today's job market, students need to realize that employers are now in the "driver's seat." Therefore, it is important to remain flexible and realistic. Although prospective employers want to know your goals and objectives, being too demanding in an uncertain economy will not be viewed favorably.

You should also make sure that you are presenting yourself in the most professional way to each prospective employer, and to all members of your network. Common mistakes that students often make in this area involve unprofessional answering machine recordings, voice mail messages, and e-mail addresses. Check to be sure that you are not projecting the wrong image through any of these means. Your answering machine message should not include music, slang terms, or anything else that might send the wrong signal to a caller. Messages such as "Yo, leave a message," or "We're not here, call back!" (which are actual messages we have encountered when calling students) are not appropriate. Although they may amuse your friends, they will certainly turn off potential employers. Similarly, voice mail messages you leave for others should be professional. Box 4.4 provides a list of simple hints to follow when using voice mail. Lastly, check your e-mail address to be sure it does not say something about you that would turn off an employer. Again, having received numerous e-mails from students, we have found this mistake to be quite common. E-mail addresses such as *partygirl*, *shotqueen*, or *beerdrinking1* are not a good idea. When in doubt, simply use your first initial and last name for your address (e.g., *jhillery@xyz.edu*).

BOX 4.4
SIMPLE HINTS WHEN USING VOICE MAIL

Whether we like it or not, voice mail is here to stay. When used properly, it actually can be a very useful tool. The following hints will help you leave clearer, more informative messages while helping you to eliminate playing the dreaded and time-wasting telephone tag.

- **Identify yourself.** Always state who you are and the company you are with, even if you assume the person already knows.
- **Speak slowly and clearly.** Leaving all the information in the world is useless if your message can't be understood.
- **Eliminate unnecessary return calls.** If you have a specific message, leave it. An informative message, such as "The package is in" or "Please send XYZ project," tells the person exactly what you want.
- **Keep your message concise.** Remember, your call may not be the only one that will be recorded, so avoid rambling and unnecessary detail.
- **Leave your phone number!** Repeat it at the end of your message, slowly. This will save time and energy in case your number has been lost or misplaced. Also leave pertinent information such as, "I will be out of the office from 2 to 4 P.M."
- **State the day and time of your call.** I think this is important. I know it helps me.

SOURCE: Heloise, international syndicated columnist, © Heloise, Inc. 2004. Reprinted with permission.

Use a Temporary Employment Agency

If, after a critical assessment of your job search, you feel you have done everything you can to find a job, yet you are still unsuccessful, there are some other options you can consider while continuing your search for that perfect job. In a tough job market, you may want to consider taking a temporary position in your area of interest. A temporary position, much like an internship, allows you to gain valuable experience and may also prove to be an "in" to the company should it need to fill a permanent position. A temporary position is also a great way to add to your network and contacts that can help you find a job. If you are hired as a "temp" for a company, it is perfectly appropriate to let everyone there know about your career goals and objectives. Many of your co-workers probably know others in the industry in which you are interested and may prove to be valuable leads for you at other companies.

Volunteer

Another option to consider is doing volunteer work. Beth Watson, a graduate of the Marketing program at Northern Illinois University, discovered first-hand how volunteering within the community can help students land their "dream" position. When the retailer of her choice came to campus to interview students, Beth was disappointed that she did not make the short-list to interview for the company's internship program. However, one month later, while she was volunteering with the Glass Slipper Project in Chicago (a nonprofit organization that distributes gently-used prom dresses to underprivileged high school girls), she met and worked with a store manager from the same retailer. Based on this experience, she began an internship with the company and is now an assistant store manager for one of the most successful retailers in the country.

Take a Job in the Service Industry

You may also need to take a job that will simply "pay the bills" while you are conducting your job search. Many college graduates continue to wait tables, bartend, or do various other service jobs until they land that perfect first job. Anyone who has worked as a server or a bartender can tell you that these jobs helped them develop valuable skills. Not only do service jobs help perfect customer-service skills, but they also develop teamwork, organizational and interpersonal communication skills, and many other skills that will be valuable in any field. They also give you the opportunity to tell a lot of people that you are looking for a job. As stated before, you never know with whom you are talking when you work with the public.

Consider Relocating to a Different Area

Because economic conditions, and resulting job opportunities, can differ greatly from one region of the country to another, you may want to consider moving. Although many recent college graduates are somewhat apprehensive about leaving all of their friends and family behind to take a job in another city or state, others find the opportunity quite rewarding and often comment that the move was the best decision they ever made concerning their professional development. In considering a move, you can start by reading financial reports, trade publications, and out-of-state newspapers (available at your university or local library) to help you identify markets where jobs are more plentiful. The Internet is also a great source for conducting research about other areas. And, don't forget about your network contacts. Many of them probably know someone who is working in another state or city, and they may provide you with a valuable link to the new area you are considering. To help you get started, the activities section at the end of the chapter contains an exercise to help you research the employment market in another area. If you find yourself somewhat anxious about making such a move, remember that you are not necessarily making a lifetime commitment to stay in the new location. Commonly, once you obtain some experience, you will be more attractive to potential employers in the market you are leaving, and you can return there if you so desire. Remember, nothing ventured, nothing gained! (See Chapter 9, page 240, which discusses how to successfully relocate to another area.)

In a tough job market, and even in a good one, it is quite common to become frustrated with a job search. If you find yourself in this situation, you may want reread this chapter, and review Table 4.2 which presents common myths about the job search today. Be sure you are not buying into any of these statements. Being persistent, optimistic, and flexible will eventually pay off! As your job search continues, one of the most important things you can do is to remain true to yourself and your passions regardless of what field you wish to enter. The majority of the time, after weeks of interviewing, sending out resumes, and networking—just when students and recent college graduates are ready to give up—their hard work comes to fruition. They may even receive multiple job offers in the same week! What a great feeling when the question then becomes, "Which job will I take?" rather than "Will I have a job to take?"

TABLE 4.2

COMMON MYTHS ABOUT THE JOB SEARCH

MYTH	FACT
If I am sending out cover letters and resumes, it will result in interviews.	You will need to follow up on every resume that you send out requesting an interview and expressing your interest in the position. You must be proactive and persistent, not passive! Opportunities will slip by if you wait for employers to contact you.
There are no positions available at the companies I am interested in because there are none advertised.	Most experts agree that only about 15–25 percent of jobs are advertised in some type of medium. An overwhelming majority of jobs are part of a "hidden" job market and are filled through referrals made through networking. Make every effort to network and find people who work at the companies you would like to work for. They can provide you with the leads you need.
I have no experience specific to my field so no employers will consider me.	Most employers, particularly when hiring for entry-level positions, will consider your enthusiasm for the position and potential to learn and advance within their organization. Sell yourself using the many transferable skills that all employers are looking for (e.g., leadership, communication skills, time management, organizational skills).
I have no control over the job search— it is the employers that are in control	You are the one who is in charge of your job search!
If I go to school, get good grades, and obtain a four-year degree, I will get a good job.	Your degree does not guarantee you, nor does it entitle you to, a well-paying job. It *prepares* you for one. Those who have the best job search and interviewing skills, and who are able to establish a good rapport with the interviewers, will usually get the best jobs.

(continued)

TABLE 4.2 continued from page 99

I do not have definite career plans so it will be hard for me to get a job.	Developing a career is a lifelong process. It is probable that you will change careers as many as four or five times over the course of your life. While you should always have a set of career goals, it is highly likely that these will change as you learn new skills and identify new areas of interest.
Most times people find their jobs through "lucky" breaks.	What often appears as luck is a matter of the person being prepared and working hard to have the chance to secure the job.
A high-paying job will make me happy.	A high-paying job that does not match your goals and interests will only result in job dissatisfaction. Having a job that pays less, but is one that you enjoy, is a far better choice. Remember, too, that you are more likely to succeed at something that you enjoy doing.
Lowering my salary requests, or not negotiating a higher salary, will make me more attractive to an employer.	As long as your demands are comparable with industry standards, you should stick to them. Agreeing to a lower salary will make you look desperate for a job and will most likely cause you to be unhappy in the position because you feel you were cheated out of the salary you deserve.
I should take the first job offer that comes along in case nothing else does.	You should only take the first offer if you are completely satisfied with it. However, there are several factors that you should critically assess before deciding on an offer. Accepting the first offer may be right for you, but you should never do so just because you think nothing else will come along. If finances are a concern, consider taking a temporary job (e.g., waiting tables), until a better offer comes your way.
Others, including my parents and friends, know what's best for me.	You know yourself better than anyone. Although you may want to consider the advice of others, you should ultimately make any decision about your career. Follow your instincts—they are usually right!

SOURCE: Based on information included at http://www.quintcareers.com, http://www.ewu.edi/~career/career_myths, and http://www.sde.state.id.us/cis/myths.htm.

PROJECTS

1. **Researching a prospective employer.** One of the most important things you need to do when embarking on a job search is to conduct research into companies that you are considering as prospective employers. Complete the following exercise for each company you are interested in pursuing. Although information is available from a variety of sources, one of the best is *http://www.hooversonline.com*. Log onto this Web site and collect the following information related to each retailing or apparel merchandising company for whom you would be interested in working.

   a. Current state of the industry and trends for the future

   b. Top companies in the industry

   c. General overview of the company

   d. Major developments, trends, and issues at the company

   e. Key executives at the company

   Summarize your findings in a 2- to 3-page report, including a discussion about implications for employment with this company. Keep your report for referral when writing a cover letter and interviewing with the firm. Remember, this information can be valuable in formulating questions to ask at an interview.

2. **Career fair and internship fair assignment.** Choose one of these fairs to attend on your campus, if possible. Before going to the fair, look over a list of the companies that will be there, review the positions they are offering (if available), and do your research. Your campus placement office should have many resources to help you with this process. You can also conduct research using the Internet at the company sites and at sites such as *http://www.hooversonline.com*, as you did for Project 1, above. At the fair, you should talk to at least three employers. Get a business card from each, and type up a brief synopsis of your conversations. The synopsis should include a summary of the conversation, a brief description of the available position, why (or why not) you would be interested in the internship, and a brief reaction to the encounter. Also note any follow-up that was agreed upon. The CD-ROM accompanying this text provides a template for this report.

3. **Visit with a professor.** Make an appointment with a professor who teaches in your major to discuss career opportunities in your field. Before your visit, prepare a list of questions. Ask about typical positions secured by graduating seniors, employers who commonly interview on campus and the types of positions they offer, the skills employers are especially interested in, and positions held by the program's alumni. You may also want to let the professor know about your career interests and ask for the names of any contacts he or she may have. Prepare a brief report to summarize the findings from your meeting.

4. **Job and internship search in a different market.** Identify a job market that interests you that is in a different location from where you currently live. Prepare a brief report, including the following:

   a. Name and description of the city or area

   b. Explanation of why you are interested in this city or area

   c. Comparison of the cost-of-living in this city or area versus your current location

   d. Major companies located in this city or area

   e. Examples of specific job opportunities you have found using the Internet, newspapers, or other sources

   f. A specific plan for conducting a job search in this city or area

   g. Advantages and disadvantages of relocating to this city or area

5. **Networking Activity.** Often, people looking for a job make the mistake of being too conservative when identifying a network for assistance. Do not limit yourselves only to professional contacts. Everyone you know should be considered a source of job leads. Using the list below, generate your own personal contact list.

People to Include in Your Network:

- **Past employers.** List all the people for and with you have previously worked, even if it was not a job that you feel is directly related to your current job search. Don't forget to include people for whom you may have done odd jobs such as lawn mowing, babysitting, or errands.

- **Your professional references.** List all those who will be serving as personal references for you (see Chapter 5 for further discussion of personal references).

- **Internship supervisors and co-workers.** List all of your supervisors, people you met, and people you worked with at your internship. If applicable, you should also include the people you know in the human resources department.

- **People you know from school.** List friends, professors, coaches, counselors, fellow students in your major, alumni, fellow members of your sorority or fraternity, and members of your professional and student organizations.

- **People who you know from volunteer activities.** List all people you have met while doing volunteer work.

- **Friends from home and their families.** List all of your friends from home and their parents and other adult family members. Also include your neighbors and their family members.

- **Current employer and co-workers.** List all the people from your current job that you consider co-workers, and your supervisors. Also include others with whom you may not work directly but who you know from this job.

- **Customers and clients.** If you have worked in a service position, your customers and clients may be of some assistance to you in your job search. List all customers and clients that you know from past and previous jobs.

- **Your family.** List family members, including your parents, adult siblings, aunts, uncles, cousins, and grandparents. Although they cannot serve as professional references for you, they can be a great help when it comes to job leads.

- **People whom you have met socially.** List all the people to whom you have been introduced at social functions. Include those you may have conversed with on the train, while standing in line with at the movies, or while shopping.

QUESTIONS FOR DISCUSSION

1. What types of services are available at your college or university placement/career services office to assist in your job search?

2. What are some questions you could ask recruiters at a job fair? What are some questions they might ask you?

3. List three organizations on your campus that you would be interested in joining. What are the requirements for membership? What are some of the activities they sponsor?

4. What are some ways that membership in student and professional organizations could help you personally (e.g., what are some skills you need to develop)?

5. List three companies which offer internships that interest you. How can you find out more about these internships?

6. What are some of the advantages to using the Internet as a job search resource? Can you think of any disadvantages?

7. What are the three job search sites on the Internet that you think are most helpful? What are the strengths of these sites over others you have visited?

8. What is the major newspaper in your area that could be useful in your job search? Under what category or categories in the classified section would you find jobs that interest you?

9. Why do you think networking is an important part of the job search? What do you think are the major advantages to networking over other job search strategies?

10. What are some of the major groups or organizations in your area that would offer you the best networking opportunities?

11. Besides those discussed in this book, can you think of other strategies for finding a job or an internship? How have your friends or classmates found jobs and internships?

12. What are some jobs you could do while searching for an entry-level career position? What transferable skills would these jobs offer you? How might one of these jobs help you find your first professional career position?

13. In reviewing the job search proverbs presented in this chapter, identify, and discuss, (a) the five that you most agree with, and (b) the five you least agree with.

ELECTRONIC ACTIVITIES

Refer to the accompanying CD-ROM. The key elements of this chapter are:

1. Summary of Chapter 4 text

2. Career search quiz

3. Career-fair attire assessment

    a. Career-fair attire critique form

4. Career-fair contact information log

5. Company contact information and career-fair report form

6. Career-fair timeline guide

REFERENCES

Donlin, K. (2003). *The last guide to cover letter and resume writing you'll ever need* (available for purchase at collegerecruiter.com). Minneapolis, MN: Adguide Publications.

Donlin, K. (2004, June 23). *Your job search network—62,500 strong* [On-line newsletter]. Available: collegerecruiter.com.

Job search proverbs [On-line]. Retrieved December 11, 2003. Available: http://www. collegegrad.com/book/1-15.shtml.

Krueger, B. (2003, January 13) *The networking by association technique: Job search tip of the week* [On-line]. Available: www.collegegrad.com.

National Association of Colleges and Employers. (2004). *Job outlook Spring 2004 update*. Bethleham, PA: NACEWeb Publications.

CHAPTER FIVE

RESUMES AND COVER LETTERS

It is always better to "underpromise and overperform" than to
"overpromise and underperform."
—JAMES H. DONNELLY, JR., IN *CLOSE TO THE CUSTOMER* (1991)

OBJECTIVES

- To identify pertinent information for preparing professional resumes and cover letters.

- To identify the appropriate format for professional resumes and cover letters.

- To construct a professional resume, reference page, and accompanying cover letter.

Cover letters and resumes create the first impression you will make on prospective employers. Therefore, their appearance and accuracy are extremely important. You will find that the extra effort involved in presenting neat, attractive, well-formatted, and high-quality (e.g., laser-printed) documents will pay off. Be sure to purchase light-colored or white premium paper appropriate for representing your professional profile. Above all, any written correspondence, and in particular the cover letter and resume, should be completely error free.

Although they are submitted together, both the letter and the resume should be able to stand alone. Each should contain relevant information for employers enabling them to know something about you and how to contact you. This chapter provides detailed information that will help you construct professional, personalized resumes and cover letters.

RESUMES

Resume writing has long been considered an arduous task. Because summarizing education, work experiences, activities, and references all at one time is overwhelming, resumes are better developed over time. A comprehensive, well-refined resume is certainly preferable to one that has been quickly compiled. You will find it helpful in the long run to begin your resume as your collegiate and work experience career begins, and to update and adjust it as new opportunities are encountered and leadership skills are enhanced. The advantages of developing a resume early in your academic career include:

- Increased accuracy in reporting dates, job duties, and specific leadership experiences (rather than writing from memory)
- The convenience of having a "work in progress" (rather than starting from scratch at the last minute)
- Time to experiment with various formats, and
- An opportunity to formulate and organize your goals as well as identify personal areas for improvement through revision.

Format of Resumes

The resume is your calling card, and should be tailored to each type of position you are seeking (e.g., management trainee, internship). Dan Bingley, coordinator for the Northern Illinois University cooperative education and internship office, advises students, "a resume is a one-page advertisement of you."

A resume should focus on educational preparation, previous work experience, leadership activities, and references. Although resume formats are not as strictly prescribed as letter formats, generally there are two types of resumes: the chronological format and the functional format (Adams & Morin, 1999).

FUNCTIONAL FORMAT. The functional format provides the opportunity to list education and work experience entries in order of importance, with the most significant, not the most recent, listed first. It generally deemphasizes places of employment and concentrates on specific skills, qualifications, and accomplishments. On a functional resume, you might find categories such as *Managerial Skills*, *Technical Skills*, and *Accomplishments*. A functional resume is best suited to people with a variety of specialized skills or many different and short-lived positions. It is not recommended for college students and recent graduates.

CHRONOLOGICAL FORMAT. The chronological format is the most common and also the most desirable type of resume for college students and recent graduates. Beginning with your most recent experience, it lists your education, followed by your employers, job titles, dates, and responsibilities (Northern Illinois University Career Planning and Placement Center, 2003–2004). Figure 5.1 provides an example of the chronological format.

Components of the Chronological Resume

Because the chronological format is preferred for college students and recent graduates, we will focus on it for our discussion. However, keep in mind that other methods of formatting resumes may also be perfectly acceptable, especially as you progress in your career. If you have questions about the preferred format for your resume, check with the career resources office at your university.

NAME AND CONTACT INFORMATION. Your name should be the first item listed on your resume with a top margin of at least three-quarters of an inch. Next, include both your current and permanent addresses and phone number. When relevant, include the precise date that you will be leaving your temporary or school address. Often employers will try to reach you after you have moved, and you do not want to miss an opportunity because the employer cannot find you. On a related note, if you place a copy of your resume on file with your career planning office, remember to update your name and contact information periodically.

Directly under your name, along with your address and phone number, you should include your e-mail address. This address should be an account that you routinely check, and the e-mail name should be professional. The best approach is to use your first initial followed by your last name (e.g., *jsmith@yahoo.com*). Michelle Fitzgibbon, store manager for Kohl's, offers the following advice: "Students should check that the e-mail address they give prospective employers is professional. In the past, I have used unprofessional e-mail addresses (e.g., *partygirl*, *cuteone*) to screen out what may have been otherwise qualified internship candidates."

OBJECTIVE. Traditionally, resumes often began with the heading *Career Objective*, or something to that effect. Although this segment may give some direction to an employer about your goals and desired position, more often the objective becomes extra baggage on the resume, and worse, too restrictive, blocking consideration of the job seeker for other opportunities that may be available within the hiring organization.

Maria Vasquez

Mvasquez1@hotmail.com

Present Address	**Permanent Address**
321 River Street	22154 Valley View Lane
Athens, OH 45701	New Concord, OH 43721
(740) 555-5505	(740) 555-5555

EDUCATION Ohio University, Athens, Ohio
Candidate for **Bachelor of Science in Human and Consumer Sciences**
Major: Fashion Retail Merchandising—Minor: Marketing
Major GPA: 3.97   Overall GPA: 3.6   Dean's List
Degree Expected: June 2005   Financing 40% of education

HONORS Mary P. Cosbey Award, 2004
—Awarded to Consumer Science Major most likely to make outstanding contribution to profession
Phi Kappa Phi Academic Honor Society, 2004
Mortar Board National Honor Society, 2004
Golden Key Honorary Society, 2003
Kappa Omicron Nu Honorary Society, 2003

PROFESSIONAL EXPERIENCE

June 2004–Aug. 2004 **Internship**
MARSHALL FIELD'S, Chicago, IL
- Gained valuable insight into the overall operations of a large retail department store
- Monitored daily departmental sales and goals
- Assistant to the Department Manager for entire departmental operations
- Assisted Manager with the hiring, training, and scheduling of sales associates
- Performed operational duties including interstore transfers, Returns-to-vendors, and seasonal markdowns
- Assisted visual merchandising team with creative merchandise displays
- Communicated weekly with buyers and vendors

Academic Breaks **Sales Associate**
2001–2005 THE LIMITED, Sunset Mall, Zanesville, OH
- Consistently met or exceeded daily sales goals while providing exceptional customer service
- Increased sales through the use of creative and unique merchandising displays

OTHER EXPERIENCE

Academic Years **Server**
2003–2005 CRAIG'S FINE DINING, Athens, OH
- Demanding clientele in a fast-paced environment provided opportunity to enhance interpersonal communication skills

LEADERSHIP ACTIVITIES

2004–2005 Phi Kappa Phi Academic Honor Society
- Vice President
2001–present Fashion Associates Student Organization
- Secretary 2004–2005

FIGURE 5.1 Chronological Resume

A poorly written objective may also work against you by turning off an employer before he or she reaches the sections of the resume that list your credentials. Recruiters, too, have indicated that an all-encompassing objective doesn't narrow the desired career path or position adequately, and a very focused objective may eliminate you from consideration of another position. Furthermore, an objective often will not provide any information about you that the employer doesn't already know. For example, consider the following objective: *Seeking a challenging position with a profitable company with opportunities for advancement.* Who doesn't want this type of position, especially if you consider the alternative—an unchallenging position with a nonprofitable company with no opportunities for advancement! It is better to tailor your cover letter to express your desired position within the given company and list your background facts in the resume. One exception to this advice is when you visit a career fair. You will not be able to write a letter to each employer, and you will want to distribute a large number of resumes. In such a situation, employers will want to know whether you are seeking an internship, an entry-level job, or summer break employment. This information should be listed in the objective section of your resume and needs to be direct. For example, a good objective would be: *Seeking an internship in retail merchandising.*

EDUCATION. The educational institutions that you have attended should be listed in order with most recent first. Generally you would include only those institutions where you received, or will receive, a degree. Likely, your university experience will be listed as current, and you should focus on your major, any minors, and the degree that you expect to earn. A notation indicating the expected date of your graduation (e.g., *Expected Graduation: June 2007*) is preferable to postdating your resume (e.g., *BS Retail Management: June 2007*). This style points out to the employer that you are currently a student seeking a work experience, an internship, or a full-time position in a future context rather than disguising the fact that your graduation has not yet occurred. Remember, plans are made, but until an event actually happens, one should not report it as fact.

Whether to list high school information is another area of confusion for many students. If you are enrolled in a university, it is implied that you have earned a high school diploma or its equivalency, so unless the high school has some particular merit toward your career preparation (such as a vocational specialization or other specialized course of study, military academy, or such), listing the high school is unnecessary. Applicants who have not engaged in education beyond the secondary level should list the high school graduation date or date the general education development (GED) degree was received to demonstrate that level of education.

Space permitting, you may also include course work that supports your career objective in this section. Additionally, if you have paid for all of, or a percentage of, your education you should include a line stating this. This percentage should include any part of your education that you have personally financed (student loans) or any grants and scholarships you have received. If you have paid for a large percentage of your education, employers will definitely ask you about this and will most likely be impressed because of it.

GRADE POINT AVERAGE.   One of the most common questions related to educational information on a resume is whether to list one's grade point average (GPA). Some employers rely on GPAs to screen potential employees, while others focus more directly on work experiences, special skills, or the interview to narrow job applicants. A good rule of thumb is that a GPA that meets or exceeds a Dean's List designation is a positive reflection of one's academic preparation and should be listed. If your overall GPA is average, or not a source of pride to you, it may be better left off of the resume. Consider, however, including your *Major* GPA if it is considerably better than your *Overall* GPA. This is often the case and occurs for a number of reasons. For example, if a student has changed majors, he or she may begin receiving higher grades in the new major because the subject matter comes more easily or is likely to be more interesting to the student. If you have done well in your required major courses, you can designate this on your resume as your *Major* GPA. If you do not list a GPA, employers who wish to know this will ask, but you should not eliminate yourself from a pool of applicants by listing on your resume a weakness rather than a strength. You should seek information regarding the expectations of the company to which you are applying before making a final determination about this item.

WORK EXPERIENCE.   The fact that you have engaged in previous work experience sends the message to the employer that you have successfully held a job and are likely to be familiar with the work environment. Be sure to list, as comprehensively as practical, the employment that you have experienced. Often entry-level applicants attempt to shorten their resumes by deleting what they consider to be nonrelated work experiences. A summer lifeguarding job or a waitressing position during the school year are representative of your work ethic, your ability to manage your time, and your willingness to accept responsibility. These seasonal and part-time jobs, while likely different in task from the job you will be seeking upon graduation, have enabled you to develop professional skills upon which you can now rely. Include as much information as space allows, and remember that if you have a good deal of "odd job" experience, on which you do not have room to expand, you can simply list the job titles and dates of employment. Although it is somewhat of a departure from the traditional chronological format, it is perfectly acceptable to separate your work experience into two sections: one titled *Relevant/Professional Experience* and one titled *Other/Work Experience* (see Figure 5.1 for an example). Under the *Relevant/Professional Experience* section, all retailing-, apparel merchandising–, and product design–related employment opportunities, including an internship, should be listed. The *Other/Work Experience* section would include positions such as a lifeguard, waitress, or camp counselor. For each job, particularly for those more directly related to the position you are seeking, include bullet statements indicating the specific tasks and responsibilities included in your duties, with your most important and relevant responsibilities listed first. Use action verbs, such as *organized, maintained, developed,* and *directed.* (See Figure 5.2 for a list of action words.) Remember to tell the employer what you did (*scheduled 25 sales personnel*) rather than listing what your responsibilities were supposed to be (*responsible for scheduling*). Use qualitative, achievement-oriented information as much as possible. When describing your responsibilities, consider too, that it is increasingly common practice for employers to electronically scan resumes that they receive. Therefore the action words that you include on your resume should be ones that are key to the field in which you are applying.

ACTIVITIES. Employers, invariably, are seeking students who have unique and outstanding professional qualities. These qualities include, but are not limited to, a willingness to accept responsibilities, an ability to prioritize, an ability to motivate others, a sense of appropriateness, mature judgment, and time and conflict management. Often the area that separates the exceptional applicant from all of the good ones is activities. A positive trend in this section is to include such activities under the heading of *Leadership Activities.* Of course, the heading must be appropriate for the individual and may be entitled *Activities/Honors,* instead, as applicable. (Note that in Figure 5.1, a separate *Honors* section has been placed directly after *Education*). If your goal is to obtain an exceptional internship or a first-rate entry-level position, it is imperative that you develop leadership skills. It is not enough to join clubs and other organizations. Rather, you must be willing to accept leadership responsibilities and up to the challenge of organizing and motivating members. Such activities not only will provide material for discussion at interviews and in cover letters, they also will enable the development of important skills such as time management, conflict resolution, creative organization, and public speaking.

If you have not yet identified activities that fit this category, begin now to develop yourself professionally as a leader. In addition to professional associations and extracurricular activities, volunteerism is a terrific way to gain leadership experience. Not only does volunteerism indicate that you are able to budget your time and organize

accelerated	demonstrated	interviewed	refined
accomplished	designed	introduced	reinforced
achieved	detected	invented	rendered
acquired	determined	investigated	reorganized
adapted	developed	judged	reported
administered	devised	launched	represented
advised	diagnosed	lectured	researched
allocated	directed	led	resolved
analyzed	dispensed	logged	responded
applied	distributed	maintained	responsible
appraised	drafted	managed	restored
approved	earned	marketed	revamped
arbitrated	edited	mediated	revised
arranged	eliminated	monitored	reviewed
assembled	encouraged	motivated	routed
assessed	enforced	negotiated	scheduled
assigned	enhanced	obtained	secured
assisted	enlarged	observed	selected
attained	ensured	opened	served
audited	entered	operated	serviced
awarded	established	ordered	set up
balanced	estimated	organized	settled
briefed	evaluated	originated	simplified
built	examined	oversaw	sold
calculated	exceeded	participated	solved
charted	executed	performed	stimulated
clarified	expanded	persuaded	streamlined
closed	expedited	planned	structured
coached	experienced	prepared	studied
coded	explored	prescribed	summarized
collaborated	facilitated	presented	supervised
collected	forecasted	prevented	supplied
compiled	formed	prioritized	supported
completed	formulated	processed	systematized
conceived	gathered	produced	surveyed
conducted	generated	programmed	synthesized
conserved	guided	projected	taught
consolidated	headed	promoted	tested
constructed	helped	proposed	trained
consulted	hired	protected	translated
contributed	identified	proved	transported
controlled	implemented	provided	tutored
converted	improved	published	updated
coordinated	increased	purchased	upgraded
counseled	influenced	received	utilized
created	initiated	recommended	validated
critiqued	inspected	reconciled	verified
debugged	installed	recorded	volunteered
decreased	instituted	recruited	wrote
defined	instructed	redesigned	
delegated	interacted	reduced	
delivered	interpreted	referred	

SOURCE: Northern Illinois University Career Planning and Placement Center, DeKalb, IL. Available: www.niu.edu/cppc. Reprinted with permission.

FIGURE 5.2 Action Words

activities, it also demonstrates that you are willing to give back to your community and provide a necessary service to others. Increasingly, employers are interested in your history of community service and, in fact, many employers have indicated that they look for these types of activities on a resume before looking for anything else. By all means, the activities section should emphasize quality over quantity!

REFERENCES. A practice has emerged in which prospective employees construct a resume and insert the final line, *References available upon request*. This is often done to keep the length of the resume at one page; however, it is advised that this statement be omitted and the author voluntarily includes a reference list as a second page accompanying the resume. This is a simple convenience on your part, and eliminates the need for employers to contact you subsequently to obtain a list of references. Virtually all employers check references, and their possession of a list of your references may accelerate your employment procedure. Because the references will need to be continued on a second page, and are considered a separate item from the resume, you may prefer to state *References Attached* at the bottom of the resume.

When listing references, be sure to identify the title and job position of each person you have selected to represent you. This is particularly important when listing gender-neutral names, as phone calls or letters from the employer will likely result in asking for Ms., Mr., or Dr. Additionally, the reference person's professional position may give an indication of the relationship between you and that person. It is also helpful to include a brief statement along with the person's contact information that delineates his or her relationship to you. If one of your references has changed jobs since working with you, you should indicate this by stating *formerly with XYZ company*. This will allow the reader of your resume to more easily identify that person's relationship to you.

In selecting references, avoid family members and purely personal references, particularly if you have work experience. It is essential to ask people whom you plan to list as references if you may use their names. Your reference people will also appreciate receiving a copy of your resume for their files. Obviously, you should seek those whom you believe will offer a favorable reference for you, and you should plan to perform to a standard that is worthy of high recommendation. Your reference list should parallel the experiences that you have listed on your resume. Intuitive employers will question the absence of supervisors representing major work experiences on your resume. Be prepared to explain the absence of a recent supervisor, should you decide to omit such a person. Furthermore, current and recent students should include an academic reference, as this is your most recent and concentrated experience. The importance of identifying professors, mentors, current and former managers, and others with whom you work and interact on a regular basis for the purpose of providing references cannot be overemphasized. If you presently are not aware of such a person, begin now to make yourself known to your professors, seek mentors who can guide your professional development and provide testament to your character, and establish positive working relationships with your supervisors.

One final comment on the reference page—be sure that the complete heading from your resume appears at the top of the reference page. Without this identifying information, it could be disastrous for the references to be separated from your resume. Additionally, the reference sheet is likely to be removed from the resume for the purpose of checking references, and it is best that you provide the necessary identification on the page. A sample reference page is provided in Figure 5.3.

OTHER RESUME ITEMS TO CONSIDER.   Avoid the following items when constructing a resume: personal criteria such as age, gender, race, marital status, family members, height, weight, and physical challenges. Mention of these criteria may eliminate you from the candidate pool or unnecessarily call attention to irrelevant information. These personal characteristics are not related to your preparation for the job, professional experiences and skills, or ability to perform the tasks necessary for the prospective position and therefore do not enhance your professional profile.

Most entry-level resumes are approximately one page long. It is easier for potential employers to scan resumes that are concise and clearly presented than those that are lengthy. Although the length should be shorter when possible, do not leave off key information that may contribute to your landing a job. When condensing descriptive information on your resume, remember that you may benefit by moving some items to your letter and expanding on certain experiences in that format. Recruiters generally emphasize a one-page limit, particularly for entry-level jobs that have numerous applicants.

Some students will have difficulty fitting their experiences and activities on one page, but others may find that they are having a hard time filling up the page. If this is the case, consider adding additional headings to the resume. For example, the resume might include the heading *Specialized Skills*, under which could be listed knowledge of particular computer programs, such as Excel or PowerPoint, or a second language that you speak, (e.g., *fluent in Spanish*.) A heading with *Related Course Work* is another option and would include any courses taken that are directly related to the position sought. Don't assume that employers know that a retailing or apparel merchandising major requires the completion of numerous business or marketing courses. This is often not the case and you may be selling yourself short by not communicating this information.

As professional experiences increase through internships or specialized opportunities, you may begin to eliminate some of the more distant unrelated experiences that had previously occupied space. Another section that may often be condensed is

REFERENCES

Maria Vasquez
Mvasquez1@hotmail.com

Present Address
321 River Street
Athens, OH 45701
(740) 555-5505

Permanent Address
22154 Valley View Lane
New Concord, OH 43721
(740) 555-5555

Ms. Ellen Sampson
Department Manager, Internship Supervisor
Marshall Field's
111 North State Street
Chicago, Illinois 60602
(312) 555-5555
esampson@marshallfields.com

Dr. Ann Paulins, Associate Professor
Director, School of Human and Consumer Sciences
Ohio University
Tupper Hall
Athens, Ohio 45701
(740) 555-5655
annpaulins@ohiou.edu

Craig Schultz, Owner
Craig's Fine Dining
444 University Avenue
Athens, Ohio 45702
(740) 505-5555
craig@eatingwell.com

Dr. Martin Panzer, Professor
Phi Kappa Phi Advisor
Department of Marketing
Barsema Hall
Athens, Ohio 45701
(740) 555-5656
mpanzer@ohiou.edu

FIGURE 5.3 Reference Page

Activities. List only those items that you can relate to specific skills that will enhance your ability to perform the position you are seeking. Many students include a good deal of "fluff" in this section that is easily spotted by employers.

Project 1 at the end of this chapter is designed to get you started on constructing your resume. A number of activities related to resumes are also included on the accompanying CD-ROM. After completing your resume, use the resume checklist provided in Figure 5.4 to evaluate your document and to make sure that it does not contain any of the "pet peeves" identified in Box 5.1.

COVER LETTERS

A cover letter should always accompany a resume. The letter is your opportunity to personalize and sell yourself to an employer. Its contents are subjective whereas the items listed on the resume are objective. According to Richard H. Beatty, author of *The Perfect Cover Letter* (1999), your letter provides a prospective employer with the opportunity to analyze your written communication skills, organization skills, overall intelligence, overall focus and priorities, personal style, social skills, business or management philosophy, operating style, management style, and technical knowledge.

The letter serves as an introduction for the writer. It should provide a rationale for the employer to peruse your resume. The letter is likely to enhance your resume, but it has the potential to detract from it. The letter can be quite revealing—or misleading—if it is not carefully constructed. Used effectively, a letter personalizes the application and allows you to point out your unique and special qualities. It, like the resume, is an important screening device, so be sure that yours represents you well.

A well-written letter is direct, providing the purpose for your correspondence early on. The tone should be confident, with specific examples offered to substantiate claims that you make about yourself. Good writing will help your letter stand out above the crowd and allow the employer to focus on the content rather than be distracted by poor sentence structure or grammar and spelling mistakes. Avoid being too wordy, but do not fill the letter with overly simple sentences. In constructing your letter, evaluate it for organization, flow of ideas, and accuracy. Above all, honesty is essential. Too many prospective employees are tempted to embellish their experiences and skills, which ultimately leads to embarrassment following reference checks or during an interview.

General Format

Proper letter-writing format should be used for all professional correspondence. The use of correct structure demonstrates an attention to detail and a willingness on your part to make the effort to present yourself professionally. Resumes are formatted to best suit the situation at hand, and it is preferable to seek opinions of respected professionals in your field of interest for feedback regarding resume styles.

_____ Objective—optional. If there is an objective, does it list specific skills you are bringing to the organization rather than mentioning what you want *from* the organization?

_____ Objective—is it excessively wordy? Is the objective vague?

_____ Is the resume 1 to 2 pages in length?

_____ Are the identification data (name, addresses, phone numbers, e-mail, URL) clearly listed?

_____ Do the addresses say "Permanent Address" and "Current Address" rather than "Home Address" and "School Address"?

_____ Does the e-mail address sound professional?

_____ Is "Education" listed first if you are a recent graduate?

_____ Is the formal name of the degree clearly spelled out rather than abbreviated (ex: Bachelor of Business Administration, Bachelor of Arts, Bachelor of Science in Communication)?

_____ Is the "expected" or "anticipated" graduation date listed?

_____ Is high school information included? High school is generally not included unless it relates to career.

_____ No other colleges or universities should be listed except for those where you received your degree(s).

_____ Are the types of categories that are included logical? Does the information relate to professional goals?

_____ Is information presented in a uniform fashion?

_____ If relevant, is the experience section broken into "Relevant/Professional Experience" and then "Other/Work Experience"?

_____ Do job descriptions begin with active verbs? Are the verbs that are used descriptive enough?

_____ Does work or internship experience include the name, city, state, position title, and tasks performed?

_____ Are activities, honors, volunteer experiences, etc., described clearly?

_____ Has a description of responsibilities or tasks been included if a leadership position is/(was) held?

_____ If an "Interests" category is included, do interests listed relate to professional goals?

_____ Is personal information left off the resume (ex: height, weight, date of birth, social security number, marital status, photograph)? Such personal information should not be included.

_____ Are all categories with dates in reverse chronological order based on when the position started?

(continued)

FIGURE 5.4   Resume Checklist

FIGURE 5.4 continued from page 119

_____ Are some work experiences listed even if they do not relate directly to career goals? Work experience is important to employers even if not directly related to career.

_____ Is the spelling perfect? Grammar? Punctuation?

_____ Is the phrase "References Available Upon Request" omitted? This phrase is generally left off the resume.

_____ Has a separate sheet been used for references? References are not included on the resume.

_____ Is the most important information listed first on the resume?

_____ Are abbreviations and acronyms spelled out? Are abbreviations used sparingly?

_____ Have too many fonts been used?

_____ Is the font professional? Is font size appropriate?

_____ Periods at the ends of fragments are optional; however, format should be consistent.

_____ Are bullets or some type of symbol used to begin sentence fragments? Do the bullets line up?

_____ If the resume uses a creative layout, is it still easy to find needed information?

_____ Does everything line up?

_____ Is similar information presented consistently?

_____ Are bolding, highlights, underlines, and any other graphic techniques used consistently?

_____ Does the layout appear crowded?

_____ Are there blank lines between categories or sections? The resume needs room "to breathe."

_____ Is there unused white space that detracts from the layout? Are margins too wide? Too narrow?

_____ If applicable, does the resume need to go onto a second page?

_____ If two pages, is the last name and "page 2" at the top of the second page?

_____ Is the layout constructed in such a manner that the reader's eye is guided to most important information?

_____ Is the resume printed on good quality paper? Is the color of the paper appropriate?

_____ Is the print quality the best possible?

_____ Are dashes and hyphens formatted consistently?

_____ If using a scannable or electronic resume format, is the resume formatted correctly?

_____ Are descriptions of jobs or other activities in fragment format? Paragraph and sentence format should be avoided.

SOURCE: Developed by Robbyn T. Matthews, Office of Career Services, Ohio University, Athens, OH. Reprinted with author's permission.

BOX 5.1

TOP TEN "PET PEEVES" FOUND ON RESUMES*

1. Misspelled words, typos, poor grammar

2. Reads like a job description rather than explaining the person's contributions and accomplishments

3. No dates included, or they are inaccurate

4. Contains missing or inaccurate contact information or unprofessional e-mail address

5. Poor formatting, including distracting boxes and graphics

6. Submitting a functional resume, rather than a chronological one

7. Resume is too long

8. Contains long paragraphs rather than bullet points

9. Candidate applying for position for which he or she is not qualified

10. Personal data listed that are not relevant to the job

*Listed in order of importance. Results are according to a recent survey of 2,500 headhunters in the United States, conducted by Resumedoctor.com.

SOURCE: Excerpt from "Love cats? That's nice but leave it off your resume." (2003, January 12). *Daily Herald*, Section 1B, p. 8.

Typos, poor sentence structure, misspelled words, and grammatical errors are unacceptable in letters and resumes and will most certainly eliminate you from consideration. Both letters and resumes should be presented in a single-spaced format when submitted as hard copies. Professional letters should be written in either full block, block, or modified block format. In this text, we chose to present full block format. The advantage of full block format is that it is simpler to format in a word processing system because there are no indents. However, regardless of the specific format selected, necessary elements in a professional letter include the heading, inside address, salutation, body, close, and signature block. Special notations may be used when you provide an attachment or enclosure (such as your resume), in the event that you send a copy of the letter to a third party, or if you have used a typist. Figures 5.5 and 5.6 provide examples of cover letters written in block format that you can refer to when reading through the following section explaining each component of the cover letter. The letter in Figure 5.5 addresses the applicant's credentials in conjunction with the specifics requirements from an advertisement, whereas the letter in Figure 5.6 takes a more general approach.

Contents and Components

HEADING. The heading provides your address, your phone number (optional), and the date. You should not include your name in the heading unless you are using personalized stationery that displays your name. If you are writing professional correspondence on behalf of a business, the heading is generally preprinted, and you simply supply the date for each letter. However, *never* use company stationery for the purpose of writing a cover letter. This is in poor taste and is probably contrary to company policy.

INSIDE ADDRESS. The inside address is that of the receiver of the letter and is the same as the address on the envelope. The inside address should contain the name, title, and position of the person whom you expect to read the letter. If you do not know the name of the appropriate individual to receive the letter, you should find out. It takes little effort to make a telephone call or consult a resource such as the career services office, the Internet, or company literature. A personalized address and salutation will demonstrate that you have made an effort to determine who will read your letter. You should include a title, such as Mr., Ms., Mrs., or Dr., in front of the name of the receiver on the inside address. Make the effort to identify the correct title, and use that in the salutation as well. The professional position of the receiver should be identified on the second line of the heading. Do your homework to ensure that the position you list is correct. Above all, take extra care to be certain that the name of your addressee is correctly spelled. In some situations, particularly with very large companies, the application process for internships or entry-level positions requires a more anonymous submission. If the contact person is not identifiable, address the letter as the advertisement for the position directs (e.g., Attention Human Resources). Similarly, if you are not able to determine the appropriate title of the receiver, use Mr. or Ms. if the gender is obvious. If in doubt, use only the name of the receiver.

SALUTATION. The salutation begins with *Dear* and includes the title of the reader, and his or her last name. The first name of the reader is not included in the salutation

95 University Terrace #3
Columbus, OH 43210

Ms. Rebecca Anderson
Hiring Manager
Unique Accessories Ltd.
1440 Chicago Apparel Center
Chicago, IL 60602

May 13, 2004

Dear Ms. Anderson:

I am writing this letter in response to your advertisement for a **Showroom Assistant** in the May 12 issue of the *Chicago Tribune*. As you will note from the attached resume, I will graduate with a **Bachelor of Science in Textiles and Clothing** from The Ohio State University in June 2004. I believe I possess all of the qualities and credentials listed in your advertisement:

Strong customer orientation and attention to detail: For the past 18 months, I have worked in J.C. Penney's Customer Service Department. In that capacity, I respond in a calm and professional manner to the complaints of dissatisfied (and often irate) customers. I also answer the telephone, issue refunds, place Internet orders, and respond to questions from vendors and warehouse personnel. In 18 months I have never received a customer complaint and have maintained a 100% accurate cash drawer.

Strong problem-solving and organizational skills: As president of my fraternity, I am constantly required to resolve difficult interpersonal and procedural problems. I plan, schedule, and moderate weekly meetings with other fraternity executive board members, and distribute and enforce fraternity rules and regulations in a "firm but fair" manner.

Self-motivated, assertive person with a positive attitude: I have maintained an above-average grade point average while attending school full-time, working an average of 20 hours per week, and participating in a number of professional and community service activities. I am equally adept at assuming leadership roles, operating in a cooperative team environment, and working independently.

You can be assured that I will apply the same level of enthusiasm and dedication as a Showroom Assistant with Unique Accessories Ltd. Your serious consideration of my qualifications is much appreciated. I look forward to the prospect of learning more about this exciting opportunity with Unique Accessories Ltd.

Sincerely,

Robert Stewart

Robert Stewart

Enclosure

FIGURE 5.5 Sample Cover Letter 1

44-A Lincoln Highway
DeKalb, IL 60115

Ms. Kim Rankin, College Recruiter
Neiman Marcus
1 LBJ Highway
Dallas, Texas 78092

June 17, 2004

Dear Ms. Rankin:

Because of my strong interest in a management career with an upscale fashion retailer, I was immediately drawn to your recent advertisement for a department manager. A background in retail management, a proven record of achieving results, and my level of enthusiasm, make me a qualified candidate to join the Neiman Marcus team.

My interest in retailing started in DECA in high school and developed further through a variety of retail and merchandising positions while I was pursuing my Textiles, Apparel, and Merchandising degree at Northern Illinois University. In researching the top retailers in the country, Neiman Marcus emerged as having an excellent training program, a reputation for exemplary customer service, and a sound market position. This is exactly the type of retailing environment I seek.

The enclosed resume highlights my qualifications, which match those you seek in a department manager. You will also note that I was recognized as the top salesperson in my store in 2004, and was instrumental in writing the new-employee handbook. Based on customer and supervisor feedback, I am confident that I have the skills needed to succeed in the retail management. Additionally, I have a true interest in working for Neiman Marcus.

Would you please consider my request for an interview so that we may discuss my qualifications further? I will call you next week to see if a meeting can be arranged. Should you need to reach me prior to that, please feel free to contact me at (815) 565-5656, or kallen@niuniv.edu.

Thank you very much for considering my application. I look forward to talking with you.

Sincerely,

Karen C. Allen

Karen C. Allen

Enclosure

FIGURE 5.6   Sample Cover Letter 2

except in the case where an appropriate title (Mr. or Ms.) cannot be determined. In this case use the full name (e.g., Dear Lee Jones). Occasionally situations dictate that a name is not available. You may find a lead via a newspaper advertisement that lists an address but no name. If you find yourself in a situation in which you cannot identify a name, use a salutation such as *Attention Human Resources Manager* or *To whom it may concern* as a last resort.

The salutation ends with a colon (:) rather than a comma. On more familiar correspondence, such as professional letters you may write to colleague or clients with whom you are acquainted, it is permissible to address the salutation using the first name and a comma. When applying for a position, however, it is always best to use a more formal approach.

BODY OF THE LETTER. The opening paragraph of your letter should begin with an introductory statement describing the position that you are seeking. It is best to state the purpose for your correspondence right away. It is frustrating for the reader to have to guess the purpose of the letter or to be unclear about the position being sought. It is helpful to include referral information, particularly if someone suggested that you contact the receiver of the letter or if you are responding to an advertisement. Briefly include background information about yourself that correlates to your compatibility with such a position.

Use the next paragraph or two to describe your specific interests and qualifications as they relate to the position announcement. This is the section of the letter in which you should highlight your achievements and elaborate on opportunities you have had that make you stand out above the crowd. Employers, as they seek to fill positions, are looking for individuals who have something to offer them that no one else has. Be sure to explain what makes you different from (and better than) all of the other job applicants. Although you may be tempted to expound your virtues, remember that the reader has only a finite amount of time. Limit the content of your letter to key items that you can relate to the necessary qualifications for the job desired.

In the closing paragraph of your letter, you will want to reiterate your excitement for and interest in the position for which you are applying, and offer information to the employer regarding your availability for an interview. Be sure that your telephone number, e-mail address, and any other relevant contact information is included in the letter as well as on your resume, and offer any necessary information that may be of use to the employer when contacting you.

If you know you will be out of town during a certain week or in the geographic area in which the company to which you are applying is located, let them know. Do not be too restrictive as to the time of day during which you may be reached. If you will not be available until late in the afternoon, rather than suggesting that the employer wait until then to call you, use an answering machine or voice mail and indicate in the letter that you would appreciate a message to which you will promptly respond. If you go this route, be sure to check your messages throughout each day. If you do not hear from the prospective employer within a week to ten days from the time you expect your letter to have arrived, it is wise for you to contact the employer. If you desire, you may indicate in your closing paragraph that you will call; however, do not be too specific about the day or time in which you plan to make the call. You will be setting yourself up for failure should an event occur that precludes you from following through on this promise. With the increasing use of electronic communication today, it is appropriate to suggest that an employer may most efficiently use electronic mail to contact you. Again, be certain to check your messages daily and, as mentioned previously, make sure your e-mail address is a professional one.

CLOSE.   The close, sometimes referred to as the "complementary close," should be appropriate for the letter. *Sincerely, Sincerely yours,* and *Respectfully yours,* are three common and suitable closes. If you use a close longer than one word, capitalize only the first word.

SIGNATURE BLOCK.   Your signature is the final personal touch of the letter, and your name appears in this section only. Your name should appear twice, once typewritten and once as a signature. Leave four single-spaced lines between the close and your typewritten name to sign the letter. Be sure that you sign the letter in blue or black ink, as this is one additional example of your attention to detail. Some suggest that it is best to sign in blue ink; otherwise your cover letter may look like a copy, and not an original cover letter. However, the choice of ink color may strictly be a matter of your preference.

General Letter-Writing Tips

Like most things in life, the adage "practice makes perfect" applies to letter writing, too. As you write your cover letter, and as you review and edit it, consider the tone being presented. The letter should be upbeat, enthusiastic, and positive. You, as the writer, should come across as confident, reliable, and capable. As you construct sentences, vary your writing style to avoid beginning sentences with and overusing the word "I." Even though, obviously, the letter focuses on you, vary the presentation of your accomplishments to make the letter interesting. Avoid wishy-washy statements such as "I feel . . . ," and "I think . . . ." These statements do not exude confidence the way a definitive statement does. ("I believe that my qualifications are acceptable for the demands of this job" versus "My qualifications are perfectly matched to the demands of the job.")

Be careful, also, to avoid slang use of English in your written communication. Common errors include statements such as, "I would like to get with you in an interview . . . ," "since I live in Chicago . . . ," and so on. Better approaches include: "I would like to arrange an interview . . . ," and "because I live in Chicago . . . ." It is not enough to communicate your message effectively; you must impress the reader with your professional style and attention to detail. Table 5.1 provides a list of word choices for cover letter writing.

Good writing style depends on variety as much as syntax, so it is helpful to refer to resources that offer ideas for words, phraseology, and structure. Seek words that imply your aptitude for management and responsibility. Label your accomplishments with words such as "challenge" and "opportunity," and reflect upon previous

TABLE 5.1

BETTER WORD CHOICES FOR COVER LETTER WRITING

INSTEAD OF	USE
Anxious	Looking forward to
Since	Because
Set up	Arrange
Starting	Beginning
Come in	Schedule
Have	Possess
Had	Completed
Had to	Had the opportunity to
Do	Complete
Get back to you	Promptly return
Hope to	Plan to or Expect to
Can	May or Shall
Would like	Expect
Feel	Believe

employment or academic opportunities as positive experiences. Use appropriately descriptive action verbs (see Figure 5.2) representing the level of responsibility that you have undertaken. You will find projects at the end of the chapter and on the accompanying CD-ROM to help you compose an effective cover letter. After completing your cover letter, use the checklist in Figure 5.7 and on the CD-ROM to evaluate your document.

SENDING YOUR LETTER.   If you are using "snail mail" to send your cover letter and resume, the size and type of envelope you select for mailing is one additional detail

_____ Is it addressed to a particular person (unless it is a response to a blind ad)?

_____ Is the salutation followed by a colon rather than a comma?

_____ Have you told the employer exactly what position you are applying for and how you found out about it?

_____ Have you stated why you are interested in the position and the organization?

_____ Have you told the employer what you can do for the organization rather than what it can do for you?

_____ Did you use specific examples to sell your skills?

_____ Have you avoided rewriting your resume in your cover letter?

_____ Is the sentence structure varied? Have you limited the use of the words "I" and "My" at the beginning of each sentence?

_____ Did you express appreciation for the employer considering your application?

_____ Is it an original letter rather than an obviously mass-produced copy?

_____ Is it neat and attractive?

_____ Did you format the letter correctly using a full or modified block layout?

_____ Did you refrain from telling the employer that you would call them to arrange an interview?

_____ Is the letter centered on the page with equal top and bottom margins?

_____ Is every word spelled correctly? Are grammar, punctuation, and capitalization correct? Is it free of typographical errors?

_____ Does the whole letter fit on one page?

_____ Have you signed your name in black or blue ink?

_____ Is it printed on high-quality paper that matches your resume? Is it printed on a high-quality printer?

SOURCE: Developed by Office of Career Services, Ohio University, Athens, OH. Reprinted with permission.

FIGURE 5.7   Cover Letter Checklist

worth considering. Cover letters and resumes should be sent in an envelope no smaller than a standard business envelope (9 by 4-inches). Most stationery available for letters and resumes will include matching business-size envelopes. The cover letter and resume should be folded together, cover letter on top, with two folds. There are two acceptable methods to follow when folding the documents. The most common is the inside-fold method: Looking down on the letter, fold from the bottom up approximately one third of the way up the page, then fold the top down over the first fold so that the documents fit into a business envelope. The top fold should be placed so that the top edge of the paper is not flush with the first fold but rather is inset about ½-inch from the folded edge. The outside-fold method produces an accordion fold. The advantage of the outside-fold is that the letter heading is immediately visible when the envelope is opened. The first fold is made identical to the first fold of the inside-fold method, but the documents are folded *back* rather than forward in the second fold. Regardless of the type of fold made, the documents should be placed in the envelope so that the letter will be face up and right side up when it is opened.

You may wish to make the extra effort to send your cover letter and resume in a large envelope. This strategy provides the advantage of delivering an unfolded cover letter and resume. In addition to the more pristine appearance of your documents, the receiver may be more apt to open a large envelope first. There is increasing acceptance among employers for receiving electronically submitted resumes and cover letters. In fact, many employers will now ask that your application materials be submitted by that method. If you find yourself in that situation, it is essential that the guidelines presented by the potential employer be followed precisely. Consider the following statement from Roland Hearns, vice president of recruitment and placement for Saks Incorporated: "I was once receiving 500 resumes per week in response to an MBA Internship advertised on our Web site. Retailing students, even at the MBA level, are facing new and increasing levels of competition in today's career marketplace."

Generally, employers will ask that you submit your resume electronically in one of two ways. Some employers will ask that you e-mail your resume and cover letter as an attached document, which is easily done through any e-mail program. (If you are not sure how to do an attachment, ask your instructor for help.) Other employers, however, will ask you to send the document(s) as an e-mail message itself. In the latter case, you should convert your material to a *plain text* (ASCII) or *text only* file so that it will transmit in an orderly fashion. Basically this conversion takes out any formatting that was previously added to make the resume look nice. Because the conversion is somewhat more complicated than simply attaching a document, the CD-ROM accompanying this text provides step-by-step instructions for converting and sending your resume in the ASCII format. Regardless of how you send your resume, you should always include a cover letter, even if that means providing it as an e-mail message.

As mentioned at the beginning of this chapter, preparing a resume and cover letter can be quite a demanding task. However, by starting early, reading through the chapter guidelines, and working through the projects we have provided, you should have both a winning resume and a cover letter that will be sure to set you apart from other candidates! Remember, once you have created a basic, strong resume and cover letter, you can easily update these documents as you expand your experiences and leadership skills throughout your career.

PROJECTS

1. **Resume development.** Prepare a resume worksheet by completing the following entries and questions. After completing the worksheet, construct a professional resume and reference page. Be sure to refer back to Figure 5.4 (Resume Checklist) and Box 5.1 ("Top Ten Pet Peeves" Found on Resumes). For your convenience, the accompanying CD-ROM provides examples, resume templates, and exercises to help you practice writing an effective resume.

   a. Current address, telephone, and e-mail address

   b. Permanent address

   c. Education
      • Institution
      • Name of major
      • Name of degree
      • Year of graduation
      • Grade point average (if desirable)
      • Percentage of education you paid for (if applicable)

   d. Work experience (for each previous job)
      • Job title
      • Duties
      • Duration (time frame) of experience
      • Major learning opportunities

    e. Activities or leadership experiences: For each of the items listed in this section, write a statement indicating how the item relates to the job opportunity you are seeking.

    f. Who can serve as references for me? Why would each person be a good reference?

2. **Cover letter development.** Locate a job or internship announcement matching your interests and qualifications. Based on the announcement, complete the following worksheet (an example is given). Once you have completed the worksheet, construct a professional cover letter based on your outline. Be sure to refer back to the examples in Table 5.1 (Better Word Choices for Cover Letter Writing), and Figure 5.7 (Cover Letter Checklist). Also note that the CD-ROM contains examples, templates for your cover letter, and drafts to help you practice writing an effective cover letter.

JOB OR INTERNSHIP REQUIREMENTS	YOUR QUALIFICATIONS
1. Two years' retail experience	1. Worked as a sales associate at The Limited; two years at the Gap as Assistant Manager
2.	2.
3.	3.

3. **Combining resume, reference page, and cover letter.** Locate a job or internship announcement matching your interests and qualifications. Based on the announcement, construct a resume, reference page, and cover letter specific to the position. You may wish to use the formats provided on the CD-ROM.

4. **Checking resume, cover letter, and reference page.** Using the checklists provided, check at least two of your classmates' resumes, cover letters, and reference pages. Provide them with positive, as well as constructive, feedback. After your classmates have checked your materials, make the changes you feel are necessary and then take the resume and cover letter to your campus career planning office to obtain additional feedback.

5. **Construct an "aspirational resume."** Refer to you goals. Construct an "aspirational resume"—that is, a resume that is a reflection of where you want to be five years in the future. What steps will you need to take to achieve this aspiration?

QUESTIONS FOR DISCUSSION

1. What are some advantages of a functional-format resume? Of a chronological format?

2. Do you agree or disagree with the idea that generally an objective is not necessary on a resume?

3. Do you think employers should consider your GPA when reviewing your resume? Why or why not?

4. What are some transferable skills you might gain from the following positions that would be important for a job in retailing or merchandising?

   a. Babysitter

   b. Lawn care person

   c. Lifeguard

   d. Restaurant server

   e. Fast-food counter help

   f. Bartender

   g. Pet or house-sitter

   h. Receptionist

   i. Caddy

   j. Office or house-cleaning person

5. Why do you think employers are interested in activities or volunteerism when reviewing your resume?

6. Do you think employers should have the freedom to call any employer you have listed on your resume for a reference? Why or why not?

7. If your resume does a great job of presenting your credentials and qualifications, why do you think it is necessary to include a cover letter with it?

8. Can you think of some strategies to enable your resume to stand out over those of other applicants?

ELECTRONIC ACTIVITIES

Refer to the accompanying CD-ROM. The key elements of this chapter are:

1. Summary of Chapter 5 text

2. Resume development

   a. Examples of resumes and references

   b. Editing the resume example

   c. Resume worksheet

   d. Resume checklist

3. Cover letter development

   a. Cover letter editing activity

   b. Cover letter worksheet

   c. Cover letter template

   d. Cover letter checklist

4. ASCII resume: e-mailing the resume

REFERENCES

Adams, B., & Morin, L. (1999). *The complete resume & job search book for college students.* Hobrook, MA: Adams Media Corporation.

Beatty, R. H. (1996). *The perfect cover letter.* New York: John Wiley & Sons.

Donnelly, J. H., Jr. (1991). *Close to the customer: 25 management tips from the other side of the counter.* Homewood, IL: Business One Irwin.

Northern Illinois University Career Planning and Placement Center. (2004–2005). *Job hunter's guide for NIU students and alumni.* Evanston, IL: Cass Communications, Inc. [On-line]. Available: http://www.niu.edu/cppc/job_hunters_guide_2004.pdf.

CHAPTER SIX

INTERVIEWING

If you can't say something nice, don't say nothin' at all!
—THUMPER, IN *BAMBI*

OBJECTIVES

- To identify telephone etiquette appropriate to requesting, scheduling, and participating in an interview.

- To identify common types of interview tests given to retailing and merchandising job candidates.

- To identify appropriate wardrobe and appearance practices for an interview.

- To recognize the importance of projecting a professional image when interviewing.

- To develop confidence with respect to interviewing situations.

- To enhance oral communication skills appropriate for a professional setting.

- To identify and implement personal strategies leading to success in interviews.

- To provide information useful in the effective evaluation of an interview.

- To provide guidelines for constructing a professional thank-you letter for follow-up after an interview.

The direct result of a successfully written cover letter and resume—and the next step in your search for employment or an internship—is an interview. The interview is your opportunity to showcase your personal style and your oral communication skills. Although you have likely made a first impression with your resume and cover letter, the first few minutes of an interview will form a lasting impression of your professional profile. Your professional "package" will be evaluated—your manners, appearance and hygiene, linguistic skills, ability to analyze situations and think on your feet, and expressed knowledge of and interest in the company.

One of the most common errors of prospective employees is too little preparation for the interview. Employers expect interviewees to have a genuine interest in their companies. This interest should extend to a knowledge of the organization's history, structure, geographic territory, subsidiaries or divisions, and information available on a recent annual report. Many employers furnish company literature to career service offices. Students and recent graduates should seek this information! Additionally, employers who visit university campuses may offer company presentations prior to interviewing opportunities. It is essential that you attend such presentations both to obtain information and to inquire informally about the nature of the company.

Keep in mind that interviewing, like anything else in life, improves with practice. Although interviewees may feel inhibited and lack confidence in early interviews, the experience gained from assessing experiences will serve as preparation to improve in the future. A recent retail merchandising student recalled that her early interviews were not positive experiences. Upon reflection, she acknowledged that she had, indeed, not prepared herself as she should have, resulting in lackluster interest by employers. As she continued to interview, however, she noticed an improved confidence in herself along with an ability to anticipate questions and better articulate responses. Following several disappointing interviews, she hit her stride and eventually landed a prestigious internship with Saks Fifth Avenue, where she is currently successfully working her way up the merchandising career ladder. The moral of the story—keep at it, keep practicing; interviewing becomes easier.

ESTABLISHING VERBAL CONTACT

If you have not previously spoken to the person with whom you will be interviewing, an initial verbal contact must be made to arrange the interview. This initial contact establishes an impression just as letters, resumes, and interviews do. A verbal impression is typically stronger and longer lasting than the impression that accompanies a letter and resume. Exhibit confidence and self-assurance as you speak with a potential employer. Likewise, provide an appropriate opportunity for the interviewer to contact you at a time that is convenient for him or her.

Telephone Etiquette

When making your initial contact by telephone, rehearse what you will say. One advantage of a telephone call compared with a face-to-face encounter is that you can use notes. Decide what you want to say and how you will say it. Your professionalism over the telephone will be evaluated.

TELEPHONE CALLS TO MAKE INITIAL CONTACT. If you have not yet determined the appropriate person to receive your letter and resume, your first telephone contact will be to establish the recipient of your correspondence. Identify yourself, then state that you are interested in contacting the person who is responsible for receiving resumes and interviewing potential hires. Be sure to request the spelling of that person's name and his or her exact job title. Use this information in your cover letter and for future telephone correspondence. As you place this initial call, be prepared to speak with this person; he or she may be the one who answers the phone, or the secretary may offer to direct your call. Take advantage of any opportunity you may have to make a positive impression, to initiate a contact, and to establish an interview opportunity.

A typical phone conversation might begin, "Hello, my name is Ann Paulins. I am interested in contacting the manager of human resources. May I have this person's name?" After receiving the name and double checking the precise spelling, be sure to obtain the correct job position title. Also identify the appropriate personal title (Ms., Mrs., Mr., Dr.), particularly if you have been given a gender-neutral name. We suggest always double checking the personal title, as names commonly don't identify gender and the person may go by another title such as doctor. The conversation should continue, "Thank you. Is that Ms. Jones?" Then, "What is Ms. Jones' job title?"

TELEPHONE CALLS TO REQUEST AN INTERVIEW. A week or so after you have sent a letter, you should follow up with a telephone call. The purpose of this call is to reinforce contact with the employer and to request an interview. You should ask for the person who has been identified as the recipient of your letter. When you place your call, one of two scenarios will most likely occur. You will either be connected to that person or you will be asked to leave a message because the person is unable to take your call. If the person is unable to take your call, you would be wise to leave a message and then ask if there is a better time for you to call again. When leaving a message, restate your name and offer to spell it, offer your telephone number and the time frame in which you will be able to receive a call, and provide a brief message such as "I am calling with regard to the status of my application for an internship." If the secretary has indicated a convenient time for you to call back, note that time and *do* call again. This will indicate a strong commitment on your part to establish contact with the potential employer.

The preferable result, of course, is to connect with the intended recipient of your call. If this is achieved, don't expect that he or she will automatically remember your letter or your resume. Approach the conversation in a manner that will allow the employer to identify your application materials and converse with you without having to be "in the dark" about who you are and what you want. Such a conversation could begin, "Hello, I am Ann Paulins. I sent a letter and resume to you last week indicating my interest in your designer's assistant position. Have you had an opportunity to review it?" The conversation from this point on will not only be an important initial contact for you but will enable you to demonstrate your ability to carry on a conversation and think on your feet. Be prepared for either event; that the person has read and is familiar with your resume or that your resume has not made it across the desk yet. As the conversation warrants, reiterate your interest in the company and your desire to visit with the employer in person. The employer may take control of the conversation, or he or she may expect you to do most of the talking. Anticipate various telephone scenarios, and even practice your responses with friends. This is another area in which practice leads to improvement, and ultimately perfection.

If you are unable to make a connection with the desired person, or if you are denied an interview, do not give up. If you are truly interested in employment opportunities with the company you should continue to correspond professionally with the appropriate representatives of the company. Listen to the reason(s) why you have not achieved your goals with the company. Are there currently no openings, are your qualifications inadequate, is their division being downsized, or is the personnel manager currently preoccupied with other business? Respond accordingly to the given reason. Set a plan for yourself to remedy any personal inadequacies (such as finishing your degree, completing a Retail Math course, or obtaining more in-store retail experience), and reposition your application to demonstrate an interest and ability in fulfilling their needs. In the event that you are unable to contact the person or if your telephone messages go unreturned, do not give up. Perseverance really does pay off. Be persistent as you go after the job of your dreams. Keep calling. Several former students have marveled that they were persistent enough to finally be invited to participate in an interview. In fact, when the interview occurred, the employer commented that the student's persistence was impressive. (The employers knew who the resilient students were!) Do not place telephone calls to the point of being a nuisance, but *do* exhibit enough perseverance to demonstrate that you are genuinely interested in the company and are committed to waiting until there is an opening or an opportunity to interview for a position. It may be helpful to remember the words of Winston Churchill, "never, never, never give up."

RECEIVING A TELEPHONE CALL. The ideal situation following distribution of your resume is receiving a telephone call from the prospective employer. Be prepared to receive a professional business telephone call after you have sent even one resume. Begin answering your telephone professionally *every time*, and encourage any roommates you may have to do the same. You are most likely to receive a business call between the hours of 8 A.M. and 5 P.M., but these hours are certainly not limited. You should be accessible when the phone call arrives, so do not fall into the habit of keeping callers waiting on the line. We often return telephone calls during the hours of 9 A.M. to noon. As you might expect, many of the recipients of our return calls are students. Although the vast majority of people with whom we speak are courteous and willing to take messages when necessary, a variety of unprofessional responses has been encountered. One common response to a request to speak with someone is "he's/(she's) asleep." Although honest, this blunt response does not contribute positively to one's professional profile. Other calls result in being placed on "hold" long enough to open and read mail and answer e-mail messages. A further frustration occurs upon requesting that a message be taken. Apparently many households do not make a practice of locating a pen and pencil near the telephone. Remember, these are *return* phone calls—the recipients of these calls have initiated contact and have requested that someone call them back! These offenses are forgivable in most contexts, but when coupled with your job search, they may be lethal.

If you have a shared number, inform your roommates or family members that you are expecting potential employers to be calling you and instruct them in the telephone etiquette to which you expect they will adhere. Begin today to practice telephone etiquette yourself, and you will easily become accustomed to speaking professionally on the phone. A simple phrase such as "Susan is unavailable right now. May I take a message?" is a catch-all for any situation that prevents the intended recipient of a call from coming to the telephone, and it is much more professional than "Susan is in the shower. Can she call you back?" Make sure that there is always paper and a writing implement by the phone.

Today, answering machines, mobile phones, and voice mail are as common as car radios. If you do not have access to such devices, make the investment now. Additionally, use the technology that mobile phones offer. Create a brief and professional greeting or message for your voice mail and check your messages often. If there is any doubt regarding the reliability of a shared land line, do not circulate that number on your resume or cover letters—use a private mobile phone instead. Once prospective employers decide to contact you, you cannot afford to miss the opportunity due to a breakdown in communication.

Be certain to make your greeting professional. A common yet perplexing experience involves unearthing the unique telephone messages that are created by students. Once you have embarked on a job search, a professional message is the only appropriate choice. A professional message identifies the telephone number to the caller and requests that a brief message be left. Whether you include your name in the message is a personal choice. For some people, the potential breach of security in identifying the occupants of the household prompts omission of a name in the message. If you are concerned that the caller may not identify that you are an occupant of the household, we suggest including your name. State your telephone number, including area code, and request the caller to leave a brief message to which you will promptly respond. A generic telephone message such as, "You have reached 000-111-2222. I am not available to take your call so please leave a brief message along with your name and telephone number when you hear the tone. I will return your call promptly." When recording your greeting, speak clearly. It is a good idea to have someone with a very nice voice record your message for you if you are uncomfortable doing it yourself.

Scheduling an Interview

If you have successfully initiated contact with a prospective employer, you will be scheduling an interview. Arrangements must be made as to where and when the interview will take place. Depending on the location of the interview, you may be responsible for making travel plans. Many students have been so excited to be offered an interview that they too readily agree to the first date and time offered by the employer. It is important to remember that you may have obligations, including classes and work, around which you must schedule. Do not be afraid to negotiate a meeting time and place that accommodates your schedule. As long as you are not too restrictive, the potential employer will respect the fact that you must follow through with previous commitments.

TELEPHONE INTERVIEWS. With time and expense for travel a major obstacle in scheduling interviews, there is a growing trend toward telephone interviews. Telephone interviews should be prepared for in the same manner as a face-to-face interview, with the exception that you do not need to plan a strategic wardrobe. Do be certain, however, that during a telephone interview you have absolute quiet in your background environment and that there will be no interruptions from your end of the telephone line. Do not respond to call waiting during a telephone interview.

If you receive a call unexpectedly, you should *never* ask the caller if he or she can call back. If you are caught off guard, ask if the caller minds holding the line while you shut the door or change phones to a quieter location. Do *not* leave the caller on hold for more than 30 seconds. Even if you do not need to change phones or locations, use the time to take a deep breath (get a grip!) and to find the notes you should have readily available. When returning to the phone, thank the caller for holding and then proceed with the interview.

Although telephone interviews do not give you the advantage of making a great "appearance" by utilizing positive and professional nonverbal behaviors, you do have the advantage of using notes. Be sure to write down, in advance, all items you wish to share with the interviewer. It is a good idea to have a copy of your resume in front of you and a list of the questions you wish to ask. Just because you have crib notes, don't make the mistake of not preparing thoroughly. You should be as well prepared for a telephone interview as you are for a face-to-face interview. During a telephone interview, take special care to speak clearly.

PREPARING FOR THE INTERVIEW

In preparation for an interview, you must familiarize yourself with the company. For retail companies and apparel (and other product) manufacturers, there is no substitute for first-person interaction with the store or the product. Visit as many Kmart stores as possible if you are going to interview with Kmart. Examine Liz Claiborne products if you are going to interview with Liz Claiborne. After a recent interview with a recruiter for a large retailing chain, a student commented that she felt confident in replying in the affirmative when asked had she ever shopped in the store. She had been stumped, however, when asked what one change she would make, given the opportunity. An interview question such as this requires an intense familiarity with the company, and the store, as well as critical thinking ability. When gathering information about a company, go beyond the written history and the informative brochures to delve into the heart of the business—the store or the product—and research the company yourself from the perspective of a consumer. Shop in the store or for the products yourself, talk to people who are frequent customers, and research the company creatively as you prepare for an interview. This firsthand knowledge of the company will impress the interviewer and will demonstrate more than a superficial awareness of current market performance and industry trends. Box 6.1 provides the guidelines for researching a company with which you have an interview. Also see Box 6.2, which illustrates that having little or no knowledge of a company is the most frequent interview and job fair mistake.

As you are preparing for the interview, identify a focus in your self-presentation. If you are interviewing for an internship or an entry-level job, define your own objectives

---

BOX 6.1

RESEARCHING A PROSPECTIVE EMPLOYER

Following is a list of information you should know about a company *before* your interview:

- Location of the company's home office
- Size of the company, including number of employees, subsidiaries, and divisions
- How long in business
- Major competition
- Reputation of the company
- Whether privately or publicly owned
- Technology systems in place
- Geographic locations
- Potential or recent growth
- Current events in the news
- Annual stock growth during the past five years
- Current stock price
- Target customers
- Price points of products
- Products and services offered
- Current employees that you know
- Formal versus on-the-job training
- Typical career path at the company

BOX 6.2

THE MOST FREQUENT INTERVIEW AND JOB FAIR MISTAKES*

1. Little or no knowledge of the company (44 percent)

2. Unprepared to discuss career plans and goals (23 percent)

3. Limited enthusiasm (16 percent)

4. Lack of eye contact (5 percent)

5. Unprepared to discuss skills or experience (3 percent)

6. Late arrival (2 percent)

7. Other (4 percent)

---

*Based on a recent survey conducted by Accountemps staffing service, which included responses from 44 percent of 150 executives with the nation's 1,000 largest companies.

SOURCE: *The most frequent interview and job fair mistake: Little or no knowledge of the company.* Handout prepared by the Career Planning and Placement Center, Northern Illinois University, DeKalb, IL. [On-line]. Available: www.niu.edu.cppc/handouts.shtml. Reprinted with permission,

for the experience. Employers want to know what you expect to learn, what you can contribute to the company, where your interests lie, and the goals you have set for yourself. Being able to confidently answer these questions will demonstrate a level of personal preparation that is in keeping with corporate expectations. Focus not only on your strengths and areas of expertise but also on the areas within the company that interest you and in which you hope to work and learn. Recruiters will have difficulty identifying a place for you if you have not defined your goals and objectives and if you are simply "willing to do anything." Even though you should be open-minded enough to pitch in and do what needs to be done on the job, in an interview you will serve yourself better when you focus on a particular job or department and are able to articulate your personal professional goals. As you plan your future, and prepare for interview questions, set realistic goals for yourself. This will be a turnoff to the employer if you are unrealistic in the accomplishments you expect for yourself. This will demonstrate that you lack knowledge in the company hierarchy and will indicate that you aren't a team player.

Most importantly in preparation for your interview, know what you have to offer the company. You are, after all, selling yourself. This sales job is for your complete "package," and you will be evaluated accordingly. No detail is too small as you plan your appearance, your responses, your questions, and your nonverbal cues, including posture, gait, eye contact, and handshake. To help you prepare further for your interview, Box 6.2 presents a list of common mistakes that candidates make during a job interview—all of which are easily avoidable with preparation.

Interview Tests

It is common, particularly for entry-level interviews, to be required to participate in a series of tests. Tests range from mandatory drug tests required of all employees to pen-and-pencil or computer-based tests that are reminiscent of academic exams. Jaimi Workman, a 2003 graduate of Ohio University's retail merchandising program, experienced a variety of testing methods during her career search. She notes that some companies favor data analysis tests whereas others prefer to administer leadership or skills inventories. Jaimi recalls that recruiters typically indicate that there is no way to prepare for the tests that will be given; however, Jaimi advises students to review information from their Retail Math course before taking analytical tests. Students should be familiar with sales reports that include this year's and last year's sales, stock-to-sales ratios, and inventory figures. In addition, knowledge of different zones—hot, warm, and cold—within the United States is important for merchandising positions.

Additionally, it is likely that you will be subjected to a leadership/skills inventory test that might include problem solving, preferences, and abilities. Your familiarity with your strengths and weaknesses should enable you to better identify your own preferences. Personal analysis of your skills and abilities may prove valuable as you navigate the questions on the interview tests. Regardless of the amount of preparation that you can undertake, your awareness of the likelihood of being subjected to a test should reduce your anxiety level before your interview.

Your Interview Wardrobe

It is universally accepted that appearance is important. When you visit the company, observe the appropriate attire and cater your wardrobe to fit the company culture. Remember that an interview is a professional occasion; when in doubt, lean toward conservative attire over casual. Several years ago an Ohio University student landed an internship with a visual merchandising department—a competitive position for which there were multiple applicants. She confided that during her interview she was quite uncomfortable when she realized that the employer and members of the visual merchandising team were all dressed in jeans and tennis shoes. Having been duly instructed as to proper interview attire, this student appeared in a conservative suit, dressed for a "corporate interview." Although this extreme difference in dress resulted in her feeling ill prepared for the interview, she later learned that her appearance had greatly impressed the director of visual merchandising. He commented to her that he was extremely impressed by her professionalism and the care that she had taken to prepare herself for the interview. Her appearance, in fact, made a lasting impression on the employer and was a deciding factor in her being offered the internship. Even though she ended up wearing jeans and tennis shoes every day of her internship, this student took comfort in the fact that she had landed the job because of her professional appearance and preparation for the interview.

When interviewing with companies that are fashion focused, it is perfectly appropriate to display a fashionable appearance. This can be accomplished, however, without compromising good taste and professional behavior. We recall a student who attended a retail career fair at Purdue University. She wore a tailored suit in a shade of green that really made her stand out in a sea of navy and black suits. Recruiters at the conference even commented to her that they appreciated her fashion sense and willingness to break out of the "corporate" appearance mold. This dress style worked— as she was remembered for exhibiting a relatively daring fashion sense while at the same time her appearance (in terms of style of her suit, grooming, and choice of accessories) was professional and appropriate.

It is a good idea to avoid clothes and accessories that will draw emphasis away from you. Be cautious of flashy clothes, dangling earrings, hair in your face, shoes you can't walk in, and other distracting items. At a panel discussion during a recent Purdue University Retail Management Career Conference, Todd Landis, the manager for college relations for Kohl's, offered this rule of thumb, "if you question what you're wearing, don't wear it." Be sure to consider the appearance of your hands, nails, teeth, and hair in addition to your wardrobe. Angela Anderson, assistant dean, career resources, the College of Business at Ohio University, notes that when your appearance or attire is noticed and might be recalled by the interviewer as a point of interest, it is not likely a good thing. It is more likely that a midriff-baring shirt, a low-cut blouse, or five-inch heels will be remembered due to their inappropriate presence during an interview than an appropriate interview suit will be recalled. It is better, however, to have your interview associated with your positive characteristics and your fit with the company than with an embarrassing faux pas. The accompanying CD-ROM provides an activity to help you discern appropriate and inappropriate interview outfits.

A last word of caution concerning your appearance for the interview. Recently there has been an increasing trend for young adults to have multiple tattoos or piercings. In fact, about 1 in every 10 Americans has a tattoo—up from 1 out of 100, 30 years ago (Schmidt, 2004). Although such body modifications are becoming somewhat more socially acceptable, you should still be discreet in revealing them in an interview or in a corporate setting. Choose an interview outfit that covers tattoos, and remove any jewelry in a nontraditional piercing (e.g., nose, tongue; earrings for men).

Behavior in the Interview

You must be aware that many nonverbal messages are likely to be communicated during your interviews. When you sit up straight and lean slightly forward, you indicate that you are an active and interested participant in the interview. Slouching back in a chair sends the opposite message. Extending your hand and offering a firm handshake exudes confidence and professionalism. Eye contact throughout the interview demonstrates your interest in the topic and your attention to the interviewer.

In addition to the nonverbal messages that you send, your behaviors should be planned with a professional strategy in mind. Never chew gum during an interview. This behavior is completely unprofessional and considered tacky and offensive to many people. Gum or any type of distraction (such as clicking a ballpoint pen or tapping your feet) will detract from the focus of the interview—you and your qualifications—and will shift the focus to your deficiencies. We do not advise smoking or drinking alcoholic beverages in an interview, even if you are offered and your interviewer chooses to imbibe.

Responding to Interview Questions

It is often said that the best interviews are essentially conversations rather than question-and-answer sessions. This is true, and your ability to communicate in a conversational manner will contribute to the effectiveness of the interview. You should be aware that the level of development in your social skills will be clearly evident in an interview. Many of the questions employers ask will direct you to offer examples of experiences you have had in which you had to solve problems, take responsibility for your actions, and evaluate your strategies. If you are able to relate such experiences to situations that will be an asset to the company, you are on the right track.

As you prepare yourself for the interview, anticipate questions that may be asked and prepare logical, insightful answers. All employers, regardless of the field, are looking for employees who know how to solve problems. You are likely to be asked questions that require you to analyze situations, plan actions, and generate results. "Behavioral interviews" or "targeted selection questions," as they are often called by recruiters, require you to draw from your personal and professional experience, your ethics, your creativity, your analytical ability, and your communication skills to respond effectively. When asked a question such as, "Give me an example of a situation in which you made a decision that you had to stand by, even though that might have been difficult," the interviewer is looking for an insightful response demonstrating that responsibility has been taken and that you have accepted ownership for your decision. You should be prepared to draw from your experiences, and relate your responses to specific tasks that you might be expected to perform on the job. Important qualities that you should strive to demonstrate via your response include leadership, the ability to motivate people, responsibility, an appreciation for conflicting opinions and an ability to resolve conflict, an ability to prioritize, and potential for personal growth. Responses to questions such as this must be well thought out and genuine. Do not feel that you must offer examples that always have "happy endings." Prospective employers will be more receptive to answers demonstrating an ability to learn from your mistakes than to responses that are simple, flip, or superficial. An interview allows you (forces you, really) to recall experiences and evaluate your actions to demonstrate how you will be effective at making decisions for the company. Your experiences may not be direct results of retailing, design, or merchandising experiences, but you should provide enough insight to explain how your experience does relate.

A student recently recounted an interview question asking her to describe an experience that she came to regret. This typically difficult question was most likely posed to give an opportunity for the student to provide insight into her character, values, and ability to learn from her mistakes and to analyze situations. Not surprisingly, she was unsure of the motive behind the question, and she was not certain how to answer. The student reflected that she had interpreted the question in a literal sense, and considered the term "regret" to mean that she dwelt on a mistake that could not be changed. The student responded in the interview that she did not make it a practice to harbor regrets, but rather to accept situations that were in the past and consequently unchangeable. Upon further analysis of the interview, the student concluded that the interview had not ended well, and likely the reason was this misinterpretation of the meaning of the "regret" question. In fact, her response had resulted in the opposite of the desired effect of a better response—she had indicated a lack of ownership for her actions and an unwillingness to learn from her mistakes. On the other hand, another student had responded to the same question that as a lifeguard manager the previous summer she had implemented a "no holidays off" policy to address the problem of having too few employees on the busiest days of the summer. She was obligated, she explained, to stand by this policy but learned as the summer wore on that a better approach could be implemented in the future. The next summer she modified the policy so that days off had to be approved by a certain date with the understanding that lifeguards were responsible for finding their own substitutes. Although she regretted the policy decision she had implemented the first year, she learned from the experience, was willing to take ownership of a decision even though it turned out not to be optimal, and did not compromise her credibility the first year on the job. The next year, she reported, morale was improved among the employees and the problem of sufficient staffing was also solved. Experiences such as lifeguarding, while not a part of the retail or apparel industry, have direct application to skills necessary for success in retail management and virtually all other job positions.

One of the mistakes many students make is to think they will not be considered for a job simply because they have no direct experience in retailing. Although it is most desirable to have some retail experience when applying for an entry-level merchandising position, if you do not have direct experience, you should at least be able to identify skills you have developed in your prior jobs that are directly related to those needed to be successful in retailing. (See Discussion Question 4 in Chapter 5, which provides the opportunity to identify transferable skills from jobs typically held by college students that are not retailing related.)

Appropriate Interview Questions

As you prepare for interviews, it is important that you be aware that there are legal limitations regarding what an interviewer may ask of you. Interview conversations should remain on a professional level at all times, and you should be alert to questions that are legal, but that lead you to make responses that reveal more information than an interviewer is legally able to ask. Personal questions such as your age, your marital status, and parenting obligations are not permissible by law. In other words, an interviewer may not ask you if you are married. An interviewer can, however, ask you "where do you see yourself in five years?"

In anticipation of interview questions and conversations, familiarize yourself with appropriate and inappropriate topics as defined by law (Table 6.1). Furthermore, develop strategies for responses to typical interview questions that are not revealing of personal information that it is not necessary for interviewers to know. Responding to illegal questions is certainly awkward, but the informed and prepared interviewee will have an advantage over one who is naive. Sometimes interviewers ask unlawful questions because they are ignorant of proper hiring procedures. Often inexperienced interviewees offer responses to legitimate questions that are more detailed than necessary. The common interview question, "Where do you see yourself in three to five years?" is innocent and legal enough, but the response may yield more information than one need offer in an interview. For example, if you reply that you hope to be settled down with a family in addition to your career aspirations, your interviewer may (even mistakenly) interpret that your priorities are not on career growth with that company. When responding to questions of this nature, it is best to stick to professional topics such as anticipated position in the company, level of responsibility related to the position, and specific accomplishments that may be achieved on the job. Avoid personal information such as anticipated change in marital status or parental responsibilities as these are not relevant to your ability to perform in the workplace. Comments made by interviewees about personal issues may legally be considered along with other applicant criteria. Experienced and productive interviewers are trained to wield as much information as possible from their interview encounters. The savvy interviewer will recognize topics on which to elaborate and on which to defer.

When you are asked inappropriate questions, you should respond at your discretion. You may reply "that is an inappropriate question that I prefer not to answer" or you may answer the question. Obviously, your experience with interview situations will inform your impression of the company and should contribute to your decision whether to continue to pursue employment there.

Duration of the Interview

You may experience interviews—particularly second interviews—that last the duration of one or two days. These interviews are typically jam-packed with activities and are likely to be exhausting. You should prepare both mentally and physically for marathon interviews. Make sure that you are in good physical shape and have the stamina to remain energetic throughout the entire interview.

Interviews that last throughout the day generally include meals and might even include an entertainment event such as attending a ball game or an "after hours"

TABLE 6.1

GUIDE TO APPROPRIATE INTERVIEWING QUESTIONS

INQUIRIES BEFORE HIRING	LAWFUL	UNLAWFUL*
1. Name	Name	Inquiry into any title that indicates race, color, religion, sex, national origin, disability, age, or ancestry
2. Address	Inquiry into place and length of current address	Inquiry into foreign address that would indicate national origin
3. Age	Any inquiry limited to establishing that applicant meets any minimum age requirements which may be established by law	a. Requiring birth certificate or baptismal record before hiring b. Any other inquiry that may reveal whether applicant is at least 40 and less than 70 years of age
4. Birthplace or national origin		a. Any inquiry into place of birth b. Any inquiry into place of birth of parents, grandparents, or spouse c. Any other inquiry into national origin
5. Race or color		Any inquiry that would indicate race or color
6. Sex		a. Any inquiry that would indicate sex b. Any inquiry made of members of one sex, but not the other
7. Religion or creed		a. Any inquiry that would indicate or identify religious denomination or custom b. Applicant may not be told any religious identity or preference of the employer c. Request for pastor's recommendation or reference

	Lawful	Unlawful
8. Disability	Inquiries necessary to determine applicant's ability to perform the essential job functions	Any other inquiry that would reveal disability
9. Citizenship	Require proof of citizenship or visa status after being offered the position	a. If native-born or naturalized b. Proof of citizenship before hiring c. Whether parents or spouse are native-born or naturalized
10. Photographs	May be required after hiring for identification purposes	Require photograph before hiring
11. Arrests and convictions	Inquiries into convictions for specific crimes related to qualifications of the job applied for	Any inquiry that would reveal arrests without convictions
12. Education	a. Inquiry into nature and extent of academic, professional, or vocational training b. Inquiry into language skills, such as reading and writing of foreign languages	a. Any inquiry that would reveal the nationality or religious affiliation of a school b. Inquiry as to what mother tongue is or how foreign language ability was acquired
13. Relatives		Any inquiry about a relative that would be unlawful if made about the applicant
14. Organizations	Inquiry into organization memberships and offices held, excluding any organization the name or character of which indicates the race, color, religion, sex, national origin, disability, age, sexual orientation, or ancestry of its members	Inquiry into all clubs and organizations where membership is held
15. Military service	a. Inquiry into service in U.S. Armed Forces when such service is a qualification for the job b. Require military discharge certificate after being hired	a. Inquiry into military service in armed service of any country but U.S. b. Request military service records c. Inquiry into type of discharge

(continued)

TABLE 6.1 continued from page 151

16. Work schedule	Inquiry into willingness to work required work schedule	Any inquiry into willingness to work any particular religious holiday
17. Other	Any question required to reveal qualifications for the specified job	Any non–job-related inquiry that may reveal information permitting unlawful discrimination
18. References	General personal and work references not relating to race, color, religion, sex, national origin, disability, age, sexual orientation, or ancestry	Request references specifically from clergy or any other persons who might reflect race, color, religion, sex, national origin, disability, age, sexual orientation, or ancestry of applicant

*Unless bona fide occupational qualification is certified in advance by the appropriate state's Civil Rights Commission.

- Employers acting under bona fide Affirmative Action Programs or acting under orders of Equal Employment law enforcement agencies of federal, state, or local governments may make some of the prohibited inquiries listed above to the extent that these inquiries are required by such programs or orders.

- Employers having federal defense contracts are exempt to the extent that otherwise-prohibited inquiries are required by federal law for security purposes.

- Any inquiry is prohibited which, although not specifically listed above, elicits information as to, or which is not job-related and may be used to discriminate on the basis of race, color, religion, sex, sexual orientation, national origin, disability, age, or ancestry in violation of law.

SOURCE: Ohio University Hiring Guide. [On-line]. Available: http://www.ohiou.edu/equity/HiringGuide.html#questions. Reprinted with permission.

get-together. Keep in mind that regardless of the activity, the interview is still going on. Your actions during events away from the corporate environment are as insightful to interviewers as your responses to their formal questions at the office. Your manners, level of professionalism, self-control, and common sense will all be evaluated. Remember that you are interviewing for a position where you may entertain clients and represent the company in a variety of contexts. Your ability to adapt to a variety of situations is being observed.

Honesty in the Interview

Ethical behavior, as discussed in Chapter 8, includes a commitment to honesty. It is necessary to be completely honest when formulating responses to anticipated questions. Do not fabricate information during an interview, particularly regarding employment history. The interviewer relies on information gathered during the interview to make placement decisions and, in some cases, to abide by company policies. Making false statements during an interview is sufficient grounds for termination, a situation that in the long run will be more detrimental to you than the advantage of making a false statement in the first place. If you anticipate some "sticky situations" that you will be expected to explain, prepare responses thoughtfully and with your, and the company's, best interest at heart. If you describe yourself as an outgoing leader who is willing to take on responsibility, what will you say when the interviewer asks what you have done to demonstrate the traits you possess?

Although you must be honest, you should present yourself and your experiences in a positive manner at all times. You should take time to evaluate your work opportunities and to identify positive aspects of bad experiences. It is much better to make lemonade than be stuck with sour lemons! We advocate a "no excuses" philosophy for assessing one's experiences. That is, do not make excuses for the mistakes, unfortunate circumstances, and problems that you have encountered. There is nothing worse in an interview than presenting an "it's not my fault" attitude. Rather, you should take ownership of the situation and demonstrate the maturity to realize and accept the benefits along with the consequences of any experience.

One important consideration in an interview is to speak well of previous employers. This demonstrates the characteristic of loyalty that we introduced in Chapter 2. If you can't honestly do this, then phrase any references to former employers in a careful manner. You will give a better impression of yourself if you comment that you "had a valuable learning opportunity as an employee of Doomsday Discounters" rather than elaborating that the manager was crazy, the employees were given no direction, and the pay was lousy. A student encountered this dilemma when interviewing for an internship position. She had had previous experience with a large, well-respected specialty retailer and was asked, "Why did you leave that job?" Wanting to be completely honest, the student replied that she did not get along well with the manager, and she felt that she could not work with this particular manager anymore. Furthermore, the student continued to discuss some of the specific circumstances surrounding the manager's performance. The interviewer, the student reported, did not seem interested in pursuing the interview any further, and the internship never materialized with this company. Providing complete, revealing information elaborating on perceptions and judgments of people extraneous to the interview is inappropriate. You must be careful about what you say and how you say it, as interpretation is the name of the game for interviewers. The student would not have compromised her honesty had she responded that the specialty-retailing job was beneficial for her, but that she hopes to expand her retail opportunities and learn about other facets of the industry. If asked specifically about management styles or previous supervisors, the student could reply that she has had opportunities to observe various management techniques, and has a good understanding of the importance of clear communication and the important role personality plays in effective management. Prospective employers expect that you will be as insightful—or disrespectful—about the opportunities they have to offer as you have been about your previous opportunities. Furthermore, as an employee of their company, you will be serving as an ambassador for them. It can be expected that you will handle delicate situations that may occur in your prospective job with the same courtesy and tact you exhibit in the interview. What you say and *how* you say it makes all the difference!

As you are responding to questions in an interview, you may feel as though you should have a quick answer for every question. Because interviews tend to be situations that make people nervous, you may tend to speak quickly as well. Do not be concerned if you need to take a few moments to collect your thoughts and develop an articulate answer. After all, you can prepare for the interview very well, but you may not be able to anticipate every single question. You will present yourself better if you concentrate on speaking clearly and reflecting on the answer momentarily before you speak than if you jump in and begin speaking before you have thought the idea through. Remember, too, that it is perfectly appropriate to ask interviewers to repeat questions or to elaborate on them if you do not fully understand what they are asking. It is better to be clear about a question rather than trying to guess at what they are asking and therefore giving an inappropriate response. For the most part, interviewers will welcome your asking for clarification, because they obviously want information from you concerning that specific question. You will also demonstrate the ability to ask questions before trying to muddle through something you do not understand. This trait is one that is highly desirable of most employees.

Take the initiative to analyze yourself by preparing responses to typical interview questions. This exercise will prevent you from fumbling over wording and ideas in the actual interview and will require that you assess your work, volunteer, club, and other leadership opportunities to identify both their intrinsic and extrinsic benefits.

Once you have thought out responses to typical questions, seek an opportunity to practice an interview on videotape. This exercise is probably the most intimidating project that our students undertake in their career search strategies courses; however, once it is completed the pain is quickly forgotten and the value of the exercise is easily realized. You will have no opportunity in a "real" interview to review your verbal interaction, nonverbal behavior, and appearance as you may in a taped practice interview. Students have observed nervous habits and other personal quirks that they would not have detected without the opportunity of viewing a videotape. Tapes also reveal the positive aspects of your interview techniques, and may serve to boost your confidence.

You will find a list of common interview questions in Box 6.3. In addition, the CD-ROM accompanying this text contains an activity that allows you to answer common interview questions. Common topics that provide the basis for many of the questions asked of recent graduates are listed below.

- Summer employment
- Jobs you liked the least
- Future plans
- Why you picked the college you attended
- How you paid for college
- How you are different from others in your major
- What you have learned in school that you can use in your job
- Your willingness to perform routine tasks
- The type of position in which you are interested
- Why you think you will like the work
- What you know about the company
- Your grades, and whether they should be considered
- Whether you have ever had problems getting along with others

Although we are not providing suggested responses for each question, the primary question that our students want to know how to answer is the "money" question, or the question about how much money you expect to be paid. Because it is extremely likely that you will have to answer this question, or have some of discussion about it, Box 6.4 provides you with the necessary guidelines for successfully responding to this question.

BOX 6.3

COMMON INTERVIEW QUESTIONS

- Are you willing to relocate?
- Describe yourself.
- Describe your ideal job.
- Describe the ideal employee–supervisor relationship.
- Describe a situation in which you learned from a mistake.
- Did you like your former place of employment?
- How have your activities contributed to your ability to do this job?
- Why did you leave your last place of employment?
- Tell me about your previous managers.
- What are your career goals?
- What are your strengths?
- What is your greatest weakness?
- What are your weaknesses?
- What do you know about this company?
- What would you change in our stores?
- What, as a customer, have you observed that is good about our merchandise?
- What have you observed that you would change about our merchandise?
- What do you expect to do in this job?
- What makes you different from the other applicants for this job?
- What is your most prized possession?
- What is your proudest achievement?
- What rewards do you expect to earn in this job?
- Where do you expect to be in 10 (or 5 or 20) years?
- When can you begin work with our company?
- Why did you select your major?
- What were your favorite courses?
- What courses did you not enjoy? Why?
- Why should I hire you?
- Do you have any questions?

BOX 6.4

"THE MONEY RESPONSE TECHNIQUE"

If the "money question" is asked early in the interview (as it often is), the best response is: "What would a person with my background and qualifications typically earn in this position with your company?" The best response if asked late in the interview process is: "I am ready to consider your very best offer." This is one time you don't want to be specific. If you give specifics, you lose—you will either be too low or too high, costing yourself thousands of dollars or possibly even keeping yourself from getting the job.

That said, if you are pressed by the interviewer for specific numbers, don't put them off with more than one "end run" response. First, make sure you have done your homework on the expected salary range for your field. The salary surveys usually are skewed toward the high end (possibly because only the best-paid graduates responded, whereas those with average or low pay did not want to admit what they were earning), so take them with a large dose of conservative adjustment. The best surveys are from those who graduated within the last year in your major from your school. You can possibly locate such information through your Career Center, Alumni Office, or your personal network of contacts. A business grad from Stanford is going to be earning a lot more than a business grad from Podunk U. Know the "going rate" for your major, your school, and the field that you are considering entering. And make sure you know it before you get propositioned with the money question.

Armed with this information, ask the interviewer: "What is the general salary range for new hires in this position?" If the entire range is acceptable, respond with: "That would be within my expected starting range, depending on the entire salary and benefits package." If only the top end of the range is acceptable, respond with: "The upper end of the range is what I have been discussing with the other companies that are currently interested." If the range is below your expected starting salary range (be careful!), respond with: "The other companies I am currently speaking with are considering me at a salary somewhat higher than that range. Of course, money is only one element and I will be evaluating the overall package." Do your best not to get pinned to specific numbers, but if the interviewer does mention a number and ask if it would be acceptable to you, respond by saying: "I would encourage you to make the formal offer. What is most important is the opportunity to work for you and your company. I am confident that your offer will be competitive." Remember, don't do any negotiating until you have a formal offer in hand. When that finally happens, go straight to the "Successful Job Offer Negotiation" section at our Web site (*www.CollegeGrad. com/offer*) for guidance on shaping it into the best offer.

Asking Questions of the Interviewer

Near the conclusion of the interview you will undoubtedly be asked whether you have any questions. Try to identify questions, as this will indicate an interest in the company, and you may be able to demonstrate that you have researched the company by asking appropriate questions. Even if you are not asked to present questions, you may certainly take your turn in the interview and seek responses from the interviewer. You will need to think on your feet (so pay attention) and be sure not to ask a question that has already been answered. This is where your notes can be especially useful.

Typical questions that are useful for prospective employees to ask pertain to daily routine, training, compensation, evaluation, career paths, and work environment. You might ask about the typical daily routine for an intern or entry-level position, and particularly whether certain activities, such as visiting the distribution center or accompanying your supervisor to a trade show, might be part of the program. Questions about the structure of the training program for entry-level employees and the evaluation process for new hires should also be of interest to you if these were not already explained. Avoid questions that would be obvious to anyone who had properly researched the company. Do not ask redundant questions about the hierarchy of the corporate ladder, as these are likely published in the company literature, but you may be interested in learning about the typical career path of current employees. Helpful information may be gained by inquiring whether employees tend to work their way up in the company or whether they tend to be hired from the outside. Similarly, you may wish to learn the average length of time a typical employee works for the company and the company's policies regarding continuing education and professional development. You may find it helpful to ask what qualities the interviewer believes are important for the job you hope to obtain. A most important question if you are interviewing for an entry-level position, as opposed to an internship, should concern the reason for the vacancy. Pay attention to the response you receive, as it will give you an insight into important information as to what you might expect if you take the position. Of course, the most desirable response from the prospective employer is that the position is available due to a promotion. If you find that the vacancy is due to a termination, your next question should be concerned with what you can do, when hired, to avoid the same fate! Box 6.5 provides you with some typical questions you could ask of your interviewer.

It is perfectly appropriate to ask when you might expect to hear from the employer regarding a decision to hire you. This shows that you are interested in following through with the interview process, and the response gives you valuable information.

BOX 6.5

QUESTIONS TO ASK YOUR INTERVIEWER

- What advice can you give me as I pursue a career as a buyer (or stylist or sales rep, etc.)?
- How can I improve my interviewing skills?
- Is there any particular experience that I can gain in the next few months that will make me a more desirable candidate for your company?
- What qualities do you believe are most important for an employee?
- How many entry-level positions are you seeking to fill?
- When will you make your hiring decision?
- Do you see a fit between my personal and professional skills and your company?
- What are the goals you set for your entry-level employees (or state the specific position for which you are applying)?
- Would you like to keep my resume (or portfolio) for review?

Some recruiters may plan to make hiring decisions in as little as a week, while others may not expect to complete their round of interviews for several months.

WHEN TO DISCUSS SALARY. As a general rule, you should refrain from asking about salary in the first interview. Recruiters know that a well-prepared interviewee will have researched the salary ranges of his or her potential employers, and the first interview is better used to establish a relationship between the company and prospective employee regarding a potential future relationship. If you feel you must inquire about salary, ask about the "range" typically offered at the entry level. The first interview is not a time to negotiate specifics. It is inappropriate to bring up questions about vacation time, holiday policies, and personal days, particularly in a first interview for an entry-level job. Bringing a focus such as this into your interview will indicate to the employer that your priorities are misguided. Although the compensation and benefits package is an important feature in your final consideration of entry-level jobs, you will be better served by keeping the focus of any interview on the mutual benefits of employment based on learning opportunities and professional skills.

EVALUATING THE INTERVIEW

A job search, and particularly an interview, is all about fit. The reason many people are unhappy in their careers or lose their jobs is not because of their inability to do the job, but rather because they are not a good fit with the company, its culture, and its employees. You will have an opportunity to familiarize yourself with the company culture in the same manner that the company is given an opportunity to evaluate you. Remember, not every job is right for every person. Do not be discouraged if an occasional interview does not "click." Keep in mind, also, that the interviewing process is comprehensive, and you can learn from your previous experiences. Furthermore, keep in mind that you are interviewing potential employment sites just as recruiters are interviewing you.

You should evaluate the interview from your perspective just as the interviewer undoubtedly will from his or hers. Take notes either during the interview or immediately after so that you can keep track of any information you wish to remember. After several interviews, the information begins to run together, so you are wise to make your notes immediately following the interview, particularly if you are participating in a job fair or some other interview-intense opportunity.

Make a list of positive and negative aspects of the company information you learned and note the way the information was presented in the interview. Reflect on your responses to the questions that were asked, and develop or refine responses to questions that you felt were difficult to answer. As you begin to make your selection regarding an employer of choice, weigh the information gathered through the interview in a manner that is consistent with your goals, values, and personal fit in that company. For your convenience, and to help you with your interview evaluations, the accompanying CD-ROM provides you with an interview evaluation form.

FOLLOWING UP AFTER THE INTERVIEW

After the interview, you should make a point of sending a thank-you letter to the interviewer. Although some employers indicate that this is a gesture that is usually not expected, other employers consider a thank-you letter to be the final component of the interview. A prompt, well-phrased thank-you letter may make the difference between a job offer and unemployment when competition is tight. That is because your thank-you letter is the last influence you can have on the interviewer's impression of you and his or her ultimate decision. In the letter, you should thank the employer for the opportunity of speaking with him or her and also refer back to the interview reiterating why you are the perfect candidate for the position. You should also address anything that you think may have been perceived as a weakness or potential objections you picked up on during your interview. Remember that the thank-you letter gives you one last chance to sell yourself, so you must tell the interviewer one more time what you can do for the company.

A separate thank-you letter should be sent to every person you met, or who participated in your interview. If you participated in a panel interview, then everyone on the panel should receive a letter. The thank-you letter should be laser printed following proper letter format or neatly handwritten. Attention to detail is just as important in the thank-you letter as it has been throughout your job search. Be sure to spell everyone's name correctly and include his or her proper title. It is more important that you send it than how it is formatted, but, as the final impression you will make on the company before any hiring decisions, it should be neatly presented and free of errors.

It has also become increasingly acceptable to send the letter via electronic mail especially if that is the form of communication you have been using with that particular employer. E-mail definitely has the advantage of being the most expedient method of delivery. However, you should also send a hard copy of the letter. To be completely effective, the thank-you letter should be sent on the same day or the day after the interview and should be kept to one page ("The Perfect Thank-You Note," 2003.) Figure 6.1 provides a sample thank-you letter to use following an initial campus interview, and Figure 6.2 provides one that can be used after a second interview. You will also find a thank-you letter template on the CD-ROM accompanying this text.

After sending your thank-you letter(s), if you do not hear back from the employer in the time frame provided to you, you can take the initiative to follow up by phone. Before doing so, however, you may want to review the guidelines presented earlier in this chapter for making telephone contacts.

As mentioned and discussed previously, interviewing is usually the area of the career search in which students experience the most anxiety. After each interview, be sure to critically evaluate the experience. In doing so, you may want to use the information in Box 6.6 which provides some general guidelines for successful interviewing. With time and practice, you will soon see each interview as a learning experience, you may even find that you enjoy interviewing. After all, remember—each interview is your opportunity to find out more about prospective employers and what they have to offer you!

123 Oak Street
Geneva, IL 60134
jjjames@yahoo.com

Ms. Rebecca Wright
College Relations Coordinator
Fashion Department Store
404 Michigan Avenue
Chicago, IL 60603

October 22, 2004

Dear Ms. Wright:

I enjoyed interviewing with you during your recruiting visit to Northern Illinois University today. The management training program you outlined sounds both challenging and rewarding and I look forward to your decision concerning an on-site visit.

As I mentioned during the interview, I will be graduating in December with a Bachelor's degree in Fashion Merchandising. Through my education and experience I have gained many skills, as well as an understanding of retailing concepts and dealing with the general public. I have worked seven years in the retail industry in various positions from Sales Clerk to Assistant Department Manager. My education and work experience would complement the Fashion Department Store's management trainee program.

Thank you again for the opportunity to interview with Fashion Department Store. The interview served to reinforce my strong interest in becoming a part of your management team. I can be reached at (630) 555-5555 or by e-mail at jjjames@yahoo.com should you need additional information.

Sincerely,

Jennifer J. James

SOURCE: Thank-you letter prepared in part by the Career Planning and Placement Center, Northern Illinois University, DeKalb, IL. This, and other effective letters, are available at www.niu.edu.cppc. Reprinted with permission.

FIGURE 6.1   Sample Thank-You Letter: Initial Campus Interview

123 Oak Street
Geneva, IL 60134
jjjames@yahoo.com

Ms. Rebecca Wright
College Relations Coordinator
Fashion Department Store
404 Michigan Avenue
Chicago, IL 60603

November 1, 2004

Dear Ms. Wright:

Thank you again for the opportunity to interview for the management training program at Fashion Department Store. I appreciated your hospitality and enjoyed meeting the members of your staff.

The on-site visit and interview convinced me of how compatible my background, interests, and skills are with the goals of Fashion Department Store. As I mentioned during our conversation, my experience as an Assistant Department Manager and as a Retail Sales Associate have prepared me well for entering your management training program. I am confidant that my work for you will result in increased profits in the Junior's department within six months of my employment.

Again, thank you for your time and consideration. I look forward to hearing from you concerning your decision.

Cordially,

Jennifer J. James

SOURCE: Thank-you letter prepared in part by the Career Planning and Placement Center, Northern Illinois University, DeKalb, IL. This, and other effective letters, are available at www.niu.edu.cppc. Reprinted with permission.

FIGURE 6.2 Sample Thank-You Letter: On-Site Visit and Second Interview

BOX 6.6

TIPS FOR SUCCESSFUL INTERVIEWING

- **Be prompt**—Arrive early and make sure *you* are the one who needs to wait.
- **Dress appropriately**—Check out the company's dress code; be conservative rather than too flashy.
- **Speak up**—Speak clearly and demonstrate your communication strengths.
- **Show interest**—Speak as though you would like to have the job. Make reference to the research you have done and the personal experiences that you have had with the company.
- **Never speak negatively about your last job or previous employer**—This will be a poor reflection on you in an interview.
- **Be honest**—References will most likely be checked. Remember that it is a relatively small industry.
- **Be enthusiastic and sincere.**
- **Take a resume with you**—You may need to distribute updated resumes or replace one that you have sent previously.
- **Bring a portfolio**—Make reference to your portfolio during the interview. Use it as a tool to demonstrate your abilities and strengths.
- **Smile**—Remember to be friendly, but don't joke and laugh too much.
- **Execute good eye contact**—Maintain eye contact without overemphasizing or staring.
- **Thank the interviewer**—At the conclusion of the interview be certain to express appreciation for the time that has been spent with you. Thank the person for meals or other amenities as well.
- **Offer to shake hands**—Be the one to offer a handshake and close the interview in a positive, professional manner.

PROJECTS

1. Participate in a practice interview on videotape. After taping the interview, evaluate your eye contact, nonverbal behavior, and appearance, as well as the delivery and quality of your responses. Discuss with others who may observe

your tape your strengths and weaknesses. Identify areas for improvement and areas that you should strive to showcase in an actual interview.

2. Visit a store location of a company for which you are interested in working. Use this opportunity to observe employees, customers, floor layout, traffic flow, and merchandise assortments. Formulate ten questions that you can ask a recruiter for that company based on your observations. Make a list of five recommendations that you could make to the recruiter if you were asked. Based on your experience, make a list of reasons that you wish to work for that company. Be prepared to share these reasons in your interview.

3. Identify a company for which you are interested in working. Follow the guidelines set forth in Box 6.1 to research the company. You may also include any other items you find interesting. Complete a brief report on your findings.

QUESTIONS FOR DISCUSSION

1. Familiarize yourself with the common interview questions listed in Box 6.3. Can you readily and coherently respond to each question? Are you able to substantiate each response? What do you consider to be appropriate and inappropriate responses to each question?

2. Consider the opportunities you are seeking in an upcoming work experience or entry-level position. What are they? What questions can you ask in an interview that will yield information you can use to determine whether the position you are seeking will provide the opportunities you want?

3. Review Box 6.1, which presents an overview of researching a prospective employer. What other things would you like to know about the company?

4. Pick five items from the list in Box 6.1 and explain why you think it is important to know the information in terms of interviewing.

5. Why do you think most people do not send a thank-you letter as a follow-up to an interview?

7. Review the list of common interview topics presented in the chapter. Provide an explanation as to what you think employers would have to gain by your talking about these subjects. For example, why would they want to know how you chose the college that you attend?

8. What are some of the most important things that you would like an employer to ask you about in an interview? What are some strategies for conveying the information in case the employer does not ask you to address these specifically?

ELECTRONIC ACTIVITIES

Refer to the accompanying CD-ROM. The key elements of this chapter are:

1. Summary of Chapter 6 text

2. Pop-up interview questions (in which students type answers)

3. "Best Practices" sections that include pictures of interview outfits to critique

4. Video interview assessments (bad versus good)

    a. Provide an opportunity to observe and assess interview segments

    b. Enable students to supply better responses based on a sample resume

    c. Video assessment form

5. Interview schedule and follow-up log

6. Interview evaluation form

7. Thank you letter template

8. Professional dress web sites

REFERENCES

Schmidt, G. (2004, February 23). "For many, tattoo doesn't work at the office." *Chicago Tribune* (Tempo Section), p. 6.

The perfect thank-you note. (2003, May 25). *Chicago Tribune* (Section 6, Career Builder), p. 1.

The most frequent interview and job fair mistake: Little or no knowledge of the company. Handout prepared by the Career Planning and Placement Center, Northern Illinois University, DeKalb, IL. [On-line]. Available: www.niu.edu.cppc/handouts.shtml.

CHAPTER SEVEN

WORK EXPERIENCES AND INTERNSHIPS

Work experiences and internships are a lot of hard work, need commitment, involve multitasking, attention to detail, and above all enthusiasm.

—RUBY ASHRAF, VICE PRESIDENT FOR MARKETING AND SALES, PRECIOUS FORMALS

OBJECTIVES

- To understand the relationship between academic preparation and work experiences in the field.

- To appreciate the value of work experiences in a variety of retailing and merchandising environments.

- To apply career search strategies to real-life situations.

- To interact in a professional manner within company structures.

- To enhance your professional profile and your resume by participating in quality work experiences.

- To learn about the retail and apparel merchandising complex through hands-on experience and training.

- To better identify your own professional strengths and weaknesses.

- To develop a better, more realistic sense of your professional goals.

Internships, cooperative education (coop), and work experiences have become commonplace for retailing and apparel merchandising students. Typically, internships are culminating work experiences that occur after a significant amount of course work has been completed toward a major—in this case a retail or apparel merchandising major.

Internships are generally "full-time" employment situations that last the duration of a quarter or semester. Some colleges and universities make arrangements with companies for students to work in conjunction with their courses. These experiences are often called *coops*. Internships and coops are, in fact, work experiences. They are formal arrangements that recognize the educational component of the work experience. Work experiences, sometimes referred to as *field experiences*, are usually shorter in duration than an internship. Work experiences, as opposed to internships, might be weekend-only, one week in duration, or project based. A work experience might be a temporary job undertaken during breaks from school. In this chapter, the terms *internship, coop,* and *work experience* will be used interchangeably.

Box 7.1 contains some useful pointers regarding internships. Table 7.1 provides a list of Web sites that are good sources of leads for internship and work experience programs.

UNDERSTANDING THE VALUE OF WORK EXPERIENCES

Work experience, whether a structured internship, temporary employment over school breaks, or a part-time job in addition to your course work, enables you to learn and practice professional behaviors, gain insight into the retailing and merchandising industries, develop leadership and time management skills, and apply knowledge that you have gained in your courses. Susan Strickler (2001) surveyed retail students who had graduated from South Dakota State University over the past 30 years to determine the value of work experiences toward their career positions. She found that three skills learned during the work experience—stress tolerance, leadership, and organization—were related to their current positions.

Retailing and apparel merchandising students are advised to take advantage of the benefits of temporary employment such as internships and summer break jobs. In addition to providing supplemental income, such work experiences allow students to explore various facets of the retailing and merchandising industries, get a foot in the door with companies where future employment is desirable, and learn firsthand practical elements of professional development. Work experiences have the potential to introduce diverse experiences that will enhance your resume and strengthen your professional profile. Your initiative to take on a variety of work experiences demonstrates your desire to learn and grow in a professional direction.

Many companies offer internship placements within their organizational structures. It is an advantage for both you and your employer to enter into a work experience

BOX 7.1

WHY, WHERE, AND HOW TO CHOOSE AN INTERNSHIP

DID YOU KNOW THAT . . . ?

- According to a survey that included manufacturers, service firms, and government nonprofits, more than 75 percent of companies said that they will employ interns, and more than 35 percent of these interns will be hired full-time by their sponsoring company (NACE Job Outlook Report, 1999).
- More than 80 percent of college seniors have completed at least one internship (VaultReports.com).

WHERE TO FIND AN INTERNSHIP

- Career centers
- The Internet
- Publications
- Alumni listings
- "Cold call" the company

TIPS TO FOLLOW IN YOUR INTERNSHIP SEARCH

- Determine your career goals.
- Identify prospective companies.
- Beef up your resume.
- Start contacting employers early.
- Prepare for your interviews.
- Interview and follow-up with employers.
- Assess which opportunity is best for you.
- Confirm you have the right information on what the job entails.
- Enjoy and make the most out of your internship!

SOURCE: *JobPostings*. (2001, January). *2*(4), p. 9. Reprinted with permission.

TABLE 7.1

WEB SITES WITH INFORMATION ON INTERNSHIPS AND WORK EXPERIENCES

www.allretailjobs.com
www.careerbuilder.com
www.coolworks.com/
www.internships.com
www.internships4america.com/
www.internships-usa.com/
www.internweb.com
www.jobgusher.com
www.jobpostings.net
www.jobtrak.com
www.monstertrak.com
www.naceweb.org
www.primeretail.com
www.superjobs.com
www.usinterns.com

arrangement that has a definite starting and ending point. Risk is reduced for the employer, who now has a "trial period" to evaluate an employee, and for you, in case you wish to change work environments in a relatively short period of time. Although many employment opportunities give preference to a full-time, permanent employee, most employers recognize the value of providing an environment in which a future professional can learn.

An internship should be viewed as a long interview. Think about the parallels: The company has a long time (typically 10 to 15 weeks) to observe and evaluate your work habits and skills, while you also have that period of time to determine whether the particular company or position is right for you. Savvy employers use internships as screening tools that can lead to entry-level positions for top performers. No brief interview can compare to the in-depth observations an employer can make of an intern. Real knowledge of an employee's work habits, attitude, and interpersonal skills is extremely valuable considering that employers will make a significant financial investment in the people they hire.

As a student who seeks a career in a competitive industry, your ability to build your resume through participation in a variety of hands-on work experiences will reflect well on your future career prospects. A temporary work experience enables you to take risks that you might not take with a permanent commitment. For example, many retailing and apparel merchandising students seek internships in New York City. The location at the heart of the industry and the pace of the city make an experience there desirable. New York City, however, is a big change of culture for many students, who might be unsure of a permanent (or at least long-term) move there. With an internship, you can forge ahead with a temporary experience that exposes you to new environments and excellent learning opportunities without the risk of being stuck in a job or a city that is not a good fit.

It is not wise to commit to a permanent employment position that you are uncertain about. In the long-run, it can be detrimental to your career to job hop too much. An internship provides a win-win situation in which you can embark on a temporary "test run"—in a certain segment of the industry, in a new city, or with an unfamiliar employer. Likewise, the employing company does not need to make a permanent or long-term commitment to you. In a competitive job market, an intern who proves that he or she is a valuable asset to the company is often first in line when a permanent position becomes available. Experience in a working relationship between the intern and the company considerably lowers the risk of an offer for both parties. The company knows whom it is hiring in terms of performance expectations and abilities, and you know what the environment is like and whether you have found a good fit for your career aspirations. Allie Henderson, who completed an internship with Escada USA in New York City during the summer of 2003, noted that the best way to get a job with a company is to secure an internship, because then you know the system and the company has a face to go with the name on your resume. When Allie took on the New York City internship, she knew that it would be a big change from her hometown experiences in rural southeastern Ohio. After graduation, Allie opted to take a full-time, store-based position in Columbus, Ohio. There, she is able to gain additional managerial experiences while using her knowledge of the "big picture" and her expertise in manufacturing and design to establish herself as a leader in her new position. The big-city experiences Allie gained during her internship offer her the advantages of knowing how to negotiate a major geographical move and anticipating related challenges as she considers further career moves. The *Careers Up Close* profile on page 174 provides a real-world look at how an internship can help identify your best fit in the industry.

ELISHA SIEPSER

ELISHA SIEPSER WANTED TO INFLUENCE THE WAY

people dress. She always pictured herself as a fashion buyer, and envisioned a career of visiting markets and buying the clothes that would be on the retail floor. As a junior Retail Merchandising major at Ohio University, Elisha began exploring opportunities in the fashion industry in earnest. She was determined to find an internship or two in New York City where she could experience the industry firsthand.

Elisha was offered multiple internships and decided to accept two of them, each offering a distinctly different experience. In the summer of 2003, she worked in the planning and buying department of men's and women's accessories at Kenneth Cole. Elisha was enthusiastic about the learning opportunities that she experienced—spending much of her time on a computer pulling sales reports, distributing merchandise, and entering orders—but she wasn't convinced that this was the way she wanted to spend her career. She was able to observe the process of product acquisition and distribution—just what she had always thought she wanted to do; however, Elisha had some doubts about her career direction.

During the fall of 2003, Elisha moved on to DKNY, where she worked in the visual department creating window displays and manuals for DKNY stores. She recalls, "The first day of the internship I went to the Madision Avenue store and participated in an overnight." She and the visual team began at 7:00 P.M. to overhaul the store. They took a pizza break around midnight, and Elisha was back in her apartment at 10:00 A.M. the next morning. Elisha's internship journal reflects her enthusiasm for this visual merchandising position: "What is so amazing about this job is that I can see my work in progress. There are no spreadsheets, Excel, or waiting to put in merchandise. It's all

Elisha states, "Do at least one internship and make it count."

hands-on. I can use my own initiative, think outside the box, and be creative. It's beyond fab!"

Elisha was fortunate to be able to discover, through a short-term internship, that her expectations of a buying career did not fit the reality that she experienced in that environment. In addition, her initiative to seek multiple internships allowed her to experience a position in the industry—visual merchandising—that turned out to be a great fit for her interests, personality, and skills. Says Elisha, "Both of my internships taught me many things about myself from what I want to do when I graduate to what I personally need in a working environment. Without both of these internships I would not have discovered that I no longer want to buy corporately and that I do want to do visual merchandising. I recommend that everyone do at least one internship and make it count." Elisha will be influencing the way people dress after all, but now she'll accomplish that with confidence and experience by pursuing a career in visual merchandising.

You have an opportunity to apply concepts that you have learned in your academic program to real-life situations on the job. Jodie Tuchman, who completed an internship with Neiman Marcus in Troy, Michigan, during the fall of 1996, notes that as a result of the job responsibilities associated with her internship, she is now better at solving problems. Jodie explains that in her position, she was responsible for customer satisfaction when assigned to the selling floor. On one occasion, Jodie had a mother-of-the-bride client who had been expecting an altered dress. The mother-of-the-bride's dress, unfortunately, was not ready when promised, and Jodie had to deal with the situation. She knew that it was her responsibility to provide a satisfactory shopping experience to the customer, so she was required to think on her feet and implement a workable solution to the dilemma at hand. Tactful reassuring communication with the customer and extra behind-the-scenes phone calls with the tailor were necessary additions to Jodie's internship tasks. Ultimately a compromise was reached where the dress was delivered late, but in time for the wedding where it was worn.

HOW TO IDENTIFY APPROPRIATE INTERNSHIPS AND WORK EXPERIENCES

You will have many decisions to make regarding career preparation in the field of retailing and apparel merchandising. As we have mentioned in previous chapters, the career niches available for employment are virtually endless. You may be curious about the work environment of a corporate office, you may be well-served to expand your experience at the store level, or you may want the opportunity to experience a showroom atmosphere or work for a well-known design house. It is important for you to refer to your short-term goals, review your resume, and identify areas of strength and weakness as you strategize your work experience and internship plans.

It is becoming commonplace for retailing and apparel merchandising students to engage in multiple internships, largely because of the great diversity of job opportunities and the interaction common among various jobs. The dynamic nature of the industry makes it a challenge for students to possess in-depth and well-rounded practical experiences. Thus, the greater the variety and quantity of work experiences and internships students secure, the more competitive they will be in their career searches. The *Careers Up Close* profile on page 174, earlier, illustrates the value of multiple internships.

Caron Billak, who completed an internship in the Fashion Office at the Atlanta Apparel Mart in 2002, noted that there are many opportunities to gain experience in the field. She suggests that students look for opportunities everywhere: Go to stores or malls and ask if you can help with fashion shows, inquire at stores about the possibility of you working there or helping with special projects that might be underway, especially seasonally. Once you have secured a work experience, Caron urges students to make their opportunities worthwhile. She suggests, "put effort into it and apply it to your future!" Caron advises students to be strategic with the experiences that are secured by giving back to the company what they gave you in an opportunity—then you can move on to other companies and new experiences. She also encourages students to document what they do during a work experience. She suggests that measurable outcomes, such as increased sales volume, press reports, and letters of commendation can be included in a portfolio and used as points of interest in an interview.

The most basic of all experiences necessary for success in the retailing and apparel merchandising industry occurs in-store. Aspiring professionals for all types of career tracks should seek significant in-store experiences. Store-based experience will provide a foundation for growth and knowledge in all other facets of the industry. The customer service, personal selling interactions, and hands-on experience with merchandise in the customer transaction phase of retailing that you can gain from working in a store are essential. Many corporate office positions—in buying, product development, merchandising, and promotions—expect, and often require, prior store experiences. In fact, some internships and entry-level corporate positions build in-store experiences into their training programs.

There is simply no replacement for the firsthand knowledge and experience of seeing merchandise effectively displayed and sold in stores. In-store work experiences provide insight into customer needs and demands, effective merchandising techniques and store layouts, and consumer product preferences. In addition, the knowledge developed in the management aspect of a store environment directly transfers to any environmental situation. Keep in mind that without the final point at which merchandise trades hands between the retailer and the consumer (traditionally in a store), all of the other aspects of merchandising would be moot. Even in this age where more and more merchandise is sold in nonstore formats, such as television, the Internet, via telephone, and through direct in-home sales, the experience of interacting with many customers in a store environment is irreplaceable and should be valued as a career-enhancing opportunity.

If you have little or no in-store experience, it is highly advisable that you seek a work experience in a store early in your academic career. Refer to Box 7.2 for a list of useful tips when applying for a work experience. There is simply no substitute for the hands-on knowledge that can be gained about the retail industry and about your personal interests and skills. Many times students are surprised by the value that is immediately apparent in a store work experience or internship. Jennifer Nichols

BOX 7.2

WORK EXPERIENCE SEARCH TIPS

WHEN ASKING FOR AN APPLICATION . . .

1. Dress nicely. Even if employees wear jeans, *you* should dress more professionally.

2. *Don't chew gum!*

3. Bring your own pen if you plan to fill out the application there.

4. Don't call. Come in person to request an application.

5. Come to get the application yourself. Don't send your parents or a friend.

6. Come in alone. Don't bring friends, children, boyfriend, etc.

7. Speak as if you would *like* to have the job.

8. Never speak negatively about your last job.

9. Bring a notebook or PDA. Write down information such as when to come back, who to talk to, and (hopefully) the date and time of an interview.

10. Bring a resume.

11. Be enthusiastic and sincere.

12. If there is a line at the desk, don't get in line, rather, *wait* until there is *no* line. If there is never no line, you have come at a *bad* time, but . . . they are likely to need your help!

13. If you don't qualify for the position, thank the manager anyway and inquire about future opportunities.

ON THE APPLICATION . . .

1. *Always* fill in something for academic and professional activities and honors if you can. If you have none, work on developing some *now!*

2. For hobbies and activities, put something constructive—*not* watching TV, going out, having fun, etc. (No kidding—these items have appeared on applications!)

3. Be honest about previous experience. References *will* be checked.

4. Print *neatly.*

5. Don't crumple the form before you return it.

noticed that while she was a retail merchandising student, some fellow students demonstrated a negative attitude regarding working in-store. In 2002, Jennifer completed an internship with Kohl's, and upon graduation in 2003 began a management training position with Target. Jennifer urges students to see the value of working in a store and to take advantage of the great opportunities for career growth there. Says Jennifer, "I know from working at Target I might do little things here and there that a sales associate would do, but the majority of my day is leading, planning, and discussing and has nothing to do with folding a million shirts or stocking shelves."

Beyond an in-store work experience, the variety and scope of other retail and apparel merchandising internships available are extensive. Virtually all of the career avenues mentioned in Chapter 1 lend themselves to work experience and internship opportunities. Your own interests and initiative set the limits for your experiences as opportunities abound.

COMPENSATION FOR WORK EXPERIENCES AND INTERNSHIPS

One of the most perplexing questions with respect to internship and work experience decisions has to do with compensation. Will the experience generate an income for you? This is often a highly personal issue—and a variety of factors play into the necessities of compensation. Negotiation of the terms of your internship, including compensation, takes thought and preparation on your part. The following are some points to consider when making a decision to embark on experiences without compensation.

Value of the Experience

Just as you are making an investment in yourself by earning an academic degree, you are afforded the opportunity to invest in yourself and your future career through completing a work experience. You should consider the value of the experience as you consider the need for compensation. Consider the return on your investment of time when you determine the level of compensation that you need to receive.

Type and Duration of Experience

By definition, a work experience is likely to be more project based and limited than a full-fledged internship. There are many possibilities for a short-term work experience that may not be worth the investment of a company to compensate you. On the other hand, an internship that involves significant preparation on your part, training and education by the company, and a relatively long-term commitment is more likely to be compensated. Both internships and work experiences can be found for varying lengths of time. In fact, you may embark upon a work experience that is a regular part-time (or even full-time) job. Experiences such as these should certainly be compensated. On the other hand, you may seek a short-term experience that complements a course you are taking (or is a requirement for a course), enhances an area of knowledge that you wish to improve, or provides a unique opportunity that will set you apart from other career candidates. In such cases you may be willing to forgo compensation.

Internships in segments of the industry such as design houses and public relations firms are almost never paid, whereas in-store internships almost always are compensated. Furthermore, a short-term, temporary work experience, such as a 40 total hour practicum experience, is much less likely to be compensated than a ten-week, 40-hour-per-week internship.

Your Expenses

The cost of living is a reality of life. If you are relocating to another city you will likely have housing, transportation, and food expenses to cover. You will need to consider whether you can afford the financial investment of these items without compensation from the internship. On the other hand, if you have the opportunity to live at home or enjoy an extended stay with relatives, your personal expenses may be reduced enough to allow you to accept an unpaid internship. Some unpaid internships provide food allowances, so be sure to find out all of the necessary details regarding your expected expenses.

Your Contribution to the Company

Consider what your contribution to the day-to-day operations of the company will be. Would the company need to pay someone else to do the job tasks you are doing if you weren't there? If you are assuming an integral role for the company, it is more appropriate to be compensated than if you are an "extra" who is provided with an opportunity to primarily observe and learn. Interns who are directly involved in sales generate direct revenue for their companies and are much more likely to receive compensation that interns who fill more peripheral roles.

Competition Level

What is the level of competition for entry-level positions in the particular segment of the industry you are targeting? When entry-level positions are scarce and the field is highly competitive, the investment in work experience without compensation is a better risk than for an industry segment in which career positions are plentiful.

Your Goals

How much do you want to engage in the work or internship experience being considered? The fit between what the work opportunity offers and your own career goals is important. The bottom line in decision making should revolve around what you want to do. If you have career aspirations that require this type of experience, you should be more willing to embark on the experience and forgo compensation. If you are offered an internship that is not of particular interest to you and you won't be compensated, you may prefer to keep looking for an alternative opportunity.

Ultimately, the decision about whether to accept a particular work experience or internship is yours to make. You will need to be strategic with your decision, and calculate the opportunity costs associated with the investment of your time. It is a decision that is a calculated risk on your part when you embark on an unpaid experience, but the advantage of getting your foot in the door may be well worth the forgone compensation. Keep in mind that any experience you undertake is an investment in your future career.

GATHERING INFORMATION

Resources abound for internship opportunities, and the field of retailing and apparel merchandising is particularly ripe with a variety of work experience possibilities. The sooner that you begin learning about internship and work experience opportunities that are available, the better equipped you will be to position yourself as a top candidate to secure the positions you desire. For short-term work experiences, a search time frame of a year in advance may be appropriate. Internship searches should generally be initiated one year in advance, and no less than six months prior to your planned experience.

A few key resources will enable you to arrive at a comprehensive choice of internships and work experiences.

- Teachers and professors
- Career services office
- Career fairs
- Internet
- Publications
- Previous students or students who are more senior than you
- Previous employers
- Friends and family members
- Firsthand inquiry

Although we believe strongly that what you know is very important and will propel you forward in your chosen career, it is true that the people whom you know are valuable resources—right at your fingertips. Take advantage of the contacts that can be made for you through personal networking. Often these are the people who know you best, and who have a good knowledge of your skills and abilities. The people who can speak well for you and recommend you in a complimentary way are the best kind of references!

Firsthand inquiry works particularly well for in-store experiences because access is so simple. Dress professionally, carry a portfolio with extra copies of your resume, be prepared to articulate what your goals are and what type of work experience you are seeking, and visit business locations to speak with managers and gather information. You have an opportunity to make a great first impression through your professional appearance and behaviors. Do be conscious of the workplace atmosphere—if it is a busy time, return when the manager can give attention to you.

Your preliminary research will yield information regarding whether or not companies that are of interest to you offer formal internship experiences. If a company doesn't offer an internship, don't pass them by. You may be able to be instrumental in starting a program or at least gain experience in a "nonstructured" internship.

Keep in mind that the search process, including information gathering and interviewing, is a two-way street. You are searching for an opportunity that fits well into your areas of interest, your career goals, and your personal needs just as the prospective companies are evaluating the fit you make in fulfilling their needs. The better the job you do in identifying what specifically you are looking for in a work experience—what your goals are, where you want to live, what type of company culture you are comfortable working in, and whether you seek compensation for your experience—the better equipped you will be to make an informed and rational choice about your future.

Making the Most of Your Contacts

There are potentially valuable contact people all around you. Your ability to identify relationships between the people you meet and your career goals is likely to improve with experience. As we suggested in Chapter 4, take every opportunity to meet people, learn what they do, and share your goals with them. Conversations often lead to discoveries of "I know someone who could help you" or "I know someone you should call about a job." Several years ago, a student who was in the midst of an internship search met a buyer on a plane. They happened to be seated next to each other, and it turned out that the plane was delayed considerably during that particular trip. Usually a plane delay is a frustrating and inconvenient experience, but this student made the most of a potentially bad experience. While sitting on the tarmac for two hours, the student struck up a conversation with her seat neighbor. It was during this conversation that the fellow traveler revealed she was a buyer for a major retail company. The student shared with the buyer her goals to enter the fashion industry and her search for an internship. As a result, the student gained valuable advice from someone who was successful in the industry and came away with her business card and a number of contacts to use toward her internship search. This particular buyer did not have an internship to offer, but she shared information with the student that eventually led to a positive internship experience. Always be prepared to meet new people, share information about yourself that will enable new contacts to understand your goals and needs, and be sure to follow up with information that is provided to you.

Keeping in Touch with Your Contacts

If you have secured a work experience several weeks or more in advance of your initial start date, it is important that you maintain contact with your future supervisor. Because turnover and change are constants in retailing and apparel merchandising, you want to become a familiar person to all of the players at your future work experience site. It is not uncommon for a supervisor who has made arrangements for your work experience, to be promoted to a new position across the country, or worse, fired! We have worked with students who have faced just such situations—finding internships in September that will start in June, only to discover in June that the manager is no longer working for the company and no one there knows anything about a student work experience. Prior to the start date of your work experience, you should maintain regular contact with the supervisor. You can establish this contact by formally acknowledging the experience and your understanding of what it will entail. This can be accomplished through a letter or e-mail. Be certain to state when you will be beginning the experience, what your goals are with respect to the learning outcomes you anticipate accomplishing, and your appreciation for the opportunity to embark on the experience with the company and the supervisor.

To eliminate the risk of living a work experience nightmare, you should establish a plan for maintaining contact with the company and the supervisor who is your contact. You can accomplish this by periodically calling, e-mailing, or stopping in. It can be somewhat awkward to make a telephone call or send an e-mail with no particular content other than "I'm just checking to make sure I still have an internship with you this summer," so we recommend that you build a strategy that will provide context for your contact with the site. Although it sounds trite, if you are "in the neighborhood" it is a good idea to stop in to say hello and meet the employees who are currently working at your prospective site. The more people who are familiar with you and who know about the plan for your future experience, the less likely you will be to fall between the cracks if changes in the management structure occur. When you make a telephone call or send an e-mail, it is better to have a reason for the contact. See Box 7.3 for some suggested agenda items that you may wish to use when maintaining contacts with future work experience sites.

As you maintain contact with a particular company representative who is the key to your work experience, do not neglect opportunities to establish additional contacts for your network. If an opportunity for work experience does fall through, be prepared to pursue new avenues using the network of contacts you are building. Remember, the more people you know, and who know you, the better your chances of being able to select ideal work experience opportunities from a range of possibilities. Furthermore, you probably want to identify multiple work experiences to complete while you are a student, so keep yourself active with a network of contacts.

IDENTIFYING A CAREER MENTOR

The people with whom you work are as important to your learning and growth as the positions and work experiences you hold. Mentors are among the most valuable resources for young professionals. As you progress in your career, the presence of a mentor who can offer you guidance, serve as a confidant, and enhance your professional network will enable you to grow with confidence. A mentor is someone who models professional behavior and is in a position to offer you honest feedback and appropriate advice with respect to your career and professional decisions.

The difference between mentors and career contacts lies in the level of the relationship you establish. A mentor must be someone you can trust and who takes a gen-

BOX 7.3

REASONS TO CONTACT FUTURE WORK EXPERIENCE SITES

- Send a copy of your goals to your supervisor.
- Request that your supervisor review your goals and offer you feedback with respect to the probability that you will be able to achieve your goals during the work experience.
- Over time, if you identify new goals, you can contact your supervisor to share the updated information.
- Send an updated resume for the company files.
- Call to arrange a meeting with your supervisor to discuss your work experience responsibilities.
- Interview your prospective supervisor for a class project.
- Forward information about your internship requirements so that your supervisor can familiarize himself or herself with it.
- Make an appointment to stop in and share your portfolio with your supervisor. Ask your supervisor if there are particular elements in your portfolio that should be enhanced prior to your work experience.
- Discuss with your supervisor the specific projects that you will be able to undertake during your internship.

uine interest in your career growth. A mentor may or may not work directly with you. Your mentors may be former or current supervisors, professors, or contacts with whom you have maintained close ties. Often a mentoring relationship develops between a senior-level professional with extensive experience and a new, entry-level employee. A supervisory relationship is not necessary, and sometimes the mentoring relationship is strengthened when there is not a supervisory component. Regardless of the specific roles that the mentor and his or her protégé assume, the relationship that they share must be one of mutual respect and trust. Potentially, your mentors will be active resources for you throughout your career.

You should actively seek mentors. Although some terrific professional contacts seem to simply happen along, you should strive to contact and cultivate potential mentors. A good place to start is with the supervisor of your work experience or a current professor. Professionals will be able to mentor you only if they believe that you are committed to your career growth, and if their areas of expertise match the goals that you have set for yourself. Your ability to communicate to potential mentors regarding your career aspirations, personal goals, and work ethic will enable prospective mentors to recognize their potential contribution toward your professional development. Be certain to let prospective mentors know who you are!

Be open-minded regarding who might serve as a mentor to you. You may not hit it off well with a supervisor, but that doesn't mean that a valuable mentor is not available in your work environment. Make a point to meet people in all divisions of the companies where you work. The ability of your mentor to offer objective feedback is important. Identifying a mentor who does not work directly with you often enables more candid and objective feedback and advice than would be the case from a mentor who works with you on a day-to-day basis. Ask successful and senior employees about their careers and for advice in yours. Follow up on all opportunities that are presented to you to learn from other professionals. Keep in touch with people so that you will be someone they remember—and perform well so that you are someone they think of fondly. Even contacts that you make while interviewing can turn into valuable mentors. Following up on every interview and each introduction to people in the industry will lead to mentoring relationships with some of the contacts that you make.

COORDINATING YOUR GOALS WITH THE JOB REQUIREMENTS

To make the most of a work experience, you must set goals for yourself. Construct a plan for your goals before beginning your work experience—you will be too busy actually working once the experience begins to identify your goals then. In addition, it is important that you communicate your goals for the work experience to your on-site supervisor. He or she should be able to offer feedback on your goals, let you know if there are any goals that are unrealistic for the experience, or alert you to goal opportunities about which you were unaware. Establishing a plan for your goals before your work experience begins allows you to optimize progress toward them during the time you are working.

Your satisfaction with your internship will depend in part on your ability to set and communicate appropriate and realistic goals during the interview. If you have not yet identified your areas of interest, you need to determine why that is, and eventually you will need to establish a direction (at least for the present) in which you wish to focus. When you are interviewing for work experience opportunities, be certain to ask questions that specifically relate to your goals so that you understand what the company has to offer and can evaluate the fit between the company and your goals. In addition to your personal career and work experience goals, you need to make sure that the work experiences you seek meet academic requirements, if applicable. Does your academic program require a certain number of hours to be worked, activities to be performed, and so on? You need to be aware of any work experience requirements and communicate them to prospective companies where you might work. You and the company will be better satisfied at the conclusion of the internship when clear goals have been established and worked toward during the duration of the experience.

MAKING THE MOST OF AN INTERNSHIP OR WORK EXPERIENCE

Begin your internship or work experience with a positive attitude. Remember, you will likely be learning as much or more than you will be contributing to the company's bottom line. Be open minded, willing to do what needs to be done, and, as Jodie Tuchman advises, "be willing to work hard and do what you do well!" In fact, a prevailing theme in most internship programs is the expectation that the intern will work hard—and must be willing to do so. This is your opportunity to demonstrate that you can and are willing to go the extra mile to enhance your professional profile and the position of the company. Internship and work experience positions often are not particularly glamorous, and almost certainly will involve completion of mundane tasks—even running errands and making coffee! Do not let the need for routine task performance deter you from making the most of your experience. In fact, you are challenged to observe the most seasoned, successful professionals in your professional environment. There are few tasks that respected professionals won't participate in themselves—and keep in mind that your job is to make things easier for them. By virtue of your junior position, you are the person doing the most learning and observing. You will gain the respect and trust of your supervisor and senior colleagues by stepping forward with a positive attitude to complete any and all tasks that need to be done.

In addition to the goals that you will be working to achieve throughout your internship, consider the professional behaviors and practices that you will portray. Your attitude and behaviors will be major components of the evaluations and assessments that your supervisor will make of your performance. A few tips for success at an internship include:

- **Seek projects.** Don't sit around waiting to be told what to do. Students who let supervisors know that they have completed tasks and are ready for another assignment will exhibit a strong work ethic and earn the respect and appreciation of their supervisors. It is likely that your supervisor won't know how long you need to complete projects, and it will be up to you to speak up when you have finished a task or project. There may be times when you have more projects underway than you have time for, too. If this happens, communicate with your supervisor and make sure that he or she knows the progress that you are making on each assignment.

· **When in doubt, ask.** It is expected that an intern who is learning will have many questions. It is far better to ask questions and confirm the nature of tasks that you are expected to complete than to make costly mistakes. Good judgment is important in this respect, however, because there is a fine line between asking timely and important questions and appearing insecure and pesky. Be aware of the corporate climate, and listen carefully when given instructions. If fact, keep a notepad or personal digital assistant (PDA) with you at all times and write information down. (See Box 7.4.) That way, you can refer to your own notes rather than ask the same question repeatedly.

BOX 7.4

INTERNSHIP TIP: CARRY A NOTEBOOK OR PDA

In a presentation to a class of aspiring interns, one former student noted that the most valuable resource she used throughout the duration of her internship was a small spiral notebook. She carried the notebook with her every place she went, and kept comprehensive notes about what tasks she was assigned, how she was instructed to go about them, and when she completed her work. She stated that she referred to the information in that notebook constantly, and it served as a source of security for her because she felt confident that she knew what she needed to do and how to do it, without having to check with her supervisor in a burdensome way. In fact, she mentioned that the process of keeping a notebook kept her organized, and the practice of keeping the notebook offered the added advantage of making a positive impression on her supervisor and the colleagues with whom she worked. She ended up making a great impression—demonstrating her self-sufficiency, organization, innovation, and commitment to learning—by creating a tool that enhanced her internship performance. In this age of technology, a personal digital assistant (PDA) works just as well—or better!

- **Continue to network throughout your internship.** The interviewing, career search, and networking skills that you have developed throughout the process of securing an internship should be continued once you have secured a site for your internship
- **Make the internship your top priority.** You need to give 100 percent to the work experience at hand, particularly when it is a full-time internship. When your attention is divided among other obligations—whether they are personal or scholastic—your performance at the internship, your ability to learn, and your evaluation will likely suffer.

Box 7.4 and the *Careers Up Close* profile on page 192 expand on two of these suggestions. Box 7.5 provides a list of expectations for merchandising internships.

EVALUATING YOUR WORK EXPERIENCES

Throughout your tenure at a work experience site, you should look for specific learning opportunities and evaluate the quality of your experience as well as your own performance. There are a number of methods that you might be required to use to accomplish your evaluation. In addition, you may wish to employ one or more of the suggestions below in preparation of your career development and future interviews. The *Careers Up Close* profile on page 194 relates the observations of one former intern in evaluating her work experience.

Keep a Journal

It is a good idea to keep a journal that you can review. By reviewing the progress that you make throughout your experience, comprehensive assessment is possible. You will be amazed at the growth and maturity you can observe in yourself. Excerpts from your journal might be used in your portfolio to document your work experiences and the knowledge you have gained. Reflecting on your journal entries should help you identify your strengths, the aspects of the industry that you particularly enjoyed, your learning throughout the experience, and a direction for your future that will optimize these.

A word of caution—be certain to keep your journal at home and write in it there. Never bring your journal to the workplace where it might become lost or, perhaps worse, found by others. It is too likely that you will record one or more entries that are not flattering to the company, your supervisor, or your co-workers.

BOX 7.5

BEST PRACTICES AND EXPECTATIONS FOR MERCHANDISING INTERNSHIPS

COMPANIES' EXPECTATIONS OF INTERNS

- Before starting the internship, learn as much about the company as possible by doing extensive company research.
- Do more than you are required to do. Be productive and stay busy. Demonstrate initiative.
- Observe everything. Watch how the "seasoned" employees operate. Analyze why some individuals are more effective and efficient than others.
- Some of the work you do will be routine, but important. Do the routine things as willingly and professionally as you do the more complex, challenging, and interesting work.
- Read and follow the company rules and policies. They are usually posted; if not, ask.
- Work with your supervisor to find out what your work includes, what your responsibilities are. Ask questions.
- Listen carefully and take notes when you are given verbal instructions. This eliminates the need to ask again at a later date and ensures accuracy during completion of assignments.
- When you are ready for more challenging work, approach your supervisor with some suggestions of potential new responsibilities rather than waiting for the supervisor to suggest new ones.
- Set high standards for yourself. Work as accurately, safely, and quickly as you can.
- Learn from your mistakes; do not try to cover up.
- Have confidence in your ideas. Present them at appropriate times.
- Be tactful; do not offend others. Be friendly, show respect, be honest, be polite.
- Learn to accept constructive criticism and implement strategies to improve performance.
- At the end of the internship, develop a draft of your updated resume listing the internship and discuss it with your supervisor.

EXPECTATIONS OF COMPANIES PROVIDING INTERNSHIPS

- Conduct an official introduction of the intern to the management team, identifying the intern's role, position, and responsibilities so other employees are aware of and understand the role of the intern.
- Meet with the intern weekly to discuss training progress and concerns, project status, and developmental opportunities. Provide the intern with specific examples of his or her strengths and weaknesses. Ask the intern for feedback on the internship experience.
- Train the intern related to company systems (computer, receiving, etc.).
- Provide the intern with opportunities for the analysis and understanding of company or departmental records.
- When possible, prepare the intern to communicate with vendors, buyers, and purchasing agents.
- Include the intern in company management and district or regional management meetings, or both.
- Include the intern in the processes of management and scheduling of sales associates.
- Expose the intern to advertising, promotion, and public relations activities.
- Assign the intern responsibility for specific projects or departments. Example: Track sales for a department for a period of time (e.g., 10 weeks), make inventory suggestions, sales technique suggestions, display suggestions, and other appropriate actions.
- Provide the intern with exposure and experience in all functional areas of the company.
- Involve the intern in pricing and markdown procedures (retail interns).
- Involve the intern in merchandising and display involvement (retail interns).
- Involve the intern with the hiring and selection process.
- Provide the intern with training in sales techniques (or other appropriate functions) and the opportunity to eventually help in the training of new hires.
- At the end of the internship, assist the intern in developing a list of appropriate responsibilities to use when updating the resume with the internship experience.

SOURCE. Linda K. Good, Professor of Merchandising Management, Michigan State University. Reprinted with permission.

WHEN MOLLY DOYLE WAS AN ASSISTANT BUYER

trainee with Shillito Rikes, she was determined to make her mark by demonstrating her retail merchandising skills and her work ethic. In particular, she recalls her first week on the job when the defective and return-to-vendor room needed to be organized. No assistant had been in the area for some time and there were hundreds of pairs of shoes to be organized, returned to vendors, and some marked out of stock. There were mismatched shoes, many worn and returned shoes, and defectives. Obviously, this was a job that no one wanted to do, but it had to be done. Molly recognized this as an opportunity to step forward and demonstrate that she was not afraid of a little hard work, and furthermore, she could approach this task with creativity and good humor. The organization and cleaning of the shoe department took the better part of four working days. The work wasn't particularly difficult, but it was messy, dusty, and tedious. It definitely wasn't part of the training program she was expecting. When her work was completed, the shoe debit room was in sparkling shape. Molly was recognized for the rest of her trainee experience as the "girl who actually got the shoe stockroom straightened out." The buyer she was assigned to looked to that accomplishment as a reference for moving forward in the program. Molly has used this example repeatedly in her professional life as a great reason to volunteer and execute the jobs no one wants to do. Now, as regional sales manager for Cejon Accessories, she regularly implements her strong work ethic and willingness to do what it takes to maintain a clean, organized showroom and offer gracious hospitality to her clients. She notes that there is always a need to serve refreshments or order lunch for buyers, clean off showroom tables, or tag samples for the designers. When interns are available to help with these tasks, she and the buyers have more time

Molly states, "Do what it takes to get the job done."

to focus on the business activities at hand and the interns have the opportunity to observe the showroom atmosphere and the buying procedures taking place. Molly stresses to the many students whom she mentors each year, "be willing to work hard and do what it takes to get the job done."

JODIE TUCHMAN

Sales Associate

H. STERN

GRADUATED IN **1997** FROM OHIO UNIVERSITY
MAJOR: FASHION AND RETAIL MERCHANDISING

Jodie says, "I thrive on constant challenges and change, which are inevitable in retail."

DURING HER INTERNSHIP EXPERIENCE WITH NEIMAN

Marcus, Jodie Tuchman observed: "Effective management is somewhat of an art in my mind. Understanding the subtle nuances of different personalities comes with time and experience. For example, associates are not all motivated in the same manner. Some associates are fiercely independent while others prefer close supervision. While some associates appreciate constructive criticism, others perceive it as a personal attack."

Jodie's assessment at the conclusion of her internship with Neiman Marcus was that "retail is not all glitz and glamour. On the whole, retail is hard work without a lot of recognition. To survive and prosper, you have to love the business and derive satisfaction from within yourself. Perhaps, my most important realization during my internship was that I thoroughly enjoyed what I was doing. I thrive on constant challenges and change, which are inevitable in retail."

Jodie pursued a career in a corporate atmosphere in a buying office at Ann Taylor, then decided that she really was most satisfied with customer interactions and selling. Her career has progressed into her current position in sales with the high-end jeweler H. Stern, on 5th Avenue in New York City. Jodie has the benefit a numerous retail experiences and is an example of a professional who has found a niche for herself that offers an exciting and satisfying career.

A journal that is left in a break room is very tempting for others to explore. Your discretion is important, but we recommend keeping the journal away from the workplace.

Ask Your Supervisor for Feedback

Few people will be as well equipped as your supervisor to offer you honest and constructive feedback regarding your on-site work performance. In fact, you will be shortchanging yourself if you do not ask your internship or work experience supervisor for an evaluation of your performance. Positive comments will reinforce your areas of strength, and a letter or copy of an evaluation instrument that is positive will be a good addition to your portfolio. There is great value in constructive criticism, as well. Advice from an on-site supervisor with respect to areas that you still need to develop, or the fit of your personality and interests and this specific work experience, is valuable as you plan for your future.

Do not avoid the opportunity to be evaluated by an expert in the field. Although aspects of evaluation are tedious at best, and painful at worst, the long-term benefits of gaining feedback about your professionalism and the success with which you implement knowledge and skills in the workplace are worth the risk. Often the anxiety that precedes an evaluation meeting is worse than that outcome of the meeting itself. Many times supervisors see more strengths in students' performance that the students expect. Regardless, an objective and informed observation of your work quality (such as can be offered by a supervisor) is invaluable toward your professional development and future goal setting. Figure 7.1 and the CD-ROM provide an example of one type of employee evaluation form that may be used to assess the performance of a retail intern or full-time employee.

Identify the Strengths and Weaknesses of Your Work Experience Site

The process of reviewing the environment in which you completed a work experience will not only enhance your self-assessment process, it will also be helpful to your professors and to other students who may wish to pursue internships or work experiences there in the future. Professors are typically very interested in understanding which companies offer outstanding experiences to students and which companies do relatively little toward student career development. Some companies are better than others with respect to organizing learning opportunities, following through with promises

Observed by: _____   Location: _____

Professional Behavior	outstanding	above average	acceptable	poor	not observed
Ethics					
Attention to tasks/customers	4	3	2	1	o
Honest feedback/communication	4	3	2	1	o
Trustworthy	4	3	2	1	o
Follows proper procedure	4	3	2	1	o
Appearance					
Follows dress code	4	3	2	1	o
Neat, clean, well-groomed	4	3	2	1	o
Attitude					
Positive toward customers/Pleasant interaction with customers	4	3	2	1	o
Balance between "too aggressive" and "not helpful"	4	3	2	1	o
Positive rapport with co-workers	4	3	2	1	o
Commitment to Company					
Knows company policy, and implements	4	3	2	1	o
Knows daily/weekly goals of company	4	3	2	1	o
Knows personal performance levels	4	3	2	1	o
Product Knowledge					
Familiar with products and inventory	4	3	2	1	o
Familiar with market competitors	4	3	2	1	o
Knows location of merchandise on floor	4	3	2	1	o
Personal Attributes					
Punctuality	4	3	2	1	o
Organization	4	3	2	1	o
Seeks and accepts responsibility	4	3	2	1	o
Helpful and friendly/approachable	4	3	2	1	o
Enthusiasm	4	3	2	1	o

FIGURE 7.1   Retail Employee Evaluation

Describe the store atmosphere:

For the employee you observed, what are his/her most positive behaviors exhibited?

For the employee you observed, what are the deficiencies and/or weaknesses you observed?

Please list recommendations you would offer for this employee to improve his/her performance.

How would you evaluate these items in the future in order to offer ongoing feedback to this employee?

of experiences in various facets of company operations, and providing access to upper-level professionals who can offer career guidance and insight into company operations. The information that you provide to your professors and peers will help future students seek and accept experiences of the highest quality. In addition, you may help realize improvements for future students if deficiencies that you observe and report are remedied as a result of intervention by professors.

It is inevitable that you will be asked in an interview to discuss what you liked and disliked about your internship experience. Your forethought on this matter will prepare you to produce thoughtful and articulate responses.

You may find that your internship site is interested in seeking feedback about its program. Your ability to construct a detailed list, with examples, of your observations of strengths and weaknesses of the site has the potential to impress the company with your observational skills. Of course, you must practice tact and diplomacy when delivering constructive criticism. Keep in mind that it is a good reflection of the company to seek information and means of improvement. This is, in fact, the type of company many individuals wish to work for, as taking the initiative for long-term improvement is certainly a quality that leads to long-term success. If your internship or work experience site is not interested in your feedback, do not take that personally. Simply keep the information you have compiled to yourself and use your knowledge of the company priorities as you seek future employment experiences.

PROJECTS

1. Set goals for your experience. Refer to Chapter 2 for guidance and use the template provided on the accompanying CD-ROM.

2. Keep a journal. Reflect on:

   a. What you learn

   b. What you apply

   c. What questions you have that can be explored during your work experience

3. Observe and reflect on the ethical environment of your work experience site.

4. Match the skills or tasks that you do as a part of your internship to the academic preparation and courses you have completed. Note the similarities and differences in your applications and expectations.

5. Case Study: Have you encountered any problems or challenges that required you to make important decisions? Describe these, and present the process of decision making that you embarked upon. Explain the advantages and disadvantages of various alternatives.

QUESTIONS FOR DISCUSSION

1. It goes with the territory in retailing that you will spend some portion of your work experience time as a sales associate. Although this position does not particularly excite a significant number of retailing and apparel merchandising or design students, it is an important learning opportunity. What could you bring to the position of sales associate to enhance your enthusiasm for the job? What could you bring to the position to enhance your professionalism as a representative of your company? How could you enhance the total shopping experience for your customers?

2. In a management capacity, how could you improve employee moral in the work situations in which you have participated? What about encouraging improved sales or production capacity?

3. After embarking on a work experience, what personal and professional strengths can you build upon?

4. Have you identified any areas of the business in which you are more interested now than before your work experience? Are there areas of the business in which you are less interested? Why?

5. What criteria contributed to a successful (and unsuccessful) work experience?

6. What criteria contributed to a successful (and unsuccessful) professional mentor?

7. What are some specific professional skills you have developed as a result of your work experience?

8. How can you effectively present the work experience that you have completed in a professional portfolio?

ELECTRONIC ACTIVITIES

Refer to the accompanying CD-ROM. The key elements of this chapter are:

1. Summary of Chapter 7 text

2. Goal setting

3. Internship evaluations

    a. Retail employee evaluation form

    b. Work supervisor's evaluation form

    c. Intern's self-evaluation form

4. Exercise that allows goal setting for work experiences and internships, and an "Opportunity Plan" that can record self-assessment of progress toward these goals.

5. Links to internship Web sites

REFERENCE

Strickler, S. (2001). What influence does a practicum experience have on a student's future? Abstract presented at the annual meeting of the International Textile and Apparel Association. Kansas City, [On-line]. Available: http://www.itaaonline.org/ITAAnew/Proceedings2001/ResearchAbstract.

CHAPTER EIGHT

PROFESSIONAL ETHICS

Do unto others as you expect others to do unto you.
— THE GOLDEN RULE

OBJECTIVES

- To identify and explore the relationship between professionalism and ethics.

- To establish awareness that benefits and consequences accompany actions.

- To develop accountability by encouraging acceptance of responsibility for actions.

- To establish awareness of the relationship, and likely conflict, between profit and ethical behavior.

- To establish awareness of the role that power plays in ethical dilemmas.

- To develop and document a personal code of ethics.

THE IMPORTANCE OF ETHICS IN BUSINESS

An important component of professional development, ethics, should be considered by students preparing for careers in any area—retailing and apparel merchandising are no exceptions. Ethics is the practice of what is "right." It is generally agreed that people know the difference between what is right and what is wrong. During the process of social development, children learn to abide by a series of rules that govern their behavior. Well-adjusted adults continue to respond and react to the standards dictated by the society in which they live. Spike Lee effectively coined the phrase, and he along with other popular advertising and media campaigns have encouraged us to "do the right thing." In the professional arena, discussions of ethics have become frequent and employees' conduct is carefully and increasingly scrutinized today.

Santa Clara University's Markkula Center for Applied Ethics provides an Internet site (*http://www.scu.edu/ethics*) that describes how the concept of ethics is often associated with feelings, religion, and the law. These associations, though, are potentially erroneous. When led only by feelings, people are as likely to make unethical choices that "feel good" as they are to choose the course that is "right." Although religions support ethical conduct in their members, ethics are not exclusive to religious people. Cultural perspective and religious beliefs can present conflicts with respect to ethics among and between people from different backgrounds. Laws, although they present behavior standards, do not always present standards that are ethical. Consider the case of pre–Civil War slavery laws as an example of unethical laws.

What, then, does it mean to be ethical? An ethical individual is one who avoids behaviors that are morally wrong. Cheating, stealing, lying, and murder are universally considered to be wrong. On the other hand, ethical individuals strive to behave in a manner that endorses virtues, including honesty and respect for others. Virtuous behaviors are universally considered to be right.

An awareness of the role of ethics in a business environment is crucial as one prepares for and enters a career. According to Michael Bugeja (1994), nationally acclaimed author and ethicist, "Ethics are easy when nothing is at stake; the difficulty is learning to live with ambiguity." One constant of life is ambiguity, and successful individuals must learn to live with the uncertainty of events that will affect them. We can, however, prepare ourselves to be better able to cope with conflict and uncertainty by exploring our own values and determining the comfort levels we associate with certain actions. When faced with ethical dilemmas, or "situations which cause internal conflict in considering what is the 'right' thing to do" (Lee, Weber, & Knaub, 1994, p. 24; Knaub, Weber, & Russ, 1994), individuals must rely on their personal sets of values, their life experiences, their feelings and emotional biases, the social context of the situation, and external influences such as parents and peers as they seek to resolve the dilemmas.

Just as ignorance is no excuse for the law, individuals are expected to perform up to the standards established by employers. Most companies provide a written set of guidelines to their employees containing operating procedures, including those for events such as emergencies and loss prevention, guidelines for dress and appearance, and standards for conduct. Individual employees are responsible for familiarizing themselves with the company's rules, and are held accountable to follow them. Ethical behavior requires that an employee live up to the standards set by an employer. Box 8.1 provides a listing of typical company guidelines.

BOX 8.1

TYPICAL COMPANY GUIDELINES FOR DRESS, APPEARANCE, AND CONDUCT

DRESS AND APPEARANCE
- Do not wear political or controversial buttons, insignias, or apparel.
- Wear a name badge at all times.
- Tattoos and piercing:
  - Some companies require no visible tattoos.
  - Some companies require no facial piercing.
  - The content of the tattoo, placement of piercing, or amount of either may be restricted.
- For women:
  - Avoid ornate and extreme styles, plunging necklines, halters, short-shorts, and extreme miniskirts.
  - Close-toe shoes are often required. If open-toe shoes are allowed, a professional pedicure may be required.
  - Capri pants are sometimes prohibited.
  - You may be required to wear hosiery.
- For men:
  - Business-like suits and a jacket at all times may be required.
  - Dress shoes with appropriate hosiery are often required.
  - Facial hair is sometimes restricted.

PROHIBITED ACTIVITIES (MAY BE GROUNDS FOR IMMEDIATE DISMISSAL)
- Any act of dishonesty or theft
- Falsification of records and documents
- Competing in business with the company
- Divulging trade secrets or proprietary information
- Engaging in conduct that may adversely affect the company or its reputation
- Carrying a weapon on company premises
- Disobeying the company's rules on smoking and/or abuse of controlled substances

(continued)

BOX 8.1 continued from page 203

- Use of alcohol or controlled substances during working hours
- Insubordination
- Tardiness or absenteeism
- Harassment of employees, colleagues, or clients
- Violation of antitrust
- Violation of employee discount policies
- Noncompliance with store security policies
- Wearing nonpurchased merchandise

DEFINING THE BOUNDARIES OF ETHICAL DILEMMAS

Many rules, or company standards, are objective. In other words, one can define easily when behaviors follow or break rules. It is the responsibility of employees to be familiar with the expectations of their employers to avoid conflict when making decisions regarding behaviors. For example, it is wrong to steal from the company, it is wrong to falsify documents, and it is wrong to dress contrary to the established dress code.

Unfortunately, there are many subjective situations in which rules or standards must be interpreted and personal opinion will vary with respect to the degree of "rightness" or "wrongness" associated with a given action. Is it wrong to take home pens or pencils from work? Is it wrong to "fudge" your timesheet when you are late—even if you stay later to make up the work? Is it wrong to make a "fashion statement" even though your appearance violates company dress policy? Is it wrong to violate company policy if you are satisfying a customer or client? Is it wrong to put your own money in the store cash register at the end of the day so that the till is balanced? Do you have a responsibility to speak up when you observe unethical behavior—even if you won't be rewarded for doing so? As individuals, people respond differently to any given stimulus, and this contributes to unique opinions and actions in situations and often to conflict. Experience, culture, religion, family relationships, generational roles, and individual value systems all contribute to one's ethical base. Thus, judgments about what constitutes ethical behavior differ. Most of us, however, will at one time in our working lives be faced with an ethical dilemma—a situation in which the best course of action is not obvious (Box 8.2).

BOX 8.2
ETHICAL DILEMMAS

Over 1,150 professionals who were members of The National Council on Family Relations and the American Home Economics Association (now the American Association of Family and Consumer Sciences) responded to a survey asking, "As a professional, have you ever faced a serious ethical dilemma relative to your role? Seventy percent replied that they had.

The following types of ethical dilemmas were identified by survey respondents:

- Confidentiality
- Lack of professionalism in colleagues
- Sexual misconduct
- Job-related issues
- Research issues
- Academic issues
- Social issues

The following factors influenced respondents' resolutions of ethical dilemmas:

FACTOR	INFLUENCE RATING*
Past experience	4.64
Code of ethics	4.61
Emotional bias	4.45
Social context	4.27
Religious background	4.03
Colleagues	4.02
Parental influence	3.91
Literature	3.68
Workshop(s)	3.43
College	3.33
Professors	3.18
Media	2.91

*rated on a scale of 1 to 5; 1 = not at all influential, 5 = very influential.

SOURCE: Knaub, P. K., Weber, M. J., & Russ, R. R. (1994). Ethical dilemmas encountered in Human Environmental Sciences: Implications for ethics education. *Journal of Family and Consumer Sciences, 86(3)*, 23–30. Copyright © *Journal of Family and Consumer* Sciences, 1994. Reprinted with permission from Table 3, page 26, and Table 4, page 27.

THE ROLE OF PERSONAL VALUES
IN ETHICAL JUDGMENTS

Individual judgments with respect to ethical behavior are directly related to individual value systems. One must be familiar with one's own personal values in order to make clear and rational judgments regarding ethics. Values are learned. Children adopt values that have been taught, consciously or not, by family members and others in their near environments. Value systems are shaped as individuals develop their personalities, and are nurtured and reinforced by the responses one receives in response to actions. Actions such as cheating and lying may be rewarded with success, power, and other positive reinforcements or may be negatively reinforced via punishment, failure, and exclusion. Personal experiences in conjunction with responses to behaviors result in decidedly varied value systems. Although there is much debate over the appropriateness of teaching values, it is clear that without a strong value system sound, well-informed, and courageous decisions in the face of ethical dilemmas cannot be made.

Michael Bugeja introduced the concept of moral absolutes in his book *Living Ethics* (1996). He presented the ideas of Christina Hoff Sommers (1993), who noted that there are some truths that are not personal judgments, but rather truths accepted by all people as clearly right or clearly wrong. These clear standards are considered to be moral absolutes. Included in her list of moral absolutes are truths such as, "it is wrong to mistreat a child," "it is wrong to humiliate someone," "it is wrong to torment an animal," "it is wrong to think only of yourself," "it is wrong to steal, to lie, to break promises," "it is right to be considerate and respectful of others," and "it is right to be charitable and generous." Bugeja added to Sommers's moral absolutes, "it is wrong to prejudge others based on physical or racial features," and "it is wrong to treat human beings like objects or property."

In order to make decisions rooted in ethics, personal values must be developed that are acceptable to those in one's immediate environment. The environment could be a family, social group, or place of employment. The organizational culture—a set of values, traditions, and customs that defines and directs employee behavior—should be explored by potential employees to clarify workplace expectations. In a professional setting, one's values must be adequately defined so that ethical decisions can be made with confidence. When decisions are made about employment options, it is helpful to keep in mind that the interview process is a two-way street. You should strive to find a workplace that has an organizational culture that dovetails well with your own ethical base.

In environments where people interact together, unique problems that do not adhere perfectly to the "rules and regulations" are bound to occur. It is within these circumstances that one must rely on one's previously developed ethical base to arrive at acceptable and appropriate decisions. Eight categories of ethical dilemmas have been identified as commonly experienced by human science professionals (Lee, Weber, & Knaub, 1994). In order of frequency, these are lack of professionalism in colleagues, social issues, job-related issues, confidentiality, academic issues, lack of professionalism in students, research issues, and sexual misconduct. Although categorized as ethical dilemmas encountered specifically by human science professionals, these situations are typical of a diverse selection of professional environments and should be considered by prospective professionals (see Box 8.2).

APPROACHES TO ETHICS

Ethics are approached in a variety of ways, depending on the circumstances surrounding a given situation (Box 8.3). The moral absolutes mentioned earlier are examples of the so-called virtue approach to ethics. Using this approach, ethical behavior is equated with virtuous behavior. As ethics are applied to larger groups of people, particularly when ethics are tied to policy making, the utility approach (also called utilitarian or utilitarianism) is often applied. This approach requires a comparison of benefits to harms, with the ethical choice being the one that provides the greatest benefit with the least amount of harm for most people. Similarly, the common good approach seeks to identify as ethical the choice that advances the common good. Additional approaches to ethics include the fairness approach and the rights approach. The fairness approach focuses on the need to treat members of a group fairly unless there is a moral reason for disparity. The rights approach relates to fundamental human rights (which may differ among cultures) and seeks to identify the choice that respects individuals and their rights to be respected and treated fairly and equally.

When faced with an ethical dilemma, one should take time to evaluate the situation, consider all sides of the given issue, and refer to appropriate ethical codes when available. Application of a specific approach to ethics may help to focus an appropriate decision. Although there are generally no "right" or "wrong" responses to ethical dilemmas, some solutions have more (or less) merit than others. To further complicate the ethics issue, one must be prepared to realize that rewards for ethical behavior are often not immediate. In fact, when unethical behavior is prevalent, ethical behavior may be associated with negative short-term feedback. Because attitudes related to ethics are rooted in value systems, the only reward for ethical behavior may be the personal satisfaction associated with doing the right thing.

BOX 8.3
COMMON ETHICAL APPROACHES

VIRTUE APPROACH

- Focuses on attitudes, dispositions, or character traits that enable us to be and to act in ways that develop our human potential.
- *Examples:* honesty, courage, faithfulness, trustworthiness, integrity, etc.
- *Principle:* "What is ethical is what develops moral virtues in ourselves and our communities."

UTILITARIAN APPROACH

- Focuses on the consequences that actions or policies have on the well-being ("utility") of all persons directly or indirectly affected by the action or policy.
- *Principle:* "Of any two actions, the most ethical one will produce the greatest balance of benefits over harms."

RIGHTS APPROACH

- Identifies certain interests or activities that our behavior must respect, especially those areas of our lives that are of such value to us that they merit protection from others.
- Holds that each person has a fundamental right to be respected and treated as a free and equal rational person capable of making his or her own decisions.
- This implies other rights (e.g., privacy, free consent, freedom of conscience, etc.) that must be protected if a person is to have the freedom to direct his or her own life.
- *Principle:* "An action or policy is morally right only if those persons affected by the decision are not used merely as instruments for advancing some goal, but are fully informed and treated only as they have freely and knowingly consented to be treated."

FAIRNESS (OR JUSTICE) APPROACH

- Focuses on how fairly or unfairly our actions distribute benefits and burdens among the members of a group.
- Fairness requires consistency in the way people are treated.
- *Principle:* "Treat people the same unless there are morally relevant differences between them."

COMMON GOOD APPROACH

- Presents a vision of society as a community whose members are joined in a shared pursuit of values and goals they hold in common.
- The community is composed of individuals whose own good is inextricably bound to the good of the whole.
- *Principle:* "What is ethical is what advances the common good."

SOURCE: Reprinted with permission of The Markkula Center for Applied Ethics at Santa Clara University, www.scu.edu/ethics.

Using Case Studies to Resolve Ethical Dilemmas

A case study approach is an effective way to go about resolving an ethical dilemma. The case study method of problem solving works well in situations in which more than one possible solution exists, and there is not necessarily a "right" versus a "wrong" solution (Granger, 1996; Rabolt & Miller, 1997; Silverman, Welty, & Lyons, 1992). The case study approach provides a system for organizing information about a problem and presenting alternative solutions to the problem that can be compared. A case study problem-solving approach requires that first the main issue, or conflict, be identified. Second, the circumstances contributing to the dilemma should be identified. Third, several alternative solutions should be developed, with advantages and disadvantages of each alternative being considered. Finally, in light of all considerations and with respect of the "rules," the solution should be reached. A considerable investment of time, for both research of the situation and thoughtful contemplation, should be devoted to successfully resolve ethical issues.

As you work through ethical dilemma cases, you should first identify whether ethical dilemmas actually exist. To be appropriately prepared to make this determination, you should be familiar with policies of your work environment, should consider what course of action is fair to all parties, and should explore your "gut reaction" to the situation. There may be specific guidelines stipulating appropriate actions and behavior of personnel. It is wise to refer to these guidelines when considering alternative decisions. Furthermore, if one employee ends up with an unfair advantage over other employees—in terms of preferential treatment by management, opportunities for career advancement, or ability to be productive while selling—overall productivity in the work environment is compromised. First reactions to situations often provide a base for further exploration, although they should not be the only consideration given to potential dilemmas. Gut reactions should be given merit; if a situation seems wrong, it probably is. Although no new employee wants to bring every decision before a mentor or manager, such people are excellent resources when particularly difficult situations present themselves. Often, it is helpful to think through a problem and seek advice from a respected person in authority before any action is taken. The J.C. Penney Business Ethics Policy offers excellent advice: "When in doubt, ask." The CD-ROM that accompanies this book provides opportunities for you to work through case studies pertaining to ethical dilemmas.

The Decision-Making Process

Once it has been determined that some choice needs to be made, a set of alternative choices should be identified. As these choices are identified, their merits and consequences should be considered. Some questions that should be considered as the process of decision-making progresses are:

- What are the positive and negative benefits and consequences that are likely to be associated with the course of action being considered?
- Do any selected courses of action violate company policy?
- Do any selected courses of action violate your own ethical standards?
- Do you personally feel comfortable with the course of action being considered?
- Does the outcome associated with the course of action result in an inappropriate advantage or disadvantage for you or any of the parties involved?
- Would you publicly stand by this course of action?

For more information about the process of ethical decision making, you may wish to review the Markkula Center for Applied Ethics at Santa Clara University Web site at *http://www.scu.edu/ethics.*

FACTORS THAT CONTRIBUTE TO ETHICAL DILEMMAS

The ability to seek information when faced with an ethical dilemma is invaluable. You can save yourself a considerable amount of stressful contemplation if you seek information and ask relevant questions. What are the circumstances surrounding the situation at hand? How will morale of company employees be affected by the actions that are taken? These and other questions will lead you to a better understanding of the situations you will face. Sufficient information is necessary to develop creative solutions to dilemmas. Considering the facts of the situation, you will be better prepared to present compromises that create outcomes that are fair to all employees and in the best interest of your company.

The Profit–Ethics Dilemma

In a business environment, the temptation of individuals to violate ethical rules is often strong due to the relationship between unfair play and profit. Profit itself is not unethical, but behaviors exhibited by individuals seeking to achieve profit may be. Companies that condone employees who capitalize on an unfair advantage, such as stockbrokers who maneuver trades based on inside information or designers who unscrupulously secure information about a competitor's upcoming line, may reap short-term profits. These profits, however, arrive at the expense of violating ethical standards, potentially damaging the firm's reputation and in some cases incurring legal retribution.

Employees must be aware of the expectations of their employers. Employers expect their employees to live up the expectations set forth. Situational dilemmas that arise with profit as a leading motivator for action should be carefully considered. Although companies expect employees to make decisions resulting in the highest possible profit margins, individual employees must remember that they alone are responsible for and must answer to decisions that they have made. Companies further expect that their "good names" will be preserved by all employees. Dr. Laura Schlessinger, a licensed marriage and family counselor, internationally syndicated radio host, and author, encourages her audience to consider, if viewed retrospectively, the choices they wish they would have made. Her approach encourages consideration of a perspective that does not necessarily provide immediate gratification, but allows one to determine the extent to which a decision involves one's character and conscience. In her book *How Could You Do That?!: The Abdication of Character, Courage, and Conscience* (1996), Dr. Schlessinger describes the situation of a woman who was distressed at witnessing racial discrimination among her co-workers at a department store. The woman's ethical dilemma—the decision about whether to speak up and voice her disapproval—was further complicated by her knowledge that doing so would likely jeopardize her career with the company.

Dr. Schlessinger relates the situation to the concept of "selling out," and shares a letter written by the woman to illustrate the important role of conscience in personal conflict:

> After speaking to you, I went back into work and spoke with my supervisor. I told her I would not "sell out" and look the other way when inappropriate behavior or injustices were displayed by her and the other executives. I also told her that I felt I had an obligation as a supervisor to set an example for my crew. I also went in and spoke with my personnel manager. During our conversation, I told him "I am not going to sell out."
>
> The next day, when I arrived at work, I was asked to report to the store manager's office. I was given a Phase I warning notice as the first step in disciplinary action. My supervisor justified this action with examples of hearsay and refused to tell me who my accusers were.
>
> However, I am not writing you to say, "poor me." I am writing to say, "thank you." You helped me to realize I would not feel wonderful if I looked the other way. I would not earn respect from my co-workers and crew if I jumped on the executive's abuse band wagon. I now realize I have a more active conscience than I gave myself credit for. And now I know, I would not and could not sell out at any job just to have a paycheck.
>
> I must admit, I was angry, hurt, and scared. I needed this job to have medical benefits and to work around my school schedule. What I didn't need from this job was the abuse and power-trip displayed by four of the six executives at my store.
>
> So, again, I want to thank you for NOT teaching me: How To Sell Out. (pp. 70–71)*

One's comfort level with the ethical environment supported by one's employer is an important measure to consider. Success and happiness can be found in very different ways, and personal values are directly related to the feelings of contentment an individual will find in any given situation. Young professionals should be aware that company environments and collective views regarding ethics differ just as individual value systems and personal ethical codes differ.

Ethics and the Role of Power

The highest proof of virtue is to possess boundless power without abusing it.
—Lord Macaulay

Power is a phenomenon that affects the environment in which decisions are made. In a business environment, the relative power one possesses is typically related to one's role as a supervisor or subordinate. Obviously, supervisors possess power over subordinate employees. Thus, one may likely believe his or her professional position and potential for growth to be at stake when actions and decisions do not reflect those of the supervisor. Herein lies the dilemma between power and ethics.

Supervisors, managers, and leaders in professional situations possess power over the employees who depend on them for evaluations, promotions, wage increases, and recommendations. Along with this power, such professionals must accept the responsibility not to abuse the power associated with their positions. In fact, the roles and responsibilities associated with both supervisors and subordinates should be carefully considered. Upcoming executives can practice good leadership ethics through responsible decision making. People in positions of power should be aware of the importance of setting a good example; theirs will be the standard to which subordinates compare their own actions.

Although employees have the responsibility to perform according to established standards within the company and to follow the direction given by the supervisor, subordinates should make certain that any conflicts between these two directives are recognized and resolved. Virtually all companies have specific policies regulating the relationships of supervisors and subordinates. Specifically, companies address issues such as discrimination, sexual harassment, and consensual relationships. Some companies prohibit two members of an immediate family from working together. Most companies discourage romantic relationships between employees, particularly among supervisors and subordinates.

Harassment of fellow employees, most often instigated by a supervisor or employee with greater power in the business organization than the victim, is particularly nonproductive in the work environment. Harassment may take the form of unwanted physical, verbal, visual, or sexual behavior directed against another because of his or her gender, race, age, religion, or disability. Most instances of harassment are illegal as well as unethical, but because of its intimidating and potentially embarrassing nature, victims often suffer through the abuse rather than report it and seek reprieve. Employees, especially executives, have the responsibility to prevent workplace harassment by setting good examples and refusing to tolerate unethical behavior. Individuals who hold positions of power over others must be aware that when workplace ethics become problematic, the supervisor is inevitably in the role of the person who "should have known better."

Figure 8.1 presents an empowerment exercise designed by Michael Bugeja (1996) that can enable you to assess your own use or abuse of power.

Instructions:

1. Recount a professional or academic dispute or situation in which you exerted power.
2. Recount a professional or academic dispute or situation in which you abused power.
3. Evaluate the disputes or situations cited above according to concepts in the Four-Step Power Process below.
4. Analyze how, if at all, would you handle each dispute or situation above differently today.

FOUR-STEP POWER PROCESS

1. *Ascertain your personal and professional power.*
   Ethical professionals acknowledge their power so they can tap or restrain it during suspected challenges or crises. To acknowledge your power base, make a list of items. Ask yourself:
   • Am I intellectually or physically powerful?
   • Do I have access to powerful tools or technology like cameras or computers?
   • Can I communicate powerful ideas?
   • Do I know or have access to powerful people?
   • Do I supervise or have authority over others?
   • What other aspects of my life involve power?

2. *Evaluate your personal or professional power.*
   After you have acknowledged your power base, determine how you have been employing that power. Analyze each item on your list. Ask yourself:
   • Do I usually abuse this type of power when I have the opportunity?
   • Do I usually exert the appropriate amount of this power to meet each challenge or problem? Or do I usually over- or underestimate situations?
   • Do I usually avoid using this type of power at all costs?

3. *Take prudent action or practice restraint.*
   Identify items on your power list that are reliable or need improvement. The goal is to meet each challenge or problem with the appropriate amount of power to suit the occasion. Ask yourself:
   • When I feel the urge to take action, do I usually (a) suppress that urge when the stakes or consequences warrant a response, (b) act on behalf of others for whom I have no responsibility, or (c) act in my own interests?
   NOTE: *If (a) or (b), seek advice from a mentor or role model whose judgment you trust to determine how to proceed or whether your participation is really required.*

FIGURE 8.1   Empowerment Assignment

- What are the usual results of my taking action: (a) bigger or more complex problems, (b) symbolic but important participation, (c) compromise to resolve a situation or dispute, or (d) total resolution of a situation or dispute?
  NOTE: *If (a), practice restraint until you can determine how your participation will be beneficial.*
- If I take action, who else might be affected: (a) innocent individuals or groups, (b) individuals or groups indirectly associated with the situation, or (c) only those directly associated with the situation?
  NOTE: *If (a) or (b), practice restraint until you can determine whether your interests are greater than the effect your actions may have on other innocent or indirectly related persons or parties.*

4. *Take responsibility for your actions.*
   Once you have ascertained and evaluated your power, you need to accept consequences for your actions. This will help you maintain or restore your personal integrity and/or professional credibility. Ask yourself:
   - Do I have anything to apologize for or correct? For instance, did I misperceive a threat or make a hasty judgment based on faulty information?
     NOTE: *If so, apologize or correct errors to match the degree of misperceptions or mistakes . . . without unduly damaging your own or other parties' interests.*
   - Does another party have anything to apologize to me for or correct? For instance, did someone else misperceive a threat by you or make a hasty judgment based on faulty information?
     NOTE: *If so, you may decide to demand an apology or a correction or some other resolution to offset the misperception or mistake.*
   - Are the consequences a direct result of (a) my actions, (b) part my and part someone else's actions over which I had no influence or control, or (c) someone else's actions over which I had no influence or control?
     NOTE: *If (b) or (c), assume responsibility for your part in the situation and/or inform other affected parties about the actions over which you had no influence or control.*

© 2003 by Michael Bugeja

ETHICS FOR INTERVIEWS

Communication between the parties in employment interviews is important, because each question and every response must be carefully considered. Often, implied meanings of questions and answers are conjectured, and perhaps misinterpreted. Those people responsible for the selection of employees are morally obligated to be familiar with the limits related to legal questions and assumptions that may be made about prospective employees (Refer to the discussion in Chapter 6 and Table 6.1). For example, interviewers should not assume that marital or parental status of individuals will affect their abilities to successfully perform their jobs. Gender, age, sexual orientation, and race discrimination, and assumptions related to these factors, are widely recognized areas in which the issue of ethics is of concern.

THE RELATIONSHIP BETWEEN ETHICS AND ETIQUETTE

Ethics and etiquette, while undeniably different entities, are related in both business and personal settings. Concepts such as fair treatment of and respect for others, honesty, and the value of charity and generosity are recognized as moral absolutes (Bugeja, 1996), or rules that apply to everyone. The idea of a moral rule is rooted in the theory of ethics, but it is obvious that the concepts of fair treatment, respect, honesty, and generosity are also inherent components of etiquette. Most often, when you carry out an action that is "right" (ethical), it is also the action that is most considerate of other people involved and affected (etiquette). Etiquette, though, goes beyond ethics to establish an environment that encourages interactions and feelings of being at ease in a given situation. According to Emily Post (1984, p. xiii), the purpose of etiquette "is to make the world a pleasanter place to live in, and you a more pleasant person to live with." This is a noble goal for which to strive and, indeed, is the "right thing to do" in both personal and professional environments.

The basic, and most familiar, rules of etiquette prevail in today's business world. It is appreciated when "please," "thank you," and "you're welcome" are used appropriately in conversation. It is good manners, and likely to result in a positive impression, to send thank-you letters and to be punctual with respect to correspondence and requests. A firm handshake is an appropriate action that demonstrates respect for an acquaintance. A smile or simply a nod or other gesture of acknowledgment is a polite way to recognize the presence or recognition of another. Respect for others and an appreciation for alternate points of view are hallmarks of both ethical behavior and good etiquette. When in the company of interviewers, colleagues, supervisors, or subordinates, your attention to good manners will be noticed and is likely to contribute to others' perceptions of your professional profile.

EXPLORING YOUR ETHICAL CONSTRUCT

Have you ever considered your own ethical base? When faced with a situation in which an ethical dilemma might arise, are you prepared to "do the right thing?"

Michael Bugeja (1996) encourages students to keep track of their behaviors by recording white lies and other nontruths. This exercise, he says, provides an opportunity for students to consider the potential consequences of their actions, and to quantify the number of times they compromise an ethical ideal. Your own history of behavior is important. Employment applications frequently include questions such as, "Have you ever been convicted of a felony?" If you have a record of shoplifting, you are not likely to be employed by a retailer. To "do the right thing," we must apply ethical principles in all aspects of our daily lives. Refer to Box 8.4, which explores seven myths about ethical principles.

Applicants for employment with retailers or in merchandising positions are often asked to complete a psychological or "attitude" questionnaire. Results of such questionnaires contribute to hiring decisions. Responses to these questionnaires offer employers information related to one's value system, beliefs, and behaviors. Although there are no right or wrong responses to the questions posed, one's ethical construct contributes to the pattern of responses. An attitude questionnaire might ask such questions as, "Do you think that it is wrong for an employee to take home a pen from work?," "If someone has stolen money before, can he/she be trusted to handle money in the future?," and "Do you think it is okay to cheat on your income taxes?" Attitude questionnaires frequently ask questions pertaining to use of alcohol, tobacco, and other substances along with pointed questions regarding one's history of convictions.

Developing a Code of Ethics

A code of ethics is a set of rules guiding the behavior of an individual or a group of people. Codes of ethics may be constructed to address philosophical issues, codes of conduct, or policies. Codes may be categorized as aspirational, educational, or regulatory. The nature of the code, whether it is a corporate code or a personal code, and the culture of the people or individuals for whom the code is constructed, dictates its purpose. Philosophical codes of ethics can also be referred to as aspirational. An aspirational code of ethics presents an individual's or group's values and ideals. The principles to which the person or group aspires are the focus of this type of code. A code of conduct could be considered an educational code of ethics. This type of code would be presented to help its readers make appropriate decisions for the organization or individual the code represents. A policy-related code of ethics is considered regulatory. Such a code of ethics contains detailed rules that govern the conduct of its author or members of the group it represents.

BOX 8.4
SEVEN MYTHS ABOUT ETHICS
By J. Edward Katz

To be ethical, one must build good habits by applying ethical principles every day, including telling the truth, not stealing, and treating others as you would want them to treat you. Start by learning the seven fundamental myths about ethics.

Myth No. 1: Business ethics. Many people talk about business ethics without realizing that there is no such thing as "business ethics." Ethical principles exist for all walks of life, and these principles do not change as one traverses different venues. Applications might differ, but the principles themselves do not.

Myth No. 2: Professional ethics can be separated from personal ethics. A variation of the first myth is that we can live however we wish in our personal lives as long as we act ethically on the job. Aristotle discards such a juvenile idea when he proclaims that my character is the sum of all my habits. If I lie habitually in my personal life, then I am not building the strength or the character to stand true at the other times.

Myth No. 3: Some things are ethical, some are not. The gist of this myth is that some issues or topics are devoid of ethical content, but this assertion can be true only if human interaction is absent. Consider the classic make-or-buy analysis taught in management accounting. At first blush, it may appear that this decision analysis is purely technical and devoid of ethical content. But ethics pervades this technical grid in several ways.

The analyst who is working for the firm is receiving compensation to perform a good investigation; doing anything less is stealing from the employer. The investigation and the recommendations presuppose reliable data and disclosure of all important assumptions; anything less is lying. The decision process itself assumes maximization of shareholder profit, constrained by various stakeholder concerns.

Myth No. 4: Ethics is a matter of education alone. To act in an ethical way, a person must understand his or her duties and obligations. Obviously, education has a role to play in instructing folks about their ethical responsibilities. I have learned, however, that education alone does not produce ethical people, for some very highly educated people act thoughtlessly, selfishly, and unethically.

Myth No. 5: Responsibility for ethical education rests with colleges and universities. The calls for more ethics training at colleges and universities makes me laugh. I wonder where were the parents, the churches, the K–12 teachers, the Little League coaches, and the Girl Scout leaders?

Myth No. 6: Ethical dilemmas are episodic. This myth takes the tack that ethical problems arise only occasionally during one's life; accordingly, individuals need education about these professional quandaries; armed with the appropriate facts, one becomes capable of solving such predicaments as they occur. Missing the ethical content of daily human interaction increases the chances of not recognizing major ethical episodes when they materialize.

Myth No. 7: You either are an ethical person or you are not. This myth has several problems. The first mistake is that this assertion presumes that education, enforcement, and habit building have no role to play. Clearly, they do. The second problem with this thought is that it assumes perfection, but all people have ethical lapses. (I silently chuckle whenever people inform me that they never lie, because they just did.) What differentiates the two groups is that an ethical person will admit the error, try to make amends, and learn from the transgression. Unethical people cover up the blunder, do not care about the consequences of their sin, and learn nothing from the experience.

J. Edward Ketz, associate professor of accounting at Pennsylvania State University, is author of *Hidden Financial Risk*, a book on accounting scandals and misdeeds.

Many corporations have adopted ethical codes by which they operate and expect their employees to abide. An ethical code is a compilation of statements or rules, or both, that offer guidance and direction to the organization that has generated the code. Members of organizations represented by codes of ethics are compelled to act professionally and within the standards of the codes. Employees often possess certain knowledge and expertise in their professions that might result in a position of disadvantage among the public should standards of ethics not be maintained. Codes of ethics therefore serve as regulatory tools for organizations, and benchmarks by which needs for disciplinary actions may weighed.

When a member of an organization faces an ethical dilemma, the code of ethics, by providing written guidelines, can be used to help that member decide the best course of action. A code of ethics' effectiveness is constrained by the circumstances under which it is administered. An effective code of ethics must be reflective of the company or organizational culture and must be enforced (Hira, 1996). The concept of creating a code of ethics has been embraced by many businesses and professional organizations. On the World Wide Web, numerous sources are dedicated to presenting information about organizations' codes of ethics and the process of creating and using codes of ethics. The Center for the Study of Ethics in the Professions of the Illinois Institute of Technology (http://www.iit.edu/departments/csep/) and the Markkula Center for Applied Ethics of Santa Clara University (http://www.scu.edu/ethics/) provide a plethora of information on the topics of ethics and ethical codes.

A code of ethics usually begins with a general statement concerning the nature of the organization and the purpose of providing the code of ethics. This introduction is followed by specific belief statements directed toward the expectations of members represented in the organization or business. Codes of ethics may be either brief and general or lengthy and considerably detailed. One of the most comprehensive codes is that of the American Marketing Association (AMA), shown in Figure 8.2. The AMA Code of Ethics addresses responsibilities of marketers with respect to honesty and fairness, rights and duties of parties in the marketing exchange process, and organizational relationships. The National Automobile Dealers Association (NADA) has adopted a code of ethics that addresses expectations of professional performance of its members (Figure 8.3).

To be optimally effective, it is essential that all members of an organization (or employees of a company) be familiar with the respective code of ethics. The code should be easily accessible to all employees, and should be shared with clients and other constituents of the organization. This reinforces the importance of accountability. The basis for discussion and awareness of ethics, and the reason for constructing a code, is that each person is responsible for his or her own actions. Individuals are expected to follow the rules of conduct set by law, company policy, and common professional courtesy. Individuals will be held accountable for decisions that they make and actions that they take in professional positions.

It is all too easy—and unfortunately fairly common—for employees to lose sight of ethical, or moral, considerations for the advancement of themselves, their division, or their company. Accountability is a reality. A helpful ethical benchmark is present

(continued on page 224)

Members of the American Marketing Association are committed to ethical professional conduct. They have joined together in subscribing to this Code of Ethics embracing the following topics:

Responsibilities of the Marketer

Marketers must accept responsibility for the consequences of their activities and make every effort to ensure that their decisions, recommendations and actions function to identify, serve and satisfy all relevant publics: customers, organizations and society.

Marketers' Professional Conduct must be guided by:

1. The basic rule of professional ethics: not knowingly to do harm;
2. The adherence to all applicable laws and regulations;
3. The accurate representation of their education, training and experience; and
4. The active support, practice and promotion of this Code of Ethics.

Honesty and Fairness

Marketers shall uphold and advance the integrity, honor and dignity of the marketing profession by:

1. Being honest in serving consumers, clients, employees, suppliers, distributors, and the public;
2. Not knowingly participating in conflict of interest without prior notice to all parties involved; and
3. Establishing equitable fee schedules including the payment or receipt of usual, customary and/or legal compensation for marketing exchanges.

Rights and Duties of Parties in the Marketing Exchange Process

Participants in the marketing exchange process should be able to expect that:

1. Products and services offered are safe and fit for their intended uses;
2. Communications about offered products and services are not deceptive;
3. All parties intend to discharge their obligations, financial and otherwise, in good faith; and
4. Appropriate internal methods exist for equitable adjustment and/or redress of grievances concerning purchases.

It is understood that the above would include, but is not limited to, the following responsibilities of the marketer:

In the area of product development and management:

- disclosure of all substantial risks associated with product or service usage;
- identification of any product component substitution that might materially change the product or impact on the buyer's purchase decision;
- identification of extra cost-added features.

(continued)

FIGURE 8.2   American Marketing Association (AMA) Code of Ethics

FIGURE 8.2 continued from page 221

In the area of promotions:

- avoidance of false and misleading advertising;
- rejection of high-pressure manipulations, or misleading sales tactics;
- avoidance of sales promotions that use deception or manipulation.

In the area of distribution:

- not manipulating the availability of a product for the purpose of exploitation;
- not using coercion in the marketing channel;
- not exerting undue influence over the reseller's choice to handle a product.

In the area of pricing:

- not engaging in price fixing;
- not practicing predatory pricing;
- disclosing the full price associated with any purchase.

In the area of marketing research:

- prohibiting selling or fundraising under the guise of conducting research;
- maintaining research integrity by avoiding misrepresentation and omission of pertinent research data;
- treating outside clients and suppliers fairly.

Organizational Relationships

Marketers should be aware of how their behavior may influence or impact the behavior of others in organizational relationships. They should not demand, encourage or apply coercion to obtain unethical behavior in their relationships with others, such as employees, suppliers, or customers.

1. Apply confidentiality and anonymity in professional relationships with regard to privileged information;
2. Meet their obligations and responsibilities in contracts and mutual agreements in a timely manner;
3. Avoid taking the work of others, in whole, or in part, and representing this work as their own or directly benefiting from it without compensation or consent of the originator or owner; and
4. Avoid manipulation to take advantage of situations to maximize personal welfare in a way that unfairly deprives or damages the organization of others.

Any AMA member found to be in violation of any provision of this Code of Ethics may have his or her Association membership suspended or revoked.

Code of Ethics for Marketing on the Internet

Preamble

The Internet, including online computer communications, has become increasingly important to marketers' activities, as they provide exchanges and access to markets worldwide. The ability

(continued on page 223)

FIGURE 8.2 continued from page 222

to interact with stakeholders has created new marketing opportunities and risks that are not currently specifically addressed in the American Marketing Association Code of Ethics. The American Marketing Association Code of Ethics for Internet marketing provides additional guidance and direction for ethical responsibility in this dynamic area of marketing. The American Marketing Association is committed to ethical professional conduct and has adopted these principles for using the Internet, including on-line marketing activities utilizing network computers.

General Responsibilities

Internet marketers must assess the risks and take responsibility for the consequences of their activities. Internet marketers' professional conduct must be guided by:

1. Support of professional ethics to avoid harm by protecting the rights of privacy, ownership and access.
2. Adherence to all applicable laws and regulations with no use of Internet marketing that would be illegal, if conducted by mail, telephone, fax or other media.
3. Awareness of changes in regulations related to Internet marketing.
4. Effective communication to organizational members on risks and policies related to Internet marketing, when appropriate.
5. Organizational commitment to ethical Internet practices communicated to employees, customers and relevant stakeholders.

Privacy

Information collected from customers should be confidential and used only for expressed purposes. All data, especially confidential customer data, should be safeguarded against unauthorized access. The expressed wishes of others should be respected with regard to the receipt of unsolicited e-mail messages.

Ownership

Information obtained from the Internet sources should be properly authorized and documented. Information ownership should be safeguarded and respected. Marketers should respect the integrity and ownership of computer and network systems.

Access

Marketers should treat access to accounts, passwords, and other information as confidential, and only examine or disclose content when authorized by a responsible party. The integrity of others' information systems should be respected with regard to placement of information, advertising or messages.

SOURCE: Reprinted with permission of the American Marketing Association, www.marketingpower.com.

As a member of the National Automobile Dealers Association, this dealership subscribes to the following principles and standards. Implicit in this Code is the requirement that NADA members comply fully with all federal, state, and local laws governing their businesses.

We pledge to:

- Operate this business in accord with the highest standards of ethical conduct.
- Treat each customer in a fair, open, and honest manner, and fully comply with all laws that prohibit discrimination.
- Meet the transportation needs of our customers in a knowledgeable and professional manner.
- Represent our products clearly and factually, standing fully behind our warranties, direct and implied, and in all other ways justifying the customer's respect and confidence.
- Advertise our products in a positive, factual, and informative manner.
- Detail charges to assist our customers in understanding repair work and provide written estimates of any service work to be performed, upon request, or as required by law.
- Resolve customer concerns promptly and courteously.
- Put our promises in writing and stand behind them.

SOURCE: Reprinted with permission of the National Automobile Dealers Association®.

FIGURE 8.3   National Automobile Dealers Association (NADA) Code of Ethics

by Kenneth Blanchard and Norman Vincent Peale in their book *The Power of Ethical Management* (1988): Ask yourself, "Is it legal?", "Is it fair?", and "How will it make me feel about myself?" A negative response to any of these questions should lead you to seriously reconsider that particular action. Consider also the ramifications of having your actions publicized for scrutiny by others. Remember, you will be held accountable for your behavior.

When faced with a simple dilemma, people undoubtedly are able to identify the difference between right and wrong. It is when the gray areas present themselves, however, that judgment can be difficult. Codes of ethics exist for these situations. Because of the individual nature of so many decisions that are made on behalf of organizations, the creation of a personal code of ethics can be an excellent beginning to exploring your ethical construct and your value system. Through the development of a personal code of ethics, you will have an opportunity to identify and prioritize your values. As you embark on a professional career, you can refer to your own code of ethics along with appropriate organizational codes of ethics to help guide your career choices and professional decisions. Examples of two students' codes of ethics are presented in Figures 8.4 and 8.5.

Foreword: As a student, and person who is part of many different relationships, I believe that there are responsibilities, as well as set standards that I have for daily living. These set standards govern how I live, as well as who I choose to share my daily life with. Responsibility, creativity, respect, and integrity are all key aspects of what I strive for, and look for in others.

Responsibility: Responsibility is defined in many different ways. My personal definition is that responsibility is a multifaceted virtue for myself that includes being accountable for your actions, taking blame if need be for your actions, and being able to complete a given task to one's best ability.

- Always strive to get a task done as completely and accurately as possible. This includes completing a task to your best ability at a given time.
- Being responsible means that you should never take on more than you can handle.
- When taking on any task you should always be accountable for your work at all times, whether complete or incomplete.
- With accountability you should be able to admit your faults and take blame for a mistake if need be.

Creativity: To be creative is to be different, artistically or otherwise. Being creative is being an individual.

- Take risks, never just settle for your first idea.
- Try and do something someone has never tried before. Be new and different.
- Use your imagination and individuality to better any project and give advice if asked.
- Have courage and take risks.

Respect:

- Make decisions that are conscientious of others.
- Never discriminate for reasons of ethnicity, gender, sexual orientation, or financial stability.
- Treat others the way you would like to be treated.
- Be thoughtful and compassionate to others. You never know when you will be in their situation or in need of help.
- Agree to disagree, try to end any conflicts easily and peacefully.
- Everyone is different in some way. See differences as adding to an individual's character, not taking away from them.

Integrity:

- Integrity means being a part of a whole. We are all integral members to our peer groups and society.
- Believe in yourself and the standards you have set for yourself.
- With integrity comes the trust of others; never put yourself in the position to jeopardize that trust.
- Trust demands fairness and equality, including honesty in all aspects of your being.

SOURCE: Reprinted with permission of Steve Kostyo © 2004.

FIGURE 8.4   Steve Kostyo's Code of Ethics

Preamble: The following are characteristics that I believe are important to have in life. I have carried them throughout my life and will continue to carry them as I enter the workforce.

- **Honesty:** Honesty is something that takes time to build. I am always honest with someone from the beginning; therefore they return the honesty to me.
- **Loyalty:** When I am loyal to others, I build a support system. It helps to have someone who values your opinions.
- **Trustworthy:** I am a trustworthy person and people are comfortable sharing information with me.
- **Dependability:** When I am given a task or job, I will work to the best of my ability and complete it in a timely manner.
- **Responsibility:** I take charge of a situation and I am responsible for the outcome. I also take full responsibility for my action.
- **Respect for yourself and others:** I always am respectful to my peers and boss no matter what the situation may be. I act in a professional manner which makes others respect me.
- **Consideration of others:** I would not ask others to do a task that I would not do myself. I am also considerate of their feelings. I always try to be understanding of others.

SOURCE: Reprinted with permission of Carrie Abbott © 2004.

FIGURE 8.5   Carrie Abbott's Code of Ethics

PROJECTS

1. Identify a list of moral absolutes. Compare your list with those of your class-mates. Do they include additional moral absolutes beyond those you originally identified? Are any moral absolutes listed that you or other classmates do not agree are moral absolutes? Discuss in class.

2. Develop a personal code of ethics. Evaluate the elements that you have included in your code and compare your code with those of your classmates. Are there any elements that you included and others did not, or vice versa? Why have you chosen to include or omit the elements that you did?

3. Complete a case study analysis that presents alternative responses to ethical dilemmas presented on the accompanying CD-ROM.

QUESTIONS FOR DISCUSSION

1. Respond to and rank the following situations identifying the level of ethi-cal acceptance you associate with each action: "5" = very unethical,

"4" = unethical, "3" = neutral or not sure, "2" = fairly ethical, and "1" = extremely ethical. Discuss whether the situation has ever been relevant for you, the circumstances associated with the situation that might affect your reaction to the degree of the potential ethical dilemma, and consequences resulting from participation in the situation.

a. Taking credit for participation in a group project in which you did no work

b. Using a false excuse for missing a mandatory class

c. Cheating on an exam

d. Turning in a paper from a "study file" as your own

e. Turning in the same term paper for two different courses in which you are enrolled

f. Copying your roommate's class notes without his or her permission

g. Giving your teacher a gift

h. Omitting a bibliographic citation in a paper

i. Inaccurately embellishing your resume

j. As a corporate buyer, accepting a personal gift from an apparel representative

k. Calling in sick to take a day off

l. Returning merchandise to a store that you have already worn

m. Using high-pressure sales to sell merchandise to a customer who you know cannot afford it

n. Scheduling more hours to employees you are friendly with and consequently cutting back hours of other employees

o. Ringing up a sale as if you were the seller when merchandise has been purchased from the "hold" rack

p. Misrepresenting the quality of the merchandise you are selling

2. How, as a manager or supervisor, would you deal with ethical dilemmas among subordinates. How might you respond to unethical behavior of a supervisor?

3. How, in an interview situation, might you deal with unethical questions? Would the existence of unethical questions in an interview affect your interest in the position? What additional factors might play into your decision?

4. Do you expect your professional behavior to be any different as a result of identifying a personal code of ethics? Why or why not?

ELECTRONIC ACTIVITIES

Refer to the accompanying CD-ROM. The key elements of this chapter are:

1. Summary of Chapter 8 text

2. Ethics "game" (three cases): Based on responses, scenarios, and dilemmas will present themselves that result in consequences (ethical versus unethical behavior)

3. Ethics case study activity

   a. Case study form

4. Links to business ethics Web sites

REFERENCES

Blanchard, K., & Peal, N. V. (1988). *The power of ethical management.* New York: Fawcett Crest.

Bugeja, M. J. (1996). *Living ethics: Developing values in mass communication.* Boston: Allyn and Bacon.

Granger, M. M. (1996). *Case studies in merchandising apparel and soft goods.* New York: Fairchild.

Hira, T. K. (1996). Ethics: Personal and professional implications. *Journal of Family and Consumer Sciences, 88*(1), 6–9.

Knaub, P. K., Weber, M. J., & Russ, R. R. (1994). Ethical dilemmas encountered in Human Environmental Sciences: Implications for ethics education. *Journal of Family and Consumer Sciences, 86*(3), 23–30.

Lee, C. L., Weber, M. J., & Knaub, P. K. (1994). Ethical dilemmas of Human Science professionals: Developing case studies for ethics education. *Journal of Family and Consumer Sciences, 86*(4), 23–29.

Post, E. L. (1984) *Emily Post's etiquette: A guide to modern manners.* (14th ed.) New York: Harper & Row.

Rabolt, N. J., & Miller, J. K. (1997). *Concepts and cases in retail and merchandise management.* New York: Fairchild.

Schlessinger, L. (1996). *How could you do that?!: The abdication of character, courage, and conscience.* New York: HarperCollins.

Silverman, R., Welty, W., & Lyon, S. (1992). *Case studies for teacher problem solving (instructor's manual).* New York: McGraw-Hill.

Sommers, C. H. (1993, September 12). Teaching the virtues. *Chicago Tribune Magazine* reprint, p. 16.

YOUR FIRST JOB AND BEYOND

> Your real education begins now.
> — UNKNOWN

OBJECTIVES

- To identify and consider key components for personally evaluating a job offer.

- To identify areas and explore tactics for the negotiation of job offers.

- To develop strategies for comparing multiple job offers.

- To identify professional methods for accepting or rejecting a job.

- To recognize the importance of professional behavior during the first few weeks at a new job.

- To consider problem-solving strategies when you find yourself in a job you do not like.

- To explore strategies for career search while working full-time in an entry-level position.

- To identify professional considerations and practices in resigning from your job.

THE JOB OFFER

After months of preparation and searching for a postgraduation entry-level position, the tendency for college students and new college graduates is to accept the first job offer that comes their way. This is especially true in times of a tight job market. Do not make this costly mistake without some careful consideration! Realize that the time between when the offer is made, and the time when you accept is a time for negotiation. Even if the job offer you receive is one that you consider your *dream* job, there may still be room for further negotiation. Following are strategies for evaluating a job offer, negotiating a job offer, dealing with multiple job offers, accepting an offer, and rejecting an offer.

Evaluating an Offer

Although you may feel that you know everything you need to about the job you are being offered, and have asked all of the important questions in your interviews, now is the time to take a critical look at the position you are being offered. By now you have identified what factors of a job are most important to you so you will want to make sure that you consider all of these key details. Common areas to examine in evaluating your offer include the base salary and performance bonuses; benefits such as medical, dental, life insurance, savings and retirement, profit sharing, and stock options; and other perks including vacation time, personal days, opportunities for volunteering, and tuition reimbursement, to name a few. To help you evaluate your job offers, the accompanying CD-ROM provides a job offer checklist, from *collegegrad.com*, that you should fill out for each job offer you receive. This comprehensive list includes such topic areas as *general benefits*, *performance review schedule*, and *training*. It also includes a list of questions to ask your prospective employer. This checklist will allow you to critically evaluate each offer and will also prove helpful for comparison, in the case that you receive multiple job offers.

Once you have considered all of the working details of the job you are being offered, perhaps the most important questions to ask yourself, are the ones listed below that are concerned with your personal feelings.

PERSONAL QUESTIONS TO ASK IN EVALUATING A JOB OFFER

- Will I like the job?
- Will I gain personal satisfaction in performing the job?
- Is the job something I am truly interested in?
- Is the job in line with my long-term career goals?
- Will I like the people I work with?
- Am I proud to represent the company?
- Will I have fun at work?
- Will I look forward to going to work at this company?

Consider a survey conducted in July 2003 by the Conference Board U.S. Job, 2003, which found that fewer than half of Americans are satisfied with their jobs. This is the highest level of discontent since the same survey was first conducted in 1995. Areas in which there was the least amount of satisfaction included promotion policies and company benefits. The same survey showed that, although income levels did tend to increase satisfaction levels, even high-end earners' satisfaction levels have fallen over time. In fact, the largest decline in job satisfaction was found among respondents who earn $50,000 or more. Therefore, in addition to considering the specific responsibilities and the salary of the job, do not forget to evaluate your personal feelings concerning the position. No matter how good an offer may seem, it will not be worth much if it is a job you will not enjoy.

Another word of caution when evaluating job offers. Do not make the mistake of letting others tell you what you *should* do. Of course you will want to consider others' opinions concerning your decision, especially those persons whom you respect, or those who also have a stake in your decision such as a spouse and any other family members. However, do not accept a job because someone else tells you to, or for reasons such as the status it may offer you in the eyes of your friends. Use the lists you have prepared, and remember that you are the best person to make the ultimate decision because you know yourself best.

Negotiating an Offer

Once you have critically evaluated all aspects of the job offer, it is now time to begin the negotiation process. For many college students and recent graduates, this is the most difficult part of the job search. However, do not make the mistake of accepting an offer without negotiation. Even if the job sounds "perfect" there may still be room for negotiation. In fact, most companies will expect you to do this. Remember, you will not receive any more than what you ask for. Although your goal is to secure the most you can; a company's goal is to hire you for the least they can.

Negotiating an offer does not always involve asking for more money. However, if you are not happy with the salary offer, this should be your first area of negotiation. In order to successfully negotiate a higher salary, you should be educated as to what you are worth. Almost all Web sites addressing career issues will offer a section of "typical" salaries for a particular job in a particular region of the country. A particularly useful site is *salary.com*, which offers a salary calculator (e.g., Salary Wizard) that lists typical entry-level positions and their average salaries. Some of the positions relating to retailing and apparel merchandising include assistant buyer, store manager, and district retail sales manager. If you plan to ask for more money, you should use this information in justifying your request. Letting the prospective employer know that you have researched this topic will lend far more credibility to your request than letting him or her think that you just invented some random number. A typical statement that you may convey in presenting your request could be: "According to my research, the average salary for a _____ (e.g., assistant buyer) in the Midwest is between _____ and _____ (range of salary). Given my experience and background I feel that a fair salary for this position would be _____."

As previously mentioned, negotiating an offer does not always involve salary. In fact, as you begin evaluating your job offer, and complete the list from your CD-ROM, you will no doubt identify numerous areas for negotiation. Some of these include benefits, vacation time, profit sharing, promised increases, training and education reimbursement, travel, and overtime. In evaluating each of these areas, if you find any aspects of the current offer that are not satisfactory, you should make note of what it would take to make each acceptable. Prepare to discuss these issues with your potential employer. In communicating your concerns, you need to keep the outlook for resolution positive. *Collegegrad.com* suggests the following dialog for an offer that is unacceptable:

> "I am still very interested in working with you and your company; however (never use the word 'but'), at this point I am not able to accept the offer for the following reason(s): state your reasoning succinctly and what part or parts of the offer are lacking). If you were able to _____ (give your proposed solution), I would gladly accept the position immediately. Are you able to help bring this about?"

Be aware, however, that you should only use this negotiation tactic for offers that are truly unacceptable, and you should be prepared to walk away entirely if no compromise can be reached. Sometimes if the company sees you are ready to walk away, they may make you a better offer. On the other hand, they may tell you they have given you their best offer and withdraw the offer completely. In addition, if the company meets your request, you should be prepared to follow through and accept the offer.

If the previous approach seems uncomfortable to you, you may approach the negotiation in a slightly different way. Be brief and straightforward and say, "I have a problem with an aspect of the offer," then stop talking and wait to see what they say. In a recent article in the *Chicago Tribune*, Joyce Fortier, a career coach based in Novi, Michigan, says: "It [this approach] works like a charm." ("*Job Offer Requires . . .*," August 3, 2003)

A last word of caution when considering the negotiation of an offer: According to Daniel Butler, vice president of retail operations for the National Retail Federation in Washington, D.C., salaries in the retail industry are usually not negotiable. For a particular job title, there is a set salary with future raises related to performance ("Opportunities in *Store for Retail Workers* . . . , 2003). Remember, though, that there still may be a salary range for each title, and if not, your negotiation does not have to involve salary. Perhaps you would be happy with an extra week of vacation. Or, would you like your first performance review done earlier than what is typical for the company? Regardless of your priorities, be assured that you must make your needs known in order for them to be considered. To help you, Box 9.1 lists some common areas that are often negotiated when considering a job offer.

BOX 9.1

ITEMS TO NEGOTIATE IN A JOB OFFER

MONEY OR MONEY-RELATED

- Salary
- Bonuses
- Initial, and subsequent, pay increases (the percentage and the timing of)
- Signing bonuses
- School scholarships and tuition reimbursement (if you are still in school at the time of the offer)
- Stock options
- Profit sharing
- Benefits
- Overtime, comp time, personal days, and vacation time
- Company car
- Expenses and reimbursement
- Relocation assistance
- College tuition reimbursement

NONMONEY

- Training and development programs
- Technology and equipment availability
- Title
- Early review dates
- Tele-commuting or working from home

SOURCE: Copyright © 2004, collegegrad.com, Inc. Based on "Items You Can Negotiate." [On-line]. Available: http://www.collegegrad.com/jobsearch/21-7.shtml. Reprinted with permission of the author and publisher.

Multiple Job Offers

Although most students do not believe it when their job search begins, it is very common for college students and recent graduates to receive multiple job offers. When this happens, the focus of the job search switches from finding a job to choosing the right one. Many of the tools you need to aid in your decisions are the ones we have previously discussed. For each job you are offered, you should fill out the job offer checklist on the accompanying CD-ROM. This will allow you to carefully evaluate the responsibilities of the job, the company itself (including the benefits package), and your projected level of job satisfaction. In reviewing your evaluations of each offer, you may be able to easily reach a decision.

In the case that you cannot reach a decision based on the evaluations you have already done, it may be helpful to do a side-by-side comparison of each position. On the left-hand side of a piece of paper, make a list of all the job factors that are most important to you. After completing the list, rank each factor in order of its importance to you. Across the top of the page, list each company from which you have an offer. Work through the list of factors and evaluate every job you are considering against that list. Which company provides the most benefits in relationship to your particular requirements?

Another strategy you can employ in evaluating your job offers is to simply list the advantages and disadvantages of each position. Look at the lists side by side. Which position offers the most advantages? Which position has more disadvantages? If, after employing these strategies, you are still unable to make a decision, you may just have to make a decision based on what *feels* best to you at the time. *Gut feelings*, or intuition, many times play an important role in decision making and will most often guide you to the right decision.

One of the most common dilemmas that students have, related to multiple job offers, is what to do if they receive a great job offer after already accepting another position. Unfortunately there is no easy solution to handling this situation. In fact the easiest solution to this problem is to avoid it. This can be done by making sure you have eliminated every other employer as a possibility before accepting any offer. In fact, receiving a job offer from one company may prompt other employers to make a quicker decision concerning your hiring.

If you receive a job offer before hearing from another employer that you have interviewed with, and are interested in, it is perfectly acceptable to tell the employer making the offer that you need more time before reaching a decision. Most employers realize that college students are interviewing with many companies and that entry-level employees want to consider all of their options before reaching a decision. Of course, some recruiters will still pressure you to make a decision right away. Remember, it is their job to get you to accept the company's offer! However, do not let them sway you into making a snap decision. Tell them that you need more time. You should then call all employers that you have interviewed with, or that you would like to interview with, and tell them of your job offer. For those companies with which you have interviewed, you might say something like this: "Ms. Jones, this is Sally Johnson. I interviewed with you last week for the _____ position you have available. I am very interested (or, most interested, if that is the case) in working for your company, however I have received another job offer for which I need to make a decision. I do not want to make any decisions before weighing all of my options. When might I expect you to make a decision concerning my candidacy with your company?" Ideally, this will prompt the second employer to make a decision regarding an offer, especially if the comany is interested in you.

If there are companies that you would like to interview with, you should call them and tell them that you currently have a job offer but would like to interview with them before making a decision. Again, this may prompt a quicker response on their part. Someone who is attractive to one company usually becomes more attractive to another. Having a job offer in hand definitely empowers you in communicating with other potential employers.

As mentioned previously, you should do everything you can to avoid the situation in which you have accepted a job offer and then receive another one that you find more attractive. In this case, you should never accept a job with Company A and then back out because Company B has given you a better offer. Once you make a decision, do not entertain any other options. This is a matter of professional ethics. Remember, in today's fast-paced world it is highly likely that at some point in your career you will encounter the people from Company A again, and they will remember that you did not honor a professional commitment with them. Remember, too, that you may never have another opportunity to work for them, and at some point in your career, that may be highly regrettable.

Accepting an Offer

Once you have evaluated all offers and reached a decision, you should call the employer and verbally accept the offer. Yate (2003) suggests that you repeat the offer back to the company to make sure you are both in agreement as to what you are accepting. You should also indicate that you will be expecting a written offer of the agreement. One word of caution: *Until you have a written agreement, you do not have an offi-*

cial job offer. If you are working for another employer, or if you are waiting to hear from other potential employers, do nothing (e.g., resigning, withdrawing your name from consideration) until you have a signed, written agreement from your new employer. Verbal agreements can be withdrawn, and it is actually common that they are, especially in tough economic conditions. Once you do receive a written offer, you will need to give your current employer sufficient notice (e.g., 2 weeks, minimum), and also notify others with whom you have interviewed that you are no longer available.

Once you have verbally accepted an offer, you will also want to prepare a brief acceptance letter to send to your new employer. Include a statement that you are accepting the offer for the specific position (e.g., assistant buyer) at the agreed-upon salary. You should also provide your start date. Close the letter by thanking the company for the opportunity, and mention that you are looking forward to becoming a productive member of its team. Figure 9.1 provides an example of an acceptance letter.

Your Street Address
City, State, Zip

Name
Title
Company Name
Street Address
City, State, Zip

Date of writing

Dear Mr./Ms.:

Thank you for the offer you have extended to me to join Claire's Corporation as an Assistant Buyer. I am pleased to accept the position with the understanding that my salary will be $XXX and that I will be located at your Hoffman Estates headquarters.

I very much look forward to a rewarding future with Claire's and am certain that the responsibilities I will have will be interesting and challenging. As indicated in your letter, I will report to work at 8:00 a.m. on (date).

Sincerely,

(Your signature)

Typed Name

FIGURE 9.1   Sample Acceptance Letter

For ease of preparation, your accompanying CD-ROM also provides you with an acceptance-letter template.

On a related note, it may be that you will not start your new job for several months, or even a full school year, after you have accepted a position. This situation usually occurs when college students complete a successful internship during their undergraduate schooling, after which the company makes a permanent offer. If you find yourself in this situation, continue to keep in touch with the company until you begin working there full-time. Of course, if you will be working at the company part-time during the school year, this will happen automatically. However, if not, you can keep in touch via e-mail, phone calls, or simply by dropping in to say hello once in a while. This is especially important in the merchandising and retailing field because people tend to move around and get promoted quickly, which means you may be working for an entirely new management team by the time you begin your permanent position. Therefore, keeping in touch is not just good P.R. on your part, but it will assure you that the new management knows you and, most importantly, knows about the offer you have been made. You may want to exercise some of the strategies presented in Table 7.3, "Reasons to Contact Future Work Experience Sites."

If you are relocating for your new job, it is never too early to start planning for your move. Although many companies will offer you help to assure a smooth process with the actual move, some new graduates find themselves somewhat homesick and at a loss as to what to do with themselves socially once they arrive in a new city. In that regard, Box 9.2 offers tips for a successful relocation strategy.

Rejecting an Offer

There are a variety of reasons for rejecting a job offer. Regardless of the reason, however, turning down a job is not easy for most job seekers. Some will even avoid this conversation by leaving voice mails after hours, or sending e-mails, neither of which are acceptable. Rejecting an offer in a more professional manner leaves the door open for future opportunities with those employers.

A best-case scenario is that you are accepting a better offer with another company. In that case, you should call all other employers with whom you have interviewed, or sent resumes, to let them know of your decision. Your communication with the companies that you are eliminating, or whose offers you are rejecting, should be straightforward and honest. Maryanne Wegerbauer (2000) suggests that you can simply say, "I've thought about the offer and have decided that my needs will best be met in another position." If you are turning down one company because you have received a

BOX 9.2

TIPS FOR A SUCCESSFUL RELOCATION STRATEGY

- **Contact a realtor.** Work with a realtor while you are seeking housing, even if you plan to live in an apartment. A realtor can give you insight into the characteristics of various neighborhoods and help you discover a fit between your interests and your new neighborhood.
- **Become active in professional organizations.** This is a great way to meet people who have similar interests and values to yours, as well as a method of establishing professional and career growth.
- **Join a faith-based organization.** If you are inclined to seek a spiritual home, the networks that are available to you through churches, synagogues, mosques, and other faith-based organizations can create a support system separate from your work acquaintances. Many social opportunities that are consistent with your spiritual beliefs and values will be available to you through this organization.
- **Volunteer.** This is another great way to meet other people—and to do good work that has a positive impact on your new community. Opportunities ranging from Big Brothers/Big Sisters to the local humane society, homeless shelters, and Habitat for Humanity are choices from which you can select.
- **Join a fitness club.** Joining a fitness club or other exercise-oriented activity is another way to meet people, and has the added benefit of fitness and improved health. Exercise is a good way to reduce the stress that builds from a day at the office and maintain your stamina as you work hard in your new career.
- **Explore a hobby.** Whether you are already an avid scrap-booker or you've always wanted to learn how to ice skate, explore opportunities to develop and become (or stay) active in a hobby. It is important to develop your interests!
- **Contact a local alumni association.** University alumni associations are often located in larger cities across the United States, and sometimes even abroad. If you are an alumni of a social organization such as a fraternity or sorority, there is likely to be an alumni association for you to join in the vicinity.

better offer in terms of salary and other benefits, you should tell them that also. Depending on how badly the other company wants you, and how much flexibility they have, they may counteroffer ("Be Tactful . . . ," 2003).

It is perfectly acceptable to keep in contact with recruiters who represent companies that you have rejected. That is, in fact, an excellent networking strategy. You never know when a particular company will be a perfect fit for you in the future. Many long-term professional relationships, in fact, have begun through an interview situation—with the job search candidate ultimately taking a position with another company. You never want to burn bridges. The professional contacts that you are making during the career search process may be able to offer opportunities that are a better fit for you a year or so down the road, but this will only happen if your initial interactions with these contact people resulted in relationships that remain mutually honest and cordial.

YOUR FIRST JOB

The impressions people form of you in the first few weeks of your new job may have everlasting effects on your long-term success. Therefore, it is critical that the image you create for yourself is positive. The way you talk, behave, make decisions, and dress are just a few of the areas in which your co-workers will immediately evaluate you. Knowing what to expect during the first day, and subsequent weeks, at a new job should help in your putting your best image forward.

What to Expect Your First Day on the Job

One of the things that may surprise you about the first day on the job is that you may find yourself bored. This is because much of the day may be filled with minor details such as being shown where you will work, how to find things that you will need (e.g., office supplies), and how to do certain tasks, most of which you may find unchallenging. You may also have to fill out numerous forms relating to your employment, health care, and liability. It is also common to be given an employee handbook to read. Even though the tasks you are completing may seem mundane to you, remember to keep a positive attitude and exhibit enthusiasm.

On your first day, and continuing for several weeks, you will probably have many questions that you need answered. In that regard, find out who you should ask when those questions do arise. For example, should you ask your immediate peers, or your supervisor? Who can answer the questions that you have? Because others will be busy doing their own tasks and may have minimal time to take away from their own responsibilities, it is important that you not repeatedly interrupt others. Although it is understandable that you will need questions answered, you do not want to be perceived as a pest. A good idea is to write your questions down in a notebook or personal digital assistant (PDA) so that if you must interrupt someone you can ask several questions at once. Also, record your answers so that you can refer back to them. Do not expect to remember everything you are going to learn in the next few months.

It is also common to be confused on your first day at a new job. You will meet many new people with many different titles. Because you will want to remember names and faces, and how the people you meet fit into the company structure, it is a good idea to record that information in a notebook or PDA for future reference. If writing things down makes you feel uncomfortable, it is perfectly acceptable to ask the person showing you around if he or she minds if you take some notes as you go through the day. Most people will perceive this as a positive sign of your willingness to learn what you can as quickly as you can. Taking a student role the first few weeks on the job is something you should expect to do and will be a good transition for you, too.

Another important aspect of your first day will be learning about the rules at your new company. For example, find out what your normal working hours will be, including any breaks or lunch times. Regardless of what you see others doing, you should adhere to those rules, especially during your first few weeks. Every company has written and "unwritten" rules that you need to identify as quickly as possible. One of the best ways to do this is to watch other employees who are successful and model their behavior. These are also the individuals you may be able to ask for direction, as needed.

How to Succeed in the First Few Weeks

The stress of transitioning from the role of a college student to that of a young professional with a brand-new job can be somewhat overwhelming. Following are a few guidelines to follow that may help ease some of the anxiety that you are almost certain to feel.

- **Identify a mentor.** One of the best things you can do to assure your success is to identify a mentor within your new company. If you do not know anyone, you may ask the human resources office if there are people willing to serve in that capacity. Or, better yet, if you can find someone who is an alumnus from your college, you will more than likely have an immediate rapport with that person by virtue of your shared alma mater. If the human resources office at your new job cannot help you identify someone, many college career offices keep records of past graduates who want to serve as mentors to new hires within their particular company.

- **Identify key players within the company.** First, and as previously mentioned, one of the best things you can do during your first few weeks at a new job is to identify key players and model their behavior. Also, get to know the successful employees and make yourself known to them. Many times these are the people who will influence your career and who can also be instrumental in helping you transition successfully into your new position. The successful people in the company are the ones that you need to impress. Carol Nicolaides (n.d.), President & Executive Coach of Progressive Leadership, suggests that you should decide, right from the beginning, the way you want to be "branded," and then take the steps necessary to become known by the brand you have chosen. Whatever you choose, being visible, and letting people know who you are will go a long way in establishing yourself as a potential star within the company.

- **Avoid gossip and office politics.** Within any company, you will find a certain amount of office politics and gossip mills. These should always be avoided. Many people at your new job will try to involve you in gossip or in "bashing" your new bosses. You must never participate in this type of behavior even though it can be quite contagious. Show respect for all of those you work with, especially your boss, and avoid becoming involved in gossip or behavior that you may later regret. Also, remember that you can be cordial to others without joining in their unprofessional behavior. In fact, taking a stand against such behavior may encourage others to do the same.

- **Dress professionally.** Dress in the retailing field can vary considerably from one company to another (e.g., upscale department store versus discount retailing) and from one aspect of the industry to another (e.g., design industry versus buying industry.) As a new employee you should find out what your company's dress code is, and adhere to it more conservatively at least for your first few weeks. Again, observe how a successful person in the company dresses if you are unsure of the appropriateness of your wardrobe. Today, many companies have adopted a business casual look; however, due to abuse by employees, or perhaps just a lack of understanding of what "business casual" means, some companies are now rethinking those guidelines. Regardless, because this trend is still extremely popular, we thought it important to include some guidelines for the business casual look for women (Box 9.3) and for men (Box 9.4). You should also note that business casual does not generally include denim jeans. However, if your company does allows you to wear denim (for example on "casual

BOX 9.3

DO'S AND DON'TS OF HEAD-TO-TOE BUSINESS CASUAL FOR WOMEN

BLOUSES

- No sheer blouses—save them for a night out
- No loud, trendy prints or peasant and poet's tops
- No floppy sleeves peeking out from under a jacket or covering the hand
- Select quality shirts made of natural fibers and in classic, timeless silhouettes
- Do wear man-tailored, button-down shirts
- Camisoles, tanks, and shells are acceptable but *only* under a jacket

JACKETS

- Do wear jackets that are tailored
- Double-breasted jackets should always be buttoned
- Loose or ill-fitting jackets give an unkempt and sloppy appearance
- Stick to basic patterns and colors—subtle plaids, checks, or stripes are fine in classic colors such as navy, black, gray, and neutrals

TROUSERS

- No capri pants—they're just too casual for the office
- Slacks should fit well—not too tight and no pantylines showing
- Avoid extremely wide pant legs
- Classic slim-cut trousers with or without cuffs are the way to go
- Make sure hems are the proper length—neither too short nor too long
- No embroidery or attention-getting embellishment
- Stick to basic patterns and colors—subtle plaids, checks, or stripes are fine in classic colors such as navy, black, gray, and neutrals

SKIRTS

- Straight slim-line skirts that fall no less than three inches above the knee to mid-calf are the correct lengths for an office environment
- Avoid extremes—skirts that are too short or too long
- No floral-patterned skirts or flowing silhouettes

DRESSES

- No floral or loud prints—they're just not appropriate for the office
- Peasant styles are out—save them for the weekend
- Do wear a sheath with a matching or coordinating jacket over it for a polished look
- As in skirts, dress length should be neither too short nor too long

ACCESSORIES

- No little-girl barrettes, scrunchies, big dangly earrings, or belts with huge buckles
- Wear classic button or small hoop earrings
- A scarf at the neck gives a finished appearance
- A tailored shawl can act as a jacket

HOSIERY

- Always buy quality hosiery—it's worth the extra investment—they wear longer and look neater and smoother
- Nude colors are best and appropriate
- Colored or lacy hosiery has no place in the office—save it for off time

SHOES

- Invest in a few good pairs of expensive shoes
- Make sure shoes are always polished with no scuffs
- No thigh-high boots—they'll make you look like a different kind of working girl
- Classic pumps are still the safest and best choice for the office
- Ankle boots work well with trousers and pantsuits
- Watch the heel height—too high or too short will make you look either too dressed up or too casual

BOX 9.4

DO'S AND DON'TS OF HEAD-TO-TOE BUSINESS CASUAL FOR MEN

SHIRTS
- Avoid loud, trendy prints
- In general, shirts should have a collar—T-shirts are too casual
- Turtleneck and mock turtleneck shirts are acceptable
- Tailored wovens such as button-down shirts and knit polo shirts are both good choices
- Shirts should always have sleeves
- Avoid shirts with brand advertising (unless, of course, it represents your company)
- Do not wear message shirts
- Select quality shirts made of natural fibers
- Tank tops are unacceptable

JACKETS
- Wear jackets that are tailored
- Always button double-breasted jackets
- Avoid loose or ill-fitting jackets that give an unkempt and sloppy appearance
- Wear basic patterns and colors—subtle plaids, checks, or stripes are fine in classic colors such as navy, black, gray, and neutrals (unless you are working in a fashion-forward environment)

TROUSERS
- Long trousers only—save the shorts for the weekends
- Slacks should fit well—not too tight
- Typically, business casual means no denim
- Classic slim-cut trousers with or without cuffs are appropriate
- Make sure hems are the proper length—neither too short nor too long
- Basic colors such as khaki, brown, black, and olive green work best; fashion forward designs such as stripes and plaids may be acceptable depending on the office culture

ACCESSORIES

- Ties need not be worn for casual dress
- Ball caps are too casual for the office
- Be aware of the culture of the office—jewelry such as earrings may not be appropriate, even on casual days
- A belt should be worn for a polished look, and preferably should match the color of your shoes

HOSIERY

- Always wear socks
- Athletic socks are typically not appropriate

SHOES

- Invest in a few good pairs of expensive shoes
- Make sure shoes are always polished with no scuffs
- Sandals are not appropriate for the office
- No tennis shoes—too casual!

GROOMING

- Clean-shaven or styled facial hair is acceptable—the scruffy look is not
- Clothing should be clean and wrinkle-free.
- Shirts should be tucked into trousers
- Generally, tattoos and piercings should not be visible

Fridays"), there are also guidelines you should follow if you choose to do so (Box 9.5). As mentioned previously, you should always err on the side of being too conservative with your dress versus being perceived as unprofessional. There are many good wardrobe-planning and professional dress books (see References at the end of this chapter) on the market to help you as needed. You can also review Chapter 6, which discusses professional dress in terms of interviewing; however, the same principles apply to your first job.

BOX 9.5

DO'S AND DON'TS OF DENIM

- Dress up jeans with a fitted blazer, interesting belt, and nice shoes
- Wearing midriff-baring low-rise jeans to the office is a definite no-no
- Pay attention to the jean's silhouette and style, so it gives a neat, flattering look and fit
- Stay away from distressed looks in jeans and embellishments such as beading and sparkle paint
- Wear dark, structured denim skirts in an appropriate length
- Avoid mixing different shades of denim on the top and bottom
- Invest in a darker-rinse, fitted jean jacket to pair with khakis, dresses, and skirts
- Novelty denim belongs at parties and nightclubs, not at the office
- Consider adding denim accessories such as watchbands, totes, and shoes to your business wardrobe
- Steer clear of extremes—too tight, too baggy, too long, too short

SOURCE: Information courtesy of Cotton Inc. Copyright © 2002. All rights reserved. Corporate dressing: The new rules. (2002, August 20) Advertising supplement to *WWD*, p. 11.

- **You cannot be everything to all people.** No matter how hard you try, there will be some people in your new environment who will not like you. Expect this to happen and do not take it personally when it does. Having others who do not like you can happen for a variety of reasons, most of which have nothing to do with you as a person. For example, maybe you are stepping into a position that another employee wanted or that a friend of that employee lost. Some people do not like new employees simply because they are new. Regardless of the reason, if you find yourself in a situation in which another employee seems less than cooperative with you, ignore the problem if possible and continue to behave in a professional manner. It is not realistic to expect that everyone in a work environment will like each other. Even so, it is important to behave professionally and respect differences with others that will no doubt occur. Even if you are unable to resolve your conflicts with some, you will gain the respect of others by behaving professionally.
- **Relax and take care of yourself.** Most employees are too hard on themselves during the first few weeks of a new job. Putting yourself under such undue stress will

not only result in your making more mistakes, but may also make you physically sick. Although you will want to do your best, do not forget that it is extremely important to take care of yourself at the same time. Your co-workers are human beings who will probably be forgiving of any minor mistakes that you are bound to make during your first few weeks. Mistakes are to be expected, and simply seeing you put your best effort forward to do the best job possible will impress your new co-workers. Therefore, do not try to do too much in the first few weeks or you will find yourself completely stressed and burned out in just a short amount of time.

Heather Holoubek, associate buyer, Claire's Accessories, Inc., International Division, notes that when she entered the "real world" from college she found herself facing some challenging situations that she was not expecting. Box 9.6 contains her list of the top ten things she wants you to know about the real world. The list also summarizes many of the important points covered in this book.

What If You Don't Like the Job

Sometimes, no matter how efficient you have been in evaluating a new job, or how hard you have tried, you may find that your new job is not living up to your expectations. Although you may ultimately decide that you should move on, this should not be your first course of action.

Before making any decisions, you should be sure that you have had time to adequately assess your job. If you have been at your job for less than six months, you probably do not yet have a realistic view of what to expect. If this is your first job after college, the stress or dissatisfaction that you are feeling may be due, in large part, to your transitioning into the different life role of a young professional. In other words, make sure that you are not blaming your new position for angst you may be feeling about other changes in your life. In that case, changing positions will not solve your problems.

However, if you do find yourself unhappy with your job, you will need to discuss your concerns with a mentor or your immediate supervisor. Ask for an appointment to speak with this person in private and be prepared to specifically state your issues. Examples of items you may want to discuss include promises that are not being kept, the lack of challenges in your position, or any situations causing you undue stress. It is a good idea to prepare a list ahead of time so that you will have an outline of all of the major points you want to cover in your meeting. This list will help to keep the meeting focused, as there is sometimes a tendency for individuals to stray from their intended

BOX 9.6

HEATHER HOLOUBEK'S TOP TEN LIST OF THINGS TO KNOW ABOUT THE REAL WORLD

1. **Never, ever sell yourself short.** Even if you are asked to do something that you do not feel particularly confident about, figure out a way to do it. If you exude confidence and believe in yourself, others will also believe in you! Sometimes it is necessary to jump in feet first and take a chance.

2. **You will do a lot of things that are not in your job description.** As a new employee you should be willing to take on any job that is asked of you. In the first few months on the job, you should say yes to almost all requests from your superiors. Although you want to protect yourself from being taken advantage of, you should have the attitude of being willing to do anything that is needed!

3. **Find a trusted mentor.** Your mentor should be someone within the company you join, and preferably in a position above yours. If you cannot identify someone within the same company, you should at least find someone in the same industry that you can turn to for advice. As you progress in your career, you should return the favor and become a mentor to someone else. Relationships with mentors can last a lifetime and will be among the most important professional relationships you have.

4. **No job is perfect.** At first the position you hold will sometimes be about what you learn in that position and where it can take you rather than about the actual position you are currently in. In other words, many entry-level positions are stepping stones to better things, but you must be willing to learn everything you can and work hard.

5. **Never forget where you came from.** As you progress into management, you should always remember what it was like, or would be like, to be in positions below you. A great rule of thumb is, "Never ask others to do something that you are not willing to do yourself." Managers should lead by example, which often means doing the most mundane jobs alongside sales associates or other entry-level personnel. When others see that you are willing to do what is necessary for the good of the team, they are more likely to take the same attitude. In the long run, this makes a better work environment for everyone!

6. **Set goals.** One of the most effective tools you can use to aid in your development is to set goals, and work toward achieving them. Once you have identified your goals, you should write them down. Generally, when you write down something, you are more likely to get it done. Remember that your goals can take various forms. They can be general or very specific, and can apply to your personal or professional life. They will also change as time goes by. However, the bottom line is that you need to set goals!

7. **Always move "up" when making job changes.** Never take a new position that is a step backward. Always move up when taking another position. Of course, this can mean many things depending on who you are, and where your priorities lie. Always ask yourself what you have to gain by taking another position (e.g., better opportunities in the long run, more money, fewer hours, etc.).

8. **Be your own advocate!** Let people know what you are doing—do not assume they know. For many young professionals, this is one of the hardest things to do. However, it is one of the most important things you can do for your professional development and advancement. In the hectic pace of today's work world, some of your work may go unnoticed if you do not point it out. Also, keep documentation of your efforts—such a record will be particularly useful at review time. Remember it's a good thing to pat yourself on the back when you have done a good job!

9. **Hold onto your friends from each position you hold.** The retail and merchandising field tends to be a very small industry, and you will no doubt encounter the same individuals throughout your career. Never "burn bridges"; instead, retain good relationships with former co-workers and supervisors. They will be a valuable network for you!

10. **Remain professional at all times.** No matter how pervasive gossip and office politics are in your work environment, you should avoid both. Although it may be difficult to remain neutral, especially when others are participating, you have nothing to gain by engaging in this conduct. It is especially important to never criticize your boss to others at work. If you have a problem with your boss, you should address it with him or her in a professional manner, rather than complaining to others. Over time, your professional behavior will earn you respect by all concerned. Remember, no matter how hard it may be, never gossip or become involved in office politics!

SOURCE: Heather Holoubek

topics, especially if they are upset or disappointed about something. Having such a list will also let your supervisor or mentor know that you have put some thought into your concerns and that you are not just acting on a whim. After you have covered all of your points, try to come to a mutual agreement on specific courses of action to solve your problems. Then, schedule another meeting within a reasonable time frame to follow up on the proposed solutions. At your next meeting, you can evaluate how the proposed solutions are, or are not, working and revise the previous strategies as necessary. If after several months, things have not changed, then you may have to consider other options.

Exploring Opportunities Beyond Your First Job

Although switching jobs after less than a year does not carry the same stigma it once did, you should still weigh your decision heavily before doing so. The ultimate decision you make may come down to asking yourself how important it is for you to honor your commitments and how much you feel you owe your employer.

Should You Stay or Should You Go?

According to Alan Goodman, chairman of the National Association of Colleges and Employers' Committee for Professional Conduct, if the company is delivering on its promises to you, it may be your ethical responsibility to stay. However, if it is not, and company representatives will not talk about it, then new hires have the right to look elsewhere.

If you find that you cannot get along with your boss, you may also have a valid reason for leaving a new job. However, be sure that you have made every effort to resolve your differences rather than simply quitting at the first sign of conflict. Sometimes, as mentioned previously, no matter what you do or how hard you try, there will be those with whom you cannot get along. If this person is your boss, it may be very difficult for you to be promoted regardless of your efforts and achievements. Before giving up entirely on the relationship, you should seek the advice of someone in the company whom you respect and can trust (e.g., your mentor). If you are having problems with your boss, chances are that others have had similar problems. If this is the case, others may have solutions that you have not considered. If, however, your repeated efforts to get along with your boss are fruitless, you may need to consider other options. Those may be with another company, or perhaps you would be happy if allowed to transfer to another area within the same company. Table 9.1 lists some important considerations to think about

TABLE 9.1
SHOULD YOU CHANGE JOBS OR STAY WHERE YOU ARE?

REMAIN WITH YOUR CURRENT EMPLOYER IF . . .	CHANGE EMPLOYERS IF . . .
You like to think about your job on weekends and decide what you might do to perform it better.	You can hardly wait until 5 o'clock rolls around.
You'd like to do this kind of work, even if you didn't need the money.	You really don't have much in common with your fellow workers, customers, or clients, or others with whom you deal.
Many of your interests are centered around the work you do.	You feel tired and irritable much of the time.
It's the kind of thing you do well, and you like the feeling of success that it provides.	It is almost impossible to lead the kind of life you want on your income and there's not much chance of improvement.
You like the feeling you get when something is completed.	The hours and kind of work interfere drastically with your preferred lifestyle.
Your colleagues are great and you enjoy the atmosphere.	Your employer isn't doing well and conditions may not get better.
What you do is identified so you have the feeling that you will be judged on your own merit.	The job stress and requirements adversely affect your self-concept.
You like the geographical area where you must live.	The work is boring and it is getting to you.
Promotional opportunities appear to be present.	There doesn't seem to be any job to which you might transfer.
You are proud, or at least not embarrassed, to tell friends where you work.	You have discussed your plans to leave with persons you respect.
Your position is compatible with your needs and values.	You have another job to go to.
Your work enables you to express your life purpose.	The work and organization are not congruent with your needs and values.
	You are unable to express your sense of purpose through your work.

SOURCE: Minichart developed by *Career Opportunities News*, P.O. Box 190, Garrett Park, MD 20896. Reprinted with permission of *Career Opportunities News*.

before making the decision to leave a job. In addition, the CD-ROM accompanying this book contains an interactive quiz to help you with such a decision.

In today's job market, another valid reason for switching jobs sooner than you may like is if you notice the company's financial rating becoming increasingly bleak. This may be evident in plunging stock values or massive layoffs, which, unfortunately, have become more commonplace these days. If you find yourself in this situation, it is a good idea to be proactive with your career. You should do everything to protect yourself, which means that it is perfectly acceptable to start looking for a new job. You do not want to wait until you are unemployed to start looking for another position. Remember the adage that "it's easier to find a job when you have a job!" In other words, you want to avoid the added stress that being unemployed brings to any job search.

Looking for Another Job While You Are Still Employed

Regardless of the reason, if you find yourself looking for another job while you are still employed, consider the following words of caution. One of the quickest ways to get fired or to be laid off from your current job prematurely is for your supervisor to find out that you looking for another job. Therefore, you should be as discrete as possible. Do *not* use the office equipment at your present job to type your resume, copy your resume, or communicate in any way with prospective employers. Invariably you will leave a copy of your resume, or a cover letter, lying around (usually in the copy machine) for the wrong person to find.

On a related note, be very careful about who you tell that you are looking for another job, and continue to perform at your highest ability. Ideally, no one at your current job should know about your new job search. However, this may not be possible, especially if you need to use some of your present co-workers as references. In this case, tell only those select few and make sure that you can trust them to keep your secret. You may also need to let your prospective employers know that they should not call anyone at your current job other than those whose names you have provided to them. You can achieve this by mentioning in your cover letter and correspondence with them that you would like your application to remain confidential at this time.

Lastly, you will need to be somewhat creative in terms of taking phone calls and scheduling interview appointments with potential employers. If you have a mobile phone, list that number on your resume and provide a voice mail letting callers know either what time you will be available to answer the phone, or what time you will return their call. You will also need to schedule interviews before or after your current working hours, or on your lunch break if that is convenient. Most prospective employers will respect the fact that you are currently working and will be flexible in scheduling around your commitments.

Resigning from Your Job

When the time comes for you to resign from your current job, you will need to do so in a professional manner. People tend to be mobile within the retail merchandising field, making it somewhat of a "small" world especially if you stay within the same region of the country. You may think that you never want to work for your present company again, but chances are extremely good that you will encounter many of your current co-workers again. Although like many people you may dream of expressing every frustration and discontentment you have had with the company when you submit your resignation, the truth of the matter is that you should not do so. It is extremely important that you continue to exhibit professional behavior when resigning and "burn no bridges" when leaving a company.

Figure 9.2 provides an example of a letter of resignation, which you should prepare for your current employer. For ease of preparation, the accompanying CD-ROM also provides you with a resignation letter template. As you will note, this letter need not be long or detailed, but rather should be short and to the point. It should simply state that you are giving your current employer notice of your resignation as of a specific effective date. Of course, you should give a minimum of two weeks' notice and be as considerate as possible concerning deadlines or projects for which you have prior commitments. The closing of the letter should be a general thank-you for the opportunities you have been given. Remember that this letter will probably become a part of your permanent record with the company, so you should say nothing negative in it that might damage your reputation. You never know when you might want to return to the company in a different capacity, or how the letter may be used when future employers request references. Nowacki and Burt (n.d.) advise that you should think of the letter as a "bridge builder" rather than a "bridge burner."

Although most employers will appreciate your willingness to stay on the job and honor the resignation date you have provided them, do not be alarmed if your employer does not. At some companies it is policy to terminate an employee immediately upon his or her resignation. In these cases, you will probably be told to pack up your belongings and leave the premises at once. This practice is common, especially where employees are in charge of a large amount of inventory, or privy to confidential

Your Street Address
City, State, Zip

Name
Title
Company Name
Street Address
City, State, Zip

Date of writing

Dear Mr./Ms.:

Please accept this letter as notice of my resignation effective _____ (a minimum of 2 weeks from current date). I appreciate the opportunity that (company name) has given me and wish you continued success.

Thank you again for allowing me to be a part of your team. I am happy to assist in any way to ensure a smooth transition.

Sincerely,

(your signature)

Typed Name

FIGURE 9.2   Sample Resignation Letter

company data. Be prepared for this to happen, and if you find yourself in this situation, continue to behave in a professional manner remaining courteous and cooperative. Once you leave, you always have the option of calling your new employer to tell them you will be available to start earlier, providing that is what you would like to do. If not, enjoy the extra, unplanned days off to relax and regenerate before starting your new and exciting job!

In the event that your employer allows you to stay to work out your notice, use that time to perform your job at an exceptional level. Save any celebration for friends and family members. Although some of your co-workers may be happy for you, there will be others who will not be. During your last weeks on the job, and as in any work situation, you should continue to behave professionally and to do everything you can to help others transition into your position or responsibilities once you leave. Some examples of things you may offer to do include giving others updates on any projects you are currently involved with, and providing co-workers with pertinent information about company clients. Remain gracious and, before leaving, be sure to thank everyone for the opportunity of working with him or her. Your behavior during the last few weeks on a job speaks volumes about your work and professional ethics. Be sure to leave on a positive note.

PROJECTS

1. By now you should have identified at least three positions that interest you. Using the Internet, look up the typical entry-level salaries for each. A particularly useful on-line tool for doing this is the Salary Wizard, which can be found at *www.quintcareers.com.* Identify salaries for each of the positions in your job market and in a different job market that interests you. Report the following:

   a. The salaries in each job market, comparing and contrasting your findings

   b. What you think might account for the differences and similarities that you found

   c. Some other factors you would need to consider in deciding which is the best salary

2. Identify someone at your college, or another young professional, who has recently accepted a job offer. Interview that person about the factors that were most important in reaching an employment decision. If multiple offers were considered, what was (were) the deciding factor(s)? Compare your results with those of your classmates. Were you able to identify any areas not listed on the job evaluation checklist on the accompanying CD-ROM? Do you agree with the factors the person used in making the decision?

3. Identify someone who has recently quit a job or changed careers. Interview him or her as to what factors led to the decision to depart. Were there any factors that could have kept this person at the position, or in the career that he or she recently left? What is your reaction to the findings?

4. Identify someone who has accepted a job that he or she later regretted. Discuss with this person how the situation may have been avoided, or what could have

been done differently when evaluating the position initially. Also talk with this person about what was learned from the experience, and what advice he or she may have for others.

5. Identify someone who has a mentor. Discuss with this person what qualities the mentor possesses that are most admired, and what some of the most important things are that the mentor has taught him or her.

6. Identify someone who is a mentor. Discuss with this person what he or she likes about being a mentor, and ask for advice regarding finding a mentor.

QUESTIONS FOR DISCUSSION

1. What are the most important job factors to you in considering an offer? Explain your answers.

2. Do you think that salary is the most important factor to consider when evaluating a job offer? Why or why not?

3. What are some concerns you may have in terms of negotiating a job offer? What could you do to lessen your concerns?

4. Do you agree that you should never accept one job offer and then back out if a better offer comes your way? Defend your position.

5. Why is it important to prepare a strategy for evaluating a job offer?

6. What would be the most likely reason that you would reject a job offer?

7. What are some qualities you would like to see in a professional mentor?

8. Do you feel it is important to have a mentor at a new job? Why or why not?

9. What are some positive things you could do to make you stand out during the first few weeks at a new job?

10. What strategies could you use to cope with the stress of transitioning from a college student to a young professional in your first career position?

11. What would you do if you found yourself in a job you did not like after a few months?

12. What are some legitimate reasons for leaving a job in a shorter time than normally expected?

13. Why is it important to not let co-workers know that you are looking for another job?

14. Why it is important not to "burn bridges" when resigning from your job? Identify three reasons.

ELECTRONIC ACTIVITIES

Refer to the accompanying CD-ROM. The key elements of this chapter are:

1. Summary of Chapter 9 text

2. "Stay or Go" quiz (parts one and two)

3. Job offer checklist

4. Sample acceptance letter template

5. Sample resignation letter template

6. Links to professional groups' Web sites

REFERENCES

Be tactful when refusing an offer. (2003, August 3). *Chicago Tribune* (Section 6, Career Builder), p. 1.

Corporate dressing: The new rules. (2002, August 20). Advertising supplement to *WWD*.

Exit stage right when switching employers. (2003, June 29). *Chicago Tribune* (Section 6, Career Builder), p. 1.

Gershman, S. (1999) *Best dressed: The born to shop lady's secrets for building a wardrobe.* New York: Clarkson, Potter.

Job offer requires examination: Negotiating salary and benefits can pay off. (2003, August 3). *Chicago Tribune* (Section 6, Career Builder), p. 1.

Johnson Gross K., & Stone, J. (1995). *Chic simple dress smart for women: Wardrobes that win in the workplace*. New York: Knopf.

Nicolaides, C. (n.d.). Successfully transitioning to your new job. [On-line]. Retrieved October 6, 2003. Available: http://www.careerbuilder.com/jobseekers/career-bytes/0201successfullytransitioning.htm.

Nowacki, S., & Burt, S. (n.d.). The resignation letter. [On-line]. Retrieved December 17, 2003. Available: http://www.worktree.com/tb/MB_resign.cfm.

Persico, L., & Duttro, K. (n.d.). Is it time to jump ship? [On-line]. Retrieved February 3, 2002. Available: http://www.careers.wsj.com/.

Opportunities in store for retail workers: Helping others a major draw for millions of employees. (2003, July 20). *Chicago Tribune* (Section 6, Career Builder), p. 1.

U.S. job satisfaction hits record low. (2003, July). *The Conference Board Reports*.

Wegerbauer, M. (2000, January). *Job offer! A how-to negotiation guide*. Indianapolis, IN: Jist Publishing.

Yate, M. (2003). *Knock 'em dead 2003*. Holbrook, MA: Adams Media Corporation.